Cases in
Public
Policy
Analysis

Cases in Public Policy Analysis

GEORGE M. GUESS
PAUL G. FARNHAM

Longman
New York & London

Cases in Public Policy Analysis

Longman Inc., 95 Church Street, White Plains, N.Y. 10601

Associated companies:
Longman Group Ltd., London
Longman Cheshire Pty., Melbourne
Longman Paul Pty., Auckland
Copp Clark Pitman, Toronto
Pitman Publishing Inc., New York

Senior editor: David J. Estrin
Production editor: Elsa van Bergen
Text design: Jill Francis Wood
Cover design: Steven August Krastin
Production coordinator: Lilieth Redman Harvey

Library of Congress Cataloging-in-Publication Data

Guess, George M.
  Cases in public policy analysis / George M. Guess, Paul G. Farnham.
    p.   cm.
  Includes index.
  ISBN 0-582-28687-5 (pbk.)
  1. Policy sciences.   I. Farnham, Paul G.   II. Title.
H97.G84 1989
361.6'1—dc 19   87-36147
                                                          CIP

ISBN 0-582-28687-5 (pbk.)

88 89 90 91 92 93 9 8 7 6 5 4 3 2 1

Contents

Acknowledgments

Since the *case analysis format* is largely a product of our classroom experiences, we would like to thank both our graduate and undergraduate students in public finance, economics, public policy, and public administration for telling us what they would like to learn in policy courses, and for providing examples of how we might inject real world decision uncertainty into our exercises. Whether our text meets faculty and student needs will ultimately be reflected in course adoptions. In the meantime, please send us your comments on the text and suggestions on how best to teach the cases.

We would also like to thank the many individuals who helped us prepare *Cases in Public Policy Analysis*. These include Jim McDonnell, Vice President of Hammer, Siler, George Associates in Atlanta; Ted Poister, Director of the Institute of Public Administration at Georgia State University; David Sjoquist, Professor of Economics at Georgia State University; and Carroll Olson, Assistant General Manager for Finance at the Metropolitan Atlanta Rapid Transit Authority (MARTA).

G. M. Guess
P. G. Farnham

CHAPTER 1

Introduction to Policy Analysis

Unlike much of political science and economics, the discipline of "policy analysis" is less interested in pure theory-building than in producing information useful in political settings to resolve practical policy problems. Akin to an applied social science that uses methods from economics, political science, sociology, and other related fields for problem-solving, policy analysis is practiced by consultants to government, decision-makers in staff government agencies, and other roles that permit analysis to inform decisions.

Though this suggests that everyone engages in policy analysis, in fact very few decisions are informed by thorough analysis given the pressures of scarce resources, mandated expenditures, and the often perverse tendency of management in large organizations to engage in protective stupidity and persistence in error. In part, the problem of uninformed decision making (intentional or not) may be due to the apparent complexity of policy analysis itself. Like other technocratic disciplines intent on carving a professional niche for their followers, policy analysis is often erroneously associated with hi-tech reports using heavy mathematics and linear programming. At least in part, the value of this kind of arcane analysis may be as a means of scaring away opponents of one's recommendations.

This book attempts to simplify the discipline and make it useful to practitioners who have little time or resources for technical or visionary sophistication. Nevertheless, it recognizes the need for basic tools to diagnose, analyze, and evaluate policy problems, and it attempts to build up those skills by providing "messy" problem settings to which the tools may be applied.

POLITICS AND TECHNICAL ANALYSIS

What is *policy analysis* and how is it carried out? Policy analysis is an applied social science discipline that attempts to produce useful information for policy decision making in political contexts (Dunn, 1981, p.ix). The distinguishing feature is practical information. Information can be produced institutionally by procedures that, for example, permit regular inventories of selected variables such as the amount of money poor people spend on food, housing, and medical care. Information may also be produced intuitively by hunch or insight. For instance, the limits of social and political life under repressive regimes are hard phenomena to measure—yet one intuitively knows the limits of his or her freedom.

But policy analysis cannot be totally technique (boiled down to mechanical knowledge and production procedures in a manual) or purely insight (a vision quest). Good policy analysis requires a mixture of both—vision to generate hypotheses and puzzles, and techniques of various kinds to order the facts and make some sense of them for decision making. The naive technocratic view of policy analysis imagines that accumulation of enough "facts" will serve to define the problem and lead toward its solution. By this view, technocrats are good because there exists only one best way to pave a street, and politicians are bad because their incessant machinations interfere with otherwise preordained neutral technical solutions. But this simplistic distinction ignores the tendency of organizations to resist analytic activities.

Thus, many line organizations become clogged with the "facts" they produce because of an inability to distinguish relevance from irrelevance. For instance, poverty is a "fact" for between 21.5 million and 30.4 million Americans. But despite development of the "poverty line" measure as a baseline, the core fact of poverty is still susceptible to extreme partisan interpretation, depending on whether one includes "in-kind" or "noncash" benefits of other programs such as food stamps and housing assistance along with cash programs like welfare (Camper, 1986).

This suggests that the facts do not simply present themselves in orderly fashion for the policy analyst. The question is: How one can design institutional incentives to encourage policy analysis where that analysis may run counter to the official line and threaten existing power relationships? Such a policy science must contain principles of economics, political science variables, and applied public management insights. Regardless of the institutional constraints to policy analysis—such as browbeating and intellectually smug, and often arrogantly indolent leadership, the available tools are rather straightforward and need to be mastered by student and practitioner alike.

BUDGETING AND PUBLIC POLICY

From what has been said it would seem that the quest for appropriate policy analysis is a function of separation of technical information from politics. Much debate still focuses on what we now know to be a false dichotomy. Where judgmental discretion exists, politics intrudes because support is required for one's viewpoint, technical or not. Discretion exists on practically any technical question—from the location of a road, how to pave it, how much it will cost, and who will benefit from it. For example, the National Railroad Passenger Corporation (Amtrak) allocates revenues and ridership across its routes on a train-by-train basis, an apparently neutral technical rule. But the allocations are "strongly influenced by analytical assumptions" (Congressional Budget Office, 1982, p. 43). For instance, how should one allocate "split-trip" passengers or those who travel on more than one route? A passenger traveling on the

"Pioneer" from Denver to Seattle also travels one-third of the way along the "Zephyr" route from Chicago to Oakland. Before April 1981, these routes were treated as separate operations with identifiable costs, revenues, and mileage. Currently, revenues associated with the Zephyr portion are attributed to the Pioneer, but only a portion of Zephyr operating costs are allocated to the Pioneer. The Pioneer's financial performance is thereby enhanced as measured by "passenger mile/train mile" and Zephyr performance is downgraded (Congressional Budget Office, 1982, p. 44). Why? Technically, the allocation can be explained by the addition of through-car service from Chicago to Seattle in April 1981. Politically, it may be explained by the rise of Bob Packwood (R-Oregon) to the chair of the Senate Commerce, Science, and Transportation Committee. The higher rate of passenger miles/train mile for the Pioneer saves the route through Packwood's home state from discontinuance (Guess, 1984, p. 388).

Similar policy problems arise through the technical act of setting prices in the hospital sector. Hospitals have discretion in determining how the prices of their services relate to the costs of production and how costs are allocated among different types of output. Resulting cost-price relationships may reflect goals ranging from the subsidization of medical care for low-income people to maximizing the income of physicians associated with the hospital. Policy analysts attempt to determine both the impact and the appropriateness of these strategies.

The budget process is both a technical and political constraint to policy discretion. Policy analysis is often considered apart from fiscal and budgetary issues as if it were simply a matter of producing the most rational input-output analysis. In the United States, public policy-making and implementation are hard to distinguish from the process of formulating, executing, and evaluating public budgets. In short, to say that personal and institutional politics intrude on analytic objectivity does not take one very far down the road to understanding.

To understand the specific role of budgetary politics in the overall relationship between policy analysis and the budget process can provide an important backdrop for making recommendations to clients. The agency analyst, of course, is constantly aware that program proposals depend almost as much on budgetary calendar timing and revenue availability as the inherent worth and justification of the proposal itself. As if by instinct, consultants and contractors recognize that indirectly the budget cycle affects their work. For example, funds to pay for development of a revenue projection model (see Chapter 3) depend in part on the accuracy of previous projections. If sales tax revenues were actually much lower than projected, funds may not exist for such items as consultants to build more models!

It may also aid comprehension to say that the budget process is ongoing while policy-making is periodic. This might seem counter-intuitive as the budget is only prepared once a year and policies are always on the drawing board. However, most nontrivial policies require public expenditures. Because the bulk of agency policy analysis is farmed out to consultants, funding support depends upon appropriations, supplemental appropriations, continuing appropriations resolutions, borrowing, and contract authority. Though agencies have authority to shift funds among expenditure categories below a congressionally specified amount, for larger shifts congressional approval must be supplied. The budget process thus drives and constrains policy analysis. The good news is that analysts know the deadlines and the actors involved, meaning that in the appropriations process the tough decisions get made. The bad news is that tough decisions are not always wise ones.

For instance, with increasing evidence that the federal student-aid program is being abused ($1.2 billion was spent by the Department of Education in fiscal year 1986 to pay off defaulted student loans), Doyle and Hartle (1986, p. 31) suggest that "the reauthorization process represents the best chance in this decade for prudent reform." But pressures for budget cutting under 1985 Gramm-Rudman-Hollings legislation in the face of powerful beneficiary pressure for the status quo (banks, student groups, research universities) means that an impersonal, across-the-board mechanism is likely to discourage careful analysis that would sensibly cut costs and address system problems. The budget process drives student-aid policy, like most others, and this inhibits analysis. Many observers, such as Barry Goldwater (1986), have noted that the present budget process excludes analysis. Because of the pressures of time, caused largely by the domination of federal budgeting by the formulation stage (first and second resolutions often take up two-thirds of the year), proper debate time is crowded out from the subsequent authorizations and appropriations stages.

Not one of the 13 appropriations bills was passed by Congress in the 1987 fiscal year session, and Congress has not passed all 13 appropriations bills on time since passage of the 1974 Congressional Budget and Impoundment and Control Act, which added the additional formulation stage to the budget process. The usual result has been a "continuing resolution" passed under great pressure for adjournment. Goldwater (1986) suggests that this is a poor substitute for policy-making: "Because debate is sharply curtailed on these resolutions...hundreds of issues are allowed to pass that would never survive in a vigorously debated appropriations bill." On the other hand, can it be demonstrated that availability of more time would stimulate the intense analysis needed? While some have argued that a two-year budget cycle (biennial) would enhance policy-making and reduce the federal budget deficit, it cannot be demonstrated that biennial systems are superior in either policy effectiveness or maintaining cash-flow balances.

SEQUENTIAL POLICY-MAKING

Despite differences in policy and budgetary cycles, most organizational policy analysis follows a similar sequence of steps: (1) diagnosis, (2) analysis, (3) implementation, and (4) evaluation. This book concentrates on diagnosis and analysis. In the *diagnostic* phase, one might isolate proximate and remote causes, state objectives clearly, and specify target groups. For instance, in Chapter 2 we use the case of cocaine abuse in an attempt to define the "messy" or inter-dependent policy problem where resources are already committed, consensus on their effectiveness is lacking, and time is short.

Additionally, the diagnostic phase requires projection of present data trends into the future so that policy alternatives can be structured with confidence. In Chapter 3 we examine how a rapid-transit agency that depends on sales tax revenues for much of its operating expenses attempts to project sales tax revenues for five years to stabilize fiscal planning. This is an extremely important area of policy analysis in that recent economic uncertainties have played havoc with technical projections. Thus, more successful policy analysts have been able to combine technique with judgment creatively to satisfy clients.

In the second or *analytic* phase, policy analysts must employ techniques to measure and compare programmatic costs and benefits. To develop realistic tradeoffs, it is essential that decision-makers understand not only the measurement of costs and benefits but also the principles of political economy on which they are calculated. In Chapter 4 we employ economic analysis to examine the issues involved with pricing hospital services. The topic of costs and prices is often erroneously viewed as the exclusive purview of accountants and of the private sector. Here we examine the question of how hospital pricing affects overall health care policy goals such as providing services to indigents while controlling the rising costs of health and hospital care.

Health care objectives are often set in advance by governmental regulators as part of an effort to establish minimal quality standards. In Chapter 5 we examine the issue of determining effective policy alternatives to attain a given objective, in this case hospital accreditation based on measures of their output or services provided. This technique, in which the costs of producing different levels of output are compared, is known as cost-effectiveness analysis (Lynch, 1985, p. 157). Finally, in Chapter 6 the strengths and weaknesses of the policy analyst's favorite (though often misused) tool, benefit-cost analysis, are examined through an application to the case of the 55 MPH speed limit.

Policy analysis is a sequence of logical steps in which messy data and conflicting information are used to structure alternatives to provide a semblance of rational choice. As noted, in this book we restrict ourselves to problem definition and trend forecasting in the diagnostic phase, and pricing, cost-effectiveness, and benefit-cost analysis in the analytic phase. It is our view that the analyst who masters these techniques through case application will be capable of anticipating problems and resolving them during the implementation and evaluation phases.

REFERENCES

Camper, Diane. (1986, October 24). Redefining poverty. *The New York Times*, p. 4.

Congressional Budget Office. (1982) *Federal subsidies for rail passenger service:*

An assessment of Amtrak. Washington, DC: U.S. Government Printing Office.

Doyle, Denis P., & Hartle, Terry W. (1986, February). Student-aid muddle. *The Atlantic Monthly*, pp. 30–34.

Dunn, Wiliam A. (1981). *Public policy analysis: An introduction*. Englewood Cliffs, NJ: Prentice-Hall.

Goldwater, Barry. (1986, October 19) Why Congress needs a kick in the budget. *The Atlanta Constitution*, p. 20A.

Guess, George M. (1984, September/October) Profitability guardians and service advocates: The evolution of Amtrak training. *Public Administration Review*, *44*(5), 384–393.

Lynch, Thomas D. (1985). *Public budgeting in America* (2nd ed.). Englewood Cliffs, NJ: Prentice-Hall.

CHAPTER 2

Problem Identification and Definition

INTRODUCTION

Let us preface the case study presented in this chapter with a more general notion of a "policy problem" and examine how it can be defined. Following the case reading, we can then more comprehensively view the "facts" through the lenses of several techniques of problem definition. These techniques, which are largely applicable to the case study presented here, will also be of use in defining other "messy" or multidimensional and interdependent problems, such as "acid rain" and the Space Shuttle *Challenger* disaster.

THE CONCEPT OF A POLICY PROBLEM

For decision-makers, what should an appropriate definition of a policy problem contain? To answer this, we need first to recognize three general features of a "problem." First, policy problems represent "unrealized values, needs or opportunities, which, however identified, may be attained through public action" (Dunn, 1981, p. 98). To produce information on the nature and solution of a problem, one must apply the "policy-analytic procedure of problem structuring," which Dunn (1981) calls the "most important but least understood aspect of policy analysis" (p. 98). Second, policy structuring cannot be a universal hard-and-fast procedure because of problem complexity and variability. Most real policy problems are "messes" or "systems of external conditions that produce dissatisfaction among different segments of the community" (Dunn, 1981, p. 99). What we are after is an "actionable" statement of issue dynamics from which expenditures can be made, personnel deployed, and procedures developed that will reduce or eliminate the undesirable state of affairs without undue harmful consequences to related activities.

"Messes," such as health care, urban mass transportation, and poverty, are difficult to resolve by using an analytic method and more often require a "holistic" approach that views problems as inseparable and unmeasurable apart from the larger system of which they are interlocking parts (Dunn, 1981, p. 99). Put another way, policy problems are not conceptual constructs like atoms or cells or parts per million of sulfur dioxide in the air. They are "problematic situations" that are the product of thought acting on the environment. They are artificial in the sense that someone subjectively judges these conditions to be problematic. Their inherent artificiality makes it easier for policy-makers to misconstrue the real problem. Separating policy problems into smaller and more manageable ones runs the risk of providing the right solution to the wrong problem. For example, the current problem of what government should do (if anything) about declining U.S. international competitiveness is frequently boiled down to one of foreign access to U.S. technology. But Reich (1987, p. 63) argues that this misconstrues the real problem: "The underlying predicament is not that the Japanese are exploiting our discoveries but that we can't turn basic inventions into new products as fast or as well as they can." Defining the problem in this way precludes the policy alternative of holding back basic inventions from foreigners and points toward solutions that give American workers and engineers experience in quickly turning basic inventions into products.

Finally, problem definition is confounded by the reality that the same information can be interpreted differently. Suppose that the number of complaints in your community about dogs roaming free has been rising annually at an increasing rate. Suppose also that the number of impoundments has been increasing at a declining rate. Based on this limited information, what is the "animal control problem"? In contrast with the "regulatory" definition, which focuses on licensing, leashes, fines, and animal contraception (that is, owner-controlled solutions), the "capital investment" definition focuses on the need for a larger and more accessible dog pound. But critics of the capital investment approach argue that a new pound would not necessarily eliminate strays (the real objective) and would merely shift the costs to the non–dog-owning public for services required by dog owners. Hence, from this perspective a more appropriate solution would be to require some combination of say, steeper fines, higher service charges or license fees, and animal contraception (a regulatory package) (Lehan, 1984, pp. 66, 67). Because policy alternatives must ultimately be traded in institutionalized settings (usually committees), "politics" will affect both initiation of the regulatory solution and its priority in relation to the capital investment (pound) solution. In general, the stakeholder with the greatest number of political resources (technical sophistication, rewards–punishment, charisma, and intense supporters) will have the most influence on problem definition and ultimate selection of alternatives.

STRUCTURING A POLICY PROBLEM

As already noted, selection of the appropriate technique for problem definition depends on a preliminary assessment of data trends, causation among variables, and relevant stakeholder positions. New information that can change our assumptions about these subjects will probably emerge during the process of problem structuring. In this event, the definition will change but the techniques for definition will not.

Of initial importance to defining a policy problem is how likely, based on the information we have, the problem can be structured for action by policy institutions. Dunn (1981, pp. 103, 104) suggests that policy problems fall into three classes: (1) well-structured, (2) moderately structured, and (3) ill-structured problems, based on their degree of complexity and interdependence. Brewer and deLeon (1983, p. 51) also recognize that a problem may remain complex because, once defined by the analyst, it is subject to competing individual, organizational, and external environmental (client) preferences.

Well-structured problems are "those which involve one or a few decision-makers and a small set of policy alternatives" (Dunn, 1981, p. 104). Low-level agency operational problems, such as the optimum point of replacing agency vehicles given age, repair, and depreciation costs, are well-structured because all consequences of all policy alternatives can be programmed in advance. *Moderately structured* problems are "those involving one or a few decision-makers and a relatively limited number of alternatives" (Dunn, 1981, p. 104). Unlike the well-structured problem, here the outcomes are not calculable within acceptable margins of error or risk. For example, the problem for the United States in its anti-cocaine war in Bolivia could be defined reasonably well as: (1) the political power of the "Coca Nostra" (the barons who supervise production of 40 percent of all cocaine in the world market and give Bolivia $600 million annually in repatriated earnings; (2) excessive cocaine supplies caused by large acreage in production in response to U.S. demand; and (3) interagency rivalry among U.S. Agency for International Development (USAID), Drug Enforcement Agency (DEA), FBI, CIA, United States Information Agency (USIA), State Department, and Bolivian governmental agencies involved in the war on drugs. According to Kline (1987, p. 27), the United States has placed its highest priority on crop control instead of going after the "handful of men, and their organizations who have such a stranglehold on the social and economic life of the nation." The problem, nevertheless, is capable of being structured, and solutions can clearly be evaluated according to that definition.

The more typical and potentially dangerous situation concerns *ill-structured* problems, or those involving "many different decision-makers whose utilities (values) are either unknown or impossible to rank in a consistent fashion" (Dunn, 1981, p. 105). Moreover, "Many of the most important policy problems are ill-structured. One of the lessons of political science, public administration, and other disciplines is that well-structured and moderately structured problems are rarely present in complex governmental settings. . . . One of the main tasks of policy analysis, therefore, is the resolution of ill-structured problems" (Dunn, 1981, p. 105).

For example, the Anti-Drug Abuse Act of 1986 (Ronald Reagan's new drug policy) attempts to define and resolve an ill-structured problem. First, there are few agreed-upon societal values, only those of conflicting individuals and groups. All would like to see drug use reduced (except suppliers), but consensus largely ends there. The bulk of the proposed $1.7 billion cost of the plan (65% or $1.04 billion) will go to drug enforcement whereas only $441 million (27.5%) will go for educational and drug-treatment activities (Brinkley, 1986b). The resultant allocation of funds suggests differences in both perspective and power resources among actors involved in drug policy. Second, policymakers tend to maximize their own values and are not motivated to act on the basis of societal preferences. The prospect of substantial enforcement money quickly turned the chance for coordinated policy into a gold rush and predictable turf battle between the Customs Service and the Coast Guard, both of which wanted new radar planes (Brinkley, 1986b).

Third, commitment of resources to existing policies and programs prevents policymakers from considering new alternatives. This is partly a fixed-cost budget problem exacerbated by an incremental budget process that provides little incentive for analysis. More powerful stakeholders in the annual budget process are able to lock in expenditure preferences with legal authority (called permanent appropriations or entitlements). This pattern, which occurs in federal, state, and local government policy processes, removes the bulk of items from policymaker discretion. In this fashion, as noted in Chapter 1, the politics of the budget process determines public policy.

There is also the problem of making choices on the basis of perceived constituent demands in the context of budget deadlines, which serves to drive out policy analysis. For instance, there is the paradox that enforcement of marijuana laws may be driving people to use cocaine and more harmful drugs. Suppliers prefer cocaine because it is easier to conceal and transport. Cocaine prices are also much higher than marijuana prices, and marijuana is bulky and harder to transport. But drug enforcers prefer going after marijuana because its bulk looks impressive before the television cameras, and seizure of a few tons increases productivity measures at lower risk than for cocaine. Thus, according to law enforcement experts, enforcement of marijuana laws contributes to higher marijuana prices and lower supplies, and this drives addicts to harder drugs (Lindsey, 1986). In this context, the 1986 recommendation of the Georgia attorney general to make possession of marijuana a felony instead of a misdemeanor (Hopkins, 1986) must be viewed as either selection of an inappropriate solution from valid and reliable data, or misguided posturing before constituents of "get tough on criminals" in general. Based on available evidence, such a law will increase the incidence of hard-drug users and make enforcement even more difficult.

These institutional features, together with the inability of policymakers to collect enough information on all possible alternatives or predict the range of consequences associated with each alternative, render the ill-structured problem largely immune from conventional definition techniques. We are faced with a difficult choice of both methods and facts to maintain our credibility as policy analysts. The wrong method or model can select the wrong facts and give us the right solution to the wrong problem (e.g., the crop eradication or "technical fix" model as a solution to the problem of cultivating cocaine in Bolivia when definition of the problem must include the dimensions of local elite power and high U.S. demand for cocaine). Despite these obstacles, let us turn to a "best available" methodology for defining the ill-structured problem.

TOWARD A TECHNIQUE FOR ILL-STRUCTURED PROBLEM DEFINITION

We are now ready to talk in greater detail about methods of gathering data to define policy problems. If public policy is really a hypothesis (Wildavsky, 1984, p. 182) waiting to be tested by programmatic expenditures clashing with the complexity of the real world, the problem(s) on which policy is based must also be considered hypotheses based on preliminary kinds of data. As the policy is implemented, the problem hypothesis is tested against data used to actually define it. In many cases, the data may prove inadequate and require a reformulation of the problem and new policy if improved results are required.

For problem definition, data gathering contains both a technical and a political dimension. Initially, data trends must be examined to determine if a problem exists. But data can become quickly politicized if analysts lack the vigilance to articulate their assumptions carefully. For instance, after more than 50 years of study and policy changes, water-fluoridation experts continue to battle it out by conducting studies with generally conflicting results. As a "messy" problem, consensus is absent both on the facts and on the relationship among key variables (Shell, 1986, p. 28). When fluoridation of the water began in the 1940s, technical data on the relation between tooth decay, fluorosis, and osteosclerosis were overwhelmed with the political interpretations by anti-communist stakeholders who believed a plot existed to take over the United States via introduction of foreign matter in our water supply.

What we need, then, is accurate, decision-applicable information that can be used for the development of public policy. Use of data that leads to a policy of crop eradication to eliminate a $600 million a year drug operation simply ignores other information, such as the U.S. demand for cocaine as a controlling variable, and the demands of competing stakeholders, such as the powerful Coca Nostra. By using such information to set artificially high and unattainable antidrug policy goals for a narrow technical definition of the problem, the United States provides probably correct solutions for only a well-structured component of the messy problem at hand.

Therefore, research must be rapid-fire, accurate, and produce useful information, not knowledge for its own sake. "As decision-related research, the problem definition must be sufficiently broad to identify the controlling variables, establish objectives, and specify performance criteria" (Lehan, 1984, p. 74). This text offers a three-step method to gather the appropriate data, classify them, and define the problem. As one might expect, even for the ill-structured problem any methodology (regardless of how much creativity or experience is combined) is going to be partly a mixture of rationality and hunchlike insights. Hence, policy-problem definition will require: (1) classification of data, (2) isolation of controlling variable(s), and (3) analysis of assumptions of competing stakeholders. When this is properly done, we should then be able to narrow the range of problem definitions.

Classification of Data

First, data should be classified according to the principles found in most statistics textbooks. Before data can be aggregated into information for decision making, it must be divided into relevant, mutually exclusive, independent, and exhaustive categories. Assuming scarce resources and a professional need to avoid waste and stimulate productivity (President Reagan signed Executive Order 12552 in February 1986 requiring that all federal agencies seek to improve the efficiency of service delivery at set levels of quality and timeliness), we need data that pertain to development of a target group and avoid cross-divisions. As will be indicated below, data on problem causation is often defined by the politics of stakeholder conflict. The policy analyst may skillfully use this fact of life to generate data on all sides of an issue as part of the winnowing process to define the problem.

For example, although single-room occupancy hotels or SROs are a "vital resource" for housing the New York City homeless, the real estate industry "portrays all SROs as inhumane and inadequate" and seeks to replace them with office buildings and luxury residential towers (Hayes, 1986). The factual issue is important here because "More than 100,000 low-rent SRO apartments have disappeared since 1971. The social fallout can be measured in the one-third of the homeless individuals in city shelters who list an SRO as their last address" (Hayes, 1986). The policy analyst would need to begin separating fact from fancy, for example, by gathering data on the percentage of SROs that could be defined (by an appropriate measure) as salvageable through maintenance and rebuilding as distinguished from those that really are "inadequate."

The question is whether we can find patterns of data that suggest public institutions (or public economic incentives for private firms to act) can feasibly act on an ill-structured problem to produce any improvement in the target groups. In most cases, data will be conflicting. For example, 1986 data on cocaine use can be classified by age group reported over a 9-year period. Based on use by ages 12–17, 18–25, and 26+, it can be demonstrated that cocaine use was higher in the middle group in 1976 (7.0% as opposed to 2.3% and 0.6% in the other groups) and also in 1985 (16.4% as opposed to 4.4% and 4.2%, respectively). Although usage is growing rapidly in all age groups, it has attained its highest mark in the middle group (Brinkley, 1986a).

Hence, data could support this as a target group. Additionally, data could be classified by ethnic group/race. Although the 18–25 high-consumption crowd is mostly white, among minorities cocaine is used most by Hispanics and least by blacks. If cocaine use is the target, then additional classification supports targeting the white 18–25 age group. Given the enforcement problems with such a strategy, it is not surprising that some enforcers would follow the path of least resistance in their regions—targeting blacks (forced by price usually to use marijuana) or Hispanics (to get at both "foreigners" and cocaine users). In the Lieber case (1986) below, it is apparent that the technical qualities of data were mixed with the budgetary demands of stakeholders for control of the ultimate policy. Decisions on anticocaine policy have been made less on the basis of hard data than in response to the shrill cry of election-year rhetoric.

TABLE 2.1. **PERCENTAGE OF PEOPLE WITHIN EACH AGE GROUP WHO REPORTED USING COCAINE WITHIN THE PREVIOUS YEAR**

	1976	*1979*	*1982*	*1985*
Age 12–17	2.3	4.2	4.1	4.4
Age 18–25	7.0	19.6	18.8	16.4
Age 26 and up	0.6	2.0	3.8	4.2

Source: National Institute of Drug Abuse. Copyright © 1986 by The New York Times Company. Reprinted by permission.

On the other hand, the data presented in Table 2.1 also indicates that cocaine use peaked around 1979 for the 18–25 age group and is growing only slightly in the other two age groups. Additional data indicate that 5.8 million people reported using cocaine at least monthly (as opposed to 18.2 million for marijuana and 113.1 million for alcohol), which represents a 38 percent increase in three years. Also, 12.2 million people reported using cocaine at least once a year, which is a "modest increase" that "contradicts the Government's tentative opinion of the last three years that cocaine use has remained stable" (Brinkley, 1986a). Thus, the data could support policies based on the conclusions that cocaine use has both leveled off and modestly increased!

But according to Kerr (1986b), much of the political excitement can be attributed to coincidence of congressional elections with the recent national realization of the "seriousness of its cocaine habit." This would suggest that, instead of a public policy issue, cocaine became an election or cyclical issue. Such problems are difficult to influence by public expenditures because they are largely matters of public perception strongly influenced by the media. This interpretation is voiced by Kerr (1986b), who suggests that "Politicians...had grabbed onto the drug issue before the elections because it was popular and easy to explain and there was no substantial pro-drug opposition." "America has gone on another of the goofy benders that so often pass for public policy debate, wrote *The New Republic* in its October 6 [1986] issue." "We are not saying that drugs aren't a problem, only that they should be addressed with some sense of logic and proportion" (Kerr, 1986b). The three-step process presented here is designed to inhibit quick-fix technical solutions (such as over-reliance on the supply-side drug policy discussed by Lieber [1986] and its Bolivian analogue of crop eradication noted in Kline [1987]) and focus holistically on the "actionable" components of ill-structured problems.

As noted, data classification and analysis can provide at least a preliminary indication that a policy problem exists. The use of statistical analysis to point toward structuring policy alternatives will be examined in Chapter 3. Here it should be noted that if differences in data can be explained, they can point to alternative problem definitions on which policy options can be based. This is especially true if data are converted from raw figures to performance data through construction of ratios (patient cures/visit; pounds of drugs seized/ attempted seizures) and other measures (e.g., changes in the street price of cocaine).

For example, the Joint Commission on Accreditation of Hospitals recently announced a fundamental shift in the way hospitals are evaluated. Whereas in the past hospital accreditation was based largely on "structure, paper work, minutes of staff and other boilerplate stuff" (Brinkley, 1986c), the agency will now examine whether hospitals actually provide care—not simply whether they have the capacity to provide such care. The policy shift was made largely because of recent improvements in statistical methodology that permit measurement of mortality and complication rates or "treatment outcomes" adjusted for the unique features of individual hospitals' patients (Brinkley, 1986c). While both the American Medical Association and the American Hospital Association supported the policy shift, the health care industry (a powerful stakeholder) strenuously objected to the new policy. This will be discussed further in Chapter 5.

It should be recalled that problem definition can be confounded by differing interpretations of the same data. Classification of data, even with the latest methodology, can inhibit problem-solving by precluding options. For example, the issue of the U.S. international competitiveness policy is often defined as one of lower productivity in producing information such as blueprints of new inventions. But according to Reich, access to this kind of information may inhibit learning. It can solve an immediate technological problem but "does not provide experience for solving the next one. It supplies answers but it does not teach.... As anyone knows who has tried to solve a puzzle with the answer book open, or tried to learn directions from here to there as a passenger rather than a driver, the ready availability of help can substitute for direct experience and thus make it more difficult to do it yourself the next time" (Reich, 1987, p. 68).

Thus, it is important that assumptions about the classification of data be made explicit at the outset of policy analysis and that data not be used to develop policy options unless alternative explanations have been formally eliminated. For example, statistical analysis can indicate whether income is more a function of education than family socioeconomic status, and whether family size or income are greater determinants of food consumption. In approaching suspected public policy problem areas, such as declining international competitiveness and low public sector productivity, data need to be gathered according to a research design that permits elimination of alternative explanations. This is done by use of a control group or agency that is subject to the same measurement. International sales of firms producing similar products that stressed blueprint production would need to be compared to those that stressed hands-on employee experience with the process of converting blueprints to applications and products. Empirical testing would then provide the basis for rigorous problem definition and development of policy alternatives.

Similarly, to examine the proposition that centralization leads to lower productivity, one could compare worker productivity in decentralized agencies with centralized agencies that are being measured for productivity. The famous 1927 studies conducted by Elton Mayo at Western Electric's Hawthorne

Plant in Illinois found that worker productivity increased less from changes in the external environment than from the effects of the primary work group (relationships between workers and their supervisors). In gathering data for a study without a control (an agency or group that experiences the same stimuli as the measurement group), the alternative explanation can only be eliminated by assuming it away, which would almost guarantee an undefined problem (Shively, 1974, p. 87).

Dunn (1981, p. 115) distinguishes (1) "surrogate" models that assume that the formal problem is a valid representation of the substantive problem, and (2) "perspective" models that merely function as one of many possible ways to structure substantive problems. This discussion emphasizes the latter type and cautions against confusing the two. In other words, given the complexity of real world ill-structured problems, it is unlikely that one model will precisely fit the exact relationship among variables. Data assumptions should be made explicit and tested according to a research design that ensures elimination of alternative explanations.

Hence, policy analysts must be careful to avoid letting the data "classify itself" in the most rational (usually familiar) manner. As illustrated by the problem of U.S. international competitiveness and public-sector productivity, classification of data in one way without controls can in practice foreclose opportunities to classify it in other ways that would produce verified alternative explanations. The policy analyst must actively work against the tendency to let perspectives become surrogates for reality.

One functional policy "analyst" who didn't allow this to happen was Antoine de Saint-Exupery, often called the Joseph Conrad of the air. "In 1940, landing a plane in pre-Occupation France, Saint-Exupery noticed that the runway lights had disappeared, indicating an obstacle on the ground (a truck, as it turned out). Instead of pulling on the stick, a maneuver that would have lifted the plane but maybe not high or soon enough, he pushed it forward. The plane nose-dived, 'wrote a witness, its wheels hitting the ground hard, and it rebounded over the obstacle, while the pilot revved the engine to gain altitude and circle the field once more'" (Drabelle, 1986, p. 177). Had Saint-Exupery followed the book, his plane would have hit the truck; using an alternative explanation of reality based on experience, he structured the problem differently, implicitly weighting data on "bounce" more profoundly than data on lift-off capacity. This produced the bizarre maneuver that saved his life. Public policy analysts can also help save the public interest by imaginative data-gathering efforts that combine depth of experience with methodological rigor.

Isolation of Controlling Variables

The second step for defining ill-structured problems is to seek the controlling variables or problem causation. In order to define a policy problem one must know its causes (or at least its correlates). Any public expenditure must be based on some order or law that can be called a policy. Policy problems such as poverty, urban transportation, and environmental protection are usually some combination of private and individual actions and preexisting public policies.

Causation will therefore be complex, and some means of distinguishing remote from more proximate causes must be provided.

In the field of tort law, according to Prosser (1964, p. 240), "There is nothing...which has called forth more disagreement, or upon which the opinions are in such a welter of confusion" than the meaning of "proximate cause." Thus, "in a philosophical sense, the consequences of an act go forward to eternity, and the causes of an event go back to the discovery of America and beyond" (Prosser, 1964, p. 240). Because, as a practical matter, legal responsibility must be limited to those causes that are closely connected with the result, tort law developed the "substantial factor" formula. That is, "the defendant's conduct is a cause of the event if it was a material element and a substantial factor in bringing it about" (Prosser, 1964, p. 244). Using the legal analogy, a problem is "caused" by factors that are substantial factors even if other factors contributed to the result. Where other factors would have caused the event anyway, one's act or omission could not be a "substantial factor" in bringing it about. Hence, "the presence of a railroad embankment may be no cause of the inundation of the plaintiff's land by a cloudburst which would have flooded it in any case" (Prosser, 1964, p. 242).

To determine the "substantial factors" in policy causation, we need to perform an analysis of the hierarchy of causes from remote to proximate or immediate. Because social science theories are often too abstract to identify immediate causes of a problematic situation, we need a "perspective" model (Dunn 1981, p. 119) to aid us. Distinguishing "possible" from "plausible" and "actionable" causes can help. *Possible causes* are more remote events or actions that contribute to a problem—unemployment and distribution of power as causes of poverty. *Plausible causes* are possible causes that have been empirically tested and found to be an important influence (substantial factor) on the problem. Distribution of power among elites, for instance, are plausible causes of poverty—but they are not directly actionable. That is, they are not "actionable" causes subject to control or manipulation by policy makers (Dunn, 1981, p. 125). In the poverty example, unemployment is both a plausible and actionable cause. The Rogers Commission found that an actionable "contributing cause" of the Space Shuttle *Challenger* accident was the decision-making process itself. "The testimony reveals failures in communication that resulted in a decision to launch 51-L based on incomplete and sometimes misleading information, a conflict between engineering data and management judgments, and a NASA management structure that permitted internal flight safety problems to bypass key shuttle managers" (Rogers Commission, 1986, p. 82). The cause therefore may be the decision structure itself. This suggests that structural problems can also lead to "major" policy problems, such as the reexamination that the entire U.S. space policy must now face as the result of this accident.

Using guidelines similar to those suggested for classification of data (mutually exclusive and exhaustive categories; relevant target group), we need to establish plausible-actionable causes for the problem situation. The causes need to be established to reduce potential unanticipated consequences from public expenditures and embarrassment for politicians, bureaucrats, and their private consultants who often make the real recommendations. Again, the search for causes must not be limited by narrow interpretations of data based on unsound technical studies without controls. Otherwise, causation may appear remote but in fact be immediate and actionable.

For instance, the State of Georgia recently suspended the licenses of two doctors for allegedly handing out thousands of improper narcotic prescriptions. In a 10-month period in 1984, the two physicians dispensed approximately 23,000 prescriptions for mood-altering or addictive drugs in a town of fewer than 20,000 inhabitants (Baum, 1986). Because many of the patients then sold the drugs on the street, practically the entire town became addicted to these drugs. After the doctors were suspended, the users substituted cocaine for the prescription drugs, and by spring a crime wave hit the town. "There is no clear line to the [doctors]," the police chief admitted. "But in talking to the people we arrested, many said they were doing it to support a drug habit. We think the suspension of the [doctors] helps explain our month of May" (Baum, 1986).

Predicting causation under such circumstances was important. Criminal-justice policy analysts would have had to know that availability of so many prescription drugs would find many willing buyers, and that once hooked, the buyers would become angry at the loss of their source. As in the case of much policy analysis, stakeholders often know the available options. But actors in such positions often prefer having the extra time available when someone else has to tell them (consultants), after which they often practice studied inaction due to larger structural limitations (political threats) that can affect careers and personal safety.

Problem definition, in such instances, may be boiled down to asking the simple question: "What is reasonably likely to happen under the circumstances?" The search for causes of a policy problem may be hindered by absence of concepts that can be measured directly. This requires the use of indirect measures and comparative analogies. For example, defining the problem of drug abuse as one of insufficient education can benefit from direct experience with control of contagious diseases.

Because disease-education programs have been historically successful, many have recommended similar programs for drug abuse (12.5% or $200 million of the Anti-Drug Abuse Act of 1986 will be spent on education and prevention; Brinkley, 1986b). Studies have found, however, that presenting the facts about the physiology and pharmacology of drug use and its legal, social, and psychological ramifications tends to encourage students to try drugs (Kerr, 1986a). While moralizing and scare tactics may work with contagious diseases, by exaggerating the immediate danger of drug use, the teacher's credibility is destroyed, which may put children at increased risk of using drugs.

Comparison of the two types of programs suggests that an important causal difference is the "patient's" skepticism of risk given other voluntary dangers in society.

Youth have rarely been accused of collective risk aversion; hence, many young people seek such thrills for peer status. Based on such comparative analysis of causes, one could conclude that programs need either to focus on enforcement or emphasize the long-term effects of drug use on individual health that will be required later in one's career, factors such as stamina, clarity of thought, and discipline. If the student cannot reconcile these character strengths with drug use, the educational program may work. If the program works, the more harmful effects on family and society may be reduced and the "cyclical social trend" of drug abuse may pass without excessive budgetary and policy hysteria. A $1.7 billion drug-abuse program based on incomplete information is, of course, one symptom of this hysteria!

Additionally, comparative analysis of actionable causes may point in the direction of related public programs. For example, an immediate cause of homeless families in New York City is the scarcity of low-income housing. But the availability of low-income housing, in turn, is a product of other public policies—rent control, enforcement of the housing code, the workings of the housing courts, city use of city-owned housing stock, and city welfare policies—all of which affect the supply of low-income housing (Hayes, 1986). Such examples suggest clearly why problems must be defined to take into account interdependencies and expenditure tradeoffs and not simply as independently functioning parts. In public policy as elsewhere in professional life, the whole is often larger than its parts. The incentives and disincentives for cooperative actions between those institutional parts that define and execute policies must not be forgotten.

Comparing Stakeholder Assumptions

Now that we have asked appropriate questions about relevant data categories and suggested the need to find "substantial factors" that contribute to the undefined problem, we are ready to move from the more technical–rational mode of analysis to the political dimension. Here we must examine the key assumptions of conflicting stakeholders in the policy arena. Since few policy areas are "originals," the stakeholders have normally been arguing their positions for a long time and this aids us in developing data categories and information on causation. In many cases, problem definition will involve almost a simultaneous conduct of the three steps. In fact, clues as to which data are relevant and what causes a problem can best be gleaned from the stakeholders who both support and stand to lose from a particular formulation of the problem.

The notion of harnessing stakeholder mutual fault-finding is an effective, time-tested method to gain policy data and information. It was used, for example, by investigators of aerospace accidents as a successful example of pluralist policy-making. The 1986 Rogers Commission investigation of the *Challenger* accident was considered by many a model of success precisely because it gained data and insight by playing neutral referee to the mutual fault-finding process waged among Morton Thiokol, Rockwell, NASA, and the media, then moving in closer to isolate the management, policy, and technical causes of the accident. As in any policy issue, each actor occupied a self-interest maximization role and stood to lose in the resource allocation game (the losers in the game usually have reduced public and private resources) against other competitors. While Cook (1986) argues that the Rogers Commission became nonadversarial in covering up the longstanding and widespread knowledge by NASA staff of the O-ring problem, the process of letting adversaries chew on each other eventually ferreted out the proximate and immediate causes of the problem. Unfortunately, policymakers have not been able to pick up the pieces and move from the detailed components of this ill-structured problem (O-rings, dependence on the shuttle, NASA organization, and contractor relations) gleaned from the adversarial process to selection of a new alternative for U.S. space policy. This is partly an analytic problem and partly a structural one (the need for annual reauthorizations and appropriations means that NASA is driven by the budget process, and this tends to drive out analysis).

In many cases, a policy problem can be more accurately defined where analysts are aware of the history of conflict among actors. What this suggests is that stakeholder analysis must take into account both the technical conflict, or battle over palpably objective data, and the reality of power imbalance among actors of different positions. Failure to do so can result in an improperly defined problem. Or it can lead to unanticipated consequences during implementation where actors exercise their political muscle (often unintentionally) to derail any chance for a reasonable solution.

For example, advocates of an enlarged definition of homelessness and an inalienable right to shelter finally achieved an "open door" policy that clogged the shelters (Main, 1986). Similarly, the real estate industry pushed for replacing SRO apartments in New York City with office buildings, which reduced available low-income housing (Hayes, 1986). As noted, the poverty problem is also a good example of stakeholder impediments to effective policy since all levels of government have grappled with it for such a long time. Varying stakeholders (who stand to gain budgetary resources, status, and power) express the views that poverty is the result of class structure, imperfections in the poor themselves, and improper delivery of poverty funds (i.e., bureaucrats take the lion's share of them and often use their discretion to allocate the rest for personal gain).

For appropriate analysis of assumptions, analysts need to: (1) take stock of the major assumptions and counterassumptions surrounding an issue, and (2) create the environment for constructive conflict by developing a list of assumptions acceptable to most of the stakeholders that permits later synthesis. In an era of declining fiscal resources for nondefense public policy projects, this is difficult to accomplish. Even if funding is virtually assured, stakeholder consensus is hard to obtain. For example, in the construction of the $1 billion Dade County Metrorail project, one might expect lots of consensus on acquisition and use of funds for rather clearly defined purposes. But, on closer inspection, contractors, subcontractors, the U.S. Urban Mass Transportation Administration (UMTA), and the Dade County Transportation Administration disagreed on most of the details of when and how to do the job, as well as who would inspect the work. The relevant stakeholders distrusted each other in a context that required sequenced cooperation for the project to be completed within budget and on time (Guess, 1985). Stakeholder analysis prior to disbursement of any funds for this project could have avoided most of the construction difficulty. Largely as the result of this "functional" policy failure, UMTA revised its own oversight policies from case-by-case examination, and random performance audits with in-house staff, to one of using private contractors outside the project to execute a performance audit of the inproject contractors.

In summary, the problem-definition process is one of harnessing competing sources of information on causation and target groups to provide appropriate data categories in order to attain consensus on data, assumptions, and solutions. Given the reality of group conflict in American politics, stakeholders can provide a ready source of this information. Proper management of the policy-analysis process can reduce unanticipated consequences later in problem formulation and policy implementation.

As you read the first case study that follows ("Coping With Cocaine," by James Lieber), bear in mind what has been said about defining policy problems. See if you can define the policy problem here (whole and parts) that can satisfy most stakeholders (parents, enforcement officials, and politicians). Each stakeholder stands to gain at the expense of other actors if the problem is defined in its favor. As noted, defining the drug problem as one of enforcement and interdiction tends to eliminate less dangerous drugs such as marijuana, which exacerbates both the enforcement and education problem (because stronger drugs intensify addiction and increase immunity from attitudinal change influences). Conversely, in a world of scarce budget resources, education may benefit from an educational definition. But this can also exacerbate enforcement problems by increasing curiosity. In short, problem definition must recognize both the analytic and political interdependencies of real-world policy problems.

Following the case study, we will help you think through the process of defining a policy problem based on what we learned from this case. (Analysis of the case study begins on page 34.)

Case Study No. 1
Coping with Cocaine

(1986, James Lieber, as originally published in the January, 1986 issue of
THE ATLANTIC MONTHLY)

Every day 5,000 Americans try cocaine for the first time—a total of 22 million so far—according to estimates by the National Institute on Drug Abuse. About five million people are believed to be using the drug at least once a month, and they are administering it to themselves in increasingly destructive ways.

The damage caused by cocaine is palpable, and much of it has been done in less than a decade. The number of people with cocaine-related problems seeking admission to federally funded drug clinics climbed by 600 percent from 1976 to 1981—the most recent period for which such a figure is available. The surge in admissions to private clinics has undoubtedly been at least as great. For example, the Benjamin Rush Center, a private psychiatric hospital in Syracuse, New York, seldom admitted cocaine abusers during the 1970s; today 40 percent of the hospital's beds are set aside for them.

There are four ways to make cocaine less available to confirmed and potential users. We can "go to the source" and try to inhibit the cultivation of coca in foreign lands. We can try to prevent the importation of the drug—"interdiction." Once it is on our shores, we can try to disrupt or destroy the dealing and money-laundering operations that make the trade profitable. And, finally, we can punish those who use cocaine, do what we can to break their habits, and try to persuade everyone else not to use it in the first place.

The Reagan Administration, early in the President's first term of office, proclaimed a war on drug trafficking, and from the outset the war has been waged primarily at the nation's borders. It has been a war, in other words, largely of interdiction. The war effort has been substantial. In 1981 the Administration endorsed successful amendments to the Posse Comitatus Act (passed as a sop to the South after the Civil War), which prohibits soldiers from policing civilians. Military personnel and equipment may now be deployed in the fight against drugs. In the spring of 1982 the Reagan Administration launched the South Florida Task Force, under the authority of Vice-President George Bush, to coordinate the activities of nine federal crime-fighting agencies. (They are the United States Attorney's Office, the Drug Enforcement Administration [DEA], the Federal Bureau of Investigation, the Customs Service, the Bureau of Alcohol, Tobacco, and Firearms, the Internal Revenue Service, the Coast Guard, the Border Patrol, and the United States Marshals.) Hundreds of federal agents poured into Miami and its environs, long known to have been the entry point of choice for illegal narcotics. Local police went into high gear.

At least on the surface Washington's efforts appear to have paid a big dividend. In November of 1982, scarcely six months after the task force got under way, Ronald Reagan came to south Florida. Speaking amid tons of seized marijuana, kilos of captured cocaine, and a small armory of impounded Uzi and Mac-10 machine guns, the President proclaimed the South Florida Task Force a "brilliant example of working federalism." During the first year of task-force activity the United States Attorney's Office in south Florida prosecuted some 664 drug-related cases—64 percent more than in the preceding year. The task force confiscated $19 million in cash and property from drug offenders—half again what had been confiscated in south Florida the year before—and interdicted enormous quantities of drugs. The quantities have increased in the years since.

From the first, the south Florida effort has been a source a pride to the Administration. But the statistics, which in themselves may seem impressive, in context tell a depressing story. For one thing, experts are convinced that the warehouses of captured contraband represent only a small fraction of the drugs being smuggled into the country. For another, the flow of imported drugs has been shifting, with cocaine occupying an increasingly important place. In 1983 government agents in south Florida seized some six tons of cocaine and 850 tons of marijuana (which tends to come in by the boatload). In 1985 the figures were twenty-five and 750 tons respectively. In other words, seizures of cocaine, a potentially lethal drug, have quadrupled while seizures of marijuana, a substance that looks benign in comparison, have fallen off. It is generally believed that the amounts of drugs seized reflect the amounts coming in. Thus, almost certainly, more cocaine is being imported now than ever before. More is also probably being consumed. The DEA has estimated that in 1981 before the South Florida Task Force existed Americans used between thirty-six and sixty-six tons of cocaine. For 1984 it increased its estimate to between sixty-one and eighty-four tons. Cocaine's price history also suggests that the supply is growing. When the task force began, dealers in Florida were paying roughly $60,000 for a kilogram of cocaine. Today they pay some 40 percent less.

Why the sudden abundance of cocaine? The government's strategy in the war on drugs may be partly to blame. The heightened risk of interdiction has prompted smugglers to favor drugs that are compact and expensive, like cocaine, over drugs that are bulky and relatively cheap, like marijuana.

During the past half decade the availability and the use of cocaine have risen sharply. The trend is disturbing—all the more so if government policies are helping to foster it. Cocaine abuse has become a public-health problem of major proportions. And, unfortunately, doctors, lawyers, and politicians disagree profoundly as to how we should attack it.

Cocaine was isolated in the laboratory more than a hundred years ago. It is an alkaloid—a member of the chemical family that includes nicotine, caffeine, and morphine—extracted from the coca plant, which grows chiefly in Latin America. When the extract is heated with hydrochloric acid, cocaine hydrochloride is created. This salt (together with various adulterants) is the stock-in-trade of most dealers, because, being water soluble, it can be taken in several different ways.

Cocaine has been produced in quantity since the 1920s. Yet even now the drug's activity is only partially understood. The cocaine molecule resembles the local anesthetics procaine (Novocain) and lidocaine (Xylocaine) in structure. All three consist of an amino group with a focal nitrogen atom and a six-carbon ring that facilitates solubility in fatty tissue (such as the tissue of the brain). Although cocaine is itself a local anesthetic, it is also a stimulant of the central nervous system—possibly the most potent in nature.

The "rush"—the sense of euphoric excitement—reported by users of the drug probably comes from the activation of nerve cells in the brain that release a chemical messenger, or neurotransmitter, called dopamine, which is associated with pleasure, alertness, and motor control. According to Mark Gold, a psychiatrist, who directs drug research at Fair Oaks Hospital, in Summit, New Jersey, cocaine tricks the brain into feeling as if it had been "totally supplied with food and sex." It is a compelling sensation. A survey conducted by 1-800-COCAINE (a national hotline for counseling and referral, set up by Gold) revealed that 70 percent of respondents had on occasion used cocaine continuously over a twenty-four-hour period. Large proportions preferred the drug to food (71 percent), sex (50 percent), family (72 percent), and friends (69 percent).

Paradoxically, chronic cocaine use eventually leads to dysphoria—a depressed, low-energy state characterized by flattened emotions, a lack of interest in sex, and physical immobility. New research by Gold and his colleague Charles Dackis suggests that after cocaine has saturated the nerve synapses and receptor neurons with dopamine, it chemically blocks the "re-uptake" sites of the original dopamine projector cells. As a result, the neurotransmitter, when its job is done, cannot return to the places where it is usually stored. Instead it is metabolized and then flushed out of the system. The dopamine stocks of heavy cocaine users are depleted more rapidly than they can be replenished. These users may be incapable of feeling pleasure without the drug.

The absence of a sense of pleasure can become all the more oppressive because cocaine hinders the brain's production of serotonin, the neurotransmitter that is chiefly responsible for sleep. In order to blunt the dysphoria, or even just to fall asleep, users of cocaine frequently resort to other drugs—alcohol, marijuana, sedatives, heroin. Or they may simply take more cocaine, hoping to regain the high. Many users conclude from the unwelcome symptoms of dopamine depletion that the cocaine is out of their systems—and that it is therefore safe to use more. Of course, this is not the case.

The physical and psychological consequences of heavy cocaine use are numerous and negative. High-dosage users can experience hallucinations and delusions, and eventually may lapse into a state that mimics schizophrenia. Many of them experience formication, the sensation that their skin is crawling with bugs. Impaired judgment and feelings of persecution are common. (One patient at the Benjamin Rush Center once drove the New York Thruway convinced that an enemy was hiding in his trunk. He repeatedly fired a gun into it, fortunately missing the gas tank.) Many cocaine users lose considerable weight and suffer from malnutrition.

Each means of administering cocaine entails a discrete set of risks. Inhaling the drug—"snorting"—eventually will cause nasal membranes to crack and bleed, and may destroy the cartilage that separates the nostrils. Those who inject cocaine intravenously invite deterioration of arteries in the muscles, kidneys, and heart; in addition, they become candidates for blood poisoning and (if they share their needles) hepatitis and AIDS. Smoking cocaine in its relatively pure "freebase" form may be more dangerous than any other method. Freebase is the alkaloid—the chemical *base*—constituent of street cocaine. According to Richard Rawson, a clinical-research psychologist affiliated with the University of California at Los Angeles Medical School and the director of the Matrix Center, a cocaine-abuse clinic in Beverly Hills, freebase is so concentrated when it reaches the brain that it produces "an explosion at the synapse." Freebase seems to be the most toxic form of cocaine and the most conducive to convulsions. Its production, which entails the use of a highly flammable solvent, such as ether, is also hazardous. It was while freebasing that the comedian Richard Pryor suffered near-fatal burns in 1980.

Like other local anesthetics, cocaine in toxic doses will cause convulsions; these may result in a rapid series of *grand mal* seizures and ultimately in death. Cocaine can also trigger sometimes fatal cardiac arrhythmia or respiratory paralysis. Tolerance for cocaine, like tolerance for alcohol, varies widely among individuals. The smallest lethal dose of cocaine was long held to be 1.2 grams ingested in a day, but clinicians have reported treating patients who have consumed ten times that amount and survived, and sending to the morgue others who had consumed only milligrams. Chronic users may experience "kindling," in which a small amount of cocaine triggers unexpectedly severe reactions—notably seizures or psychotic behavior. Kindling may be the result of drug-provoked alterations in the brain's physiology, such as, perhaps, the creation of new receptor sites that become fresh targets of neurotransmitters.

Cocaine is among the most "reinforcing" of drugs. In an experiment reported in the journal *Psychopharmacologia* in 1969, monkeys were allowed to self-administer intravenously a variety of chemical substances, including cocaine, caffeine, amphetamines, and nicotine. The monkeys went on binges with each of these substances, but only with cocaine did their use become so compulsive that they reached a lethal dose and died. Although there is some disagreement about whether cocaine produces psychological dependence or physical addiction, the dopamine-depletion model suggests that at least there is a physical component. And chronic users do experience withdrawal: craving, extreme irritability, fuzzy thinking, sluggishness, and heavy sleeping—symptoms lasting from days to weeks.

Richard Rawson considers cocaine to be addictive and says that the probability of getting hooked is different for different people. "If two people walk into a room with plutonium in it, only one may get cancer, because of differences in their immune systems," he says. "There is a genetic factor involved. Similarly, the propensity for cocaine addiction may involve an underlying neurophysiological vulnerability."

That vulnerability may run in families. About 80 percent of those being treated for cocaine addiction at the Benjamin Rush Center and the Matrix Center have families in which alcoholism has been a problem. Studies have long shown that children of alcoholics are far more likely than others to develop a problem with alcohol or other drugs; children of alcoholics who are raised by non-alcoholic foster parents are just as likely to become alcoholics as if they had remained with their biological parents. The evidence points persuasively to the existence of a genetic risk factor in addiction to any substance, including cocaine.

The risk to the user of becoming addicted to cocaine seems to be linked most closely with how the user administers the drug and how much of it he consumes. Smoking freebase carries the greatest risk. The least risk is posed by the method of consumption that was used exclusively for nearly 5,000 years: chewing on coca leaves. According to Ronald Siegel, a psychopharmacologist at UCLA who is a consultant to President Reagan's Commission on Organized Crime, until ways of ingesting more concentrated doses were found, "there was no cocaine problem." Siegel has studied Peruvian Indians, who chew coca for the mild stimulation it provides as well as for its appetite-suppressing effect. They do so without apparent damage to their health. A one-hundred-gram sample of coca leaves, Siegel points out, contains more than 300 calories and significant quantities of vitamins A and B_2. The Indians, who traffic in coca, know that cocaine is snorted and taken intravenously by others, and they deem these practices repulsive.

According to Siegel, cocaine did not become a health hazard until 1860, when European scientists succeeded in extracting the cocaine alkaloid from the coca leaf. The drug thus became available in a pure and puissant form and its many useful qualities were hailed by physicians. Because it works simultaneously as a pain-killer and a vasoconstrictor, cocaine became a popular anesthetic for procedures (such as eye and throat surgery) in which clearing away blood was difficult. Because it anesthetizes the body but keeps the mind sharp, doctors prescribed it for the terminally ill. Cocaine was used in cough medicines, hemorrhoid balms, nasal sprays, and wines (one of which bore the endorsements of President William McKinley, Thomas Edison, and Pope Leo XIII). And, of course, the drug was once an ingredient in Coca-Cola.

The darker side of cocaine was exposed within decades: many people became habitual users of the drug, which commonly they administered with a hypodermic needle, or of products that contained it; some experienced toxic reactions; a few died of overdoses. Cocaine represented a greater threat to society than either opium or morphine. By the 1880s some states had outlawed it for other than medicinal purposes. Interstate shipment of cocaine was prohibited by the Pure Food and Drug Act of 1906. The Harrison Narcotics Act of 1914 imposed a nationwide ban on the use of both cocaine and heroin (except, again, for medicinal purposes). International agreements in 1925 and 1931 outlawed trade in cocaine. Because the principal sources of coca at the time, including Peru and Bolivia, lacked the capacity to refine coca leaves, and because the leaves themselves were too bulky to smuggle, the prohibition was not difficult to enforce. In the 1930s amphetamines were first used clinically and quickly captured much of the underground market for stimulants. By the onset of the Second World War cocaine was no longer a menace.

Cocaine reappeared as a significant recreational drug in the late 1960s and early 1970s. It did so at least in part because of a successful crackdown by police on amphetamine laboratories and the trafficking networks sustaining them, which created a place in the market for a new stimulant. But cocaine was given a better press than amphetamines, probably because it was far more expensive and thus kept better company.

Snorting cocaine predominated over intravenous injection when the drug made its comeback. That preference helped to keep the problems associated with cocaine to a minimum. Contrary to popular belief, the nose is not a short route to the brain. After being snorted, cocaine sustains a three- or four-minute passage through the circulatory system before arriving at the receptors. It is being diluted all the while. Two other circumstances also gave users some protection against the drug's ill effects. In 1979 Robert Byck, who with Craig Van Dyke was in

the midst of a six-year study of cocaine at the Yale University School of Medicine, testified before Congresss that cocaine posed a severe threat to public health but one mitigated by the drug's "adulteration" and "exceedingly high price." While Byck spoke, an adulterated gram of cocaine could sell for $100 or more.

The conditions identified by Byck no longer obtain. In the past five years, as more and more cocaine has entered the United States and the price has dropped, purity has increased. Much of the cocaine now sold is at least twice as pure as the cocaine sold a decade ago. Meanwhile, the price of cocaine has plummeted. Today a gram can often be had for $50, making it less expensive than an ounce of marijuana. Cocaine is within reach of the suburban middle class and, increasingly, the urban poor. Indeed, users can now procure cocaine in such large amounts that the tiny coke spoon—the principal item of paraphernalia in the 1970s—is an object of nostalgia.

There is some evidence that more and more people are choosing to inject a cocaine solution directly into their bloodstreams (a fifteen-second route to the brain) or to smoke freebase (a seven-second route). One source is the reports of federally funded drug-treatment programs to the National Institute of Drug Abuse (NIDA), a division of the Department of Health and Human Services. These show that 25 percent of cocaine users admitted for treatment in 1977 were shooting up or smoking freebase, whereas 41 percent were in 1984. Another source of evidence is the 1-800-COCAINE hotline. In 1983 among 500 callers surveyed at random 39 percent were shooting up or smoking freebase. The 1985 figure is 48 percent. One might expect problem users to favor the most potent ways of taking cocaine. But these statistics are not the only indication that a change is occurring. There are also death statistics.

Alcohol contributes to as many as 200,000 deaths annually in the United States; tobacco contributes to another 350,000. There is no comparable figure on the long-term lethal effect of cocaine abuse, but some comparative data does exist on "crisis deaths." The NIDA maintains a Drug Abuse Warning Network (DAWN), which collects information on drug overdoses from emergency rooms and medical examiners in twenty-six metropolitan areas. Sketchy as the DAWN data are, they are perhaps the best indication we have of the relative dangerousness of various drugs. In 1984 cocaine (implicated in 604 deaths) was third on the list, behind heroin and morphine (1,072 deaths) and alcohol used in combination with other drugs (1,131 deaths). More alarming than the number of cocaine-related deaths is the rate at which the number may have been increasing. In the first half of this decade the number of deaths reported to DAWN in which cocaine was implicated increased by 324 percent—considerably faster than the reported number of deaths involving alcohol or other drugs.

A poll limited to southern California, which the Matrix Center conducted last year, showed that 58 percent of callers to the center chose smoking freebase over any other method. Users in California can now buy $10 chunks of freebase (thus avoiding the danger of preparing it themselves) at places called rock houses. This has helped to create a market for cocaine among the very poor. As Rawson explains, "A person may get a two-hundred-dollar welfare check and think he'll spend twenty dollars on freebase and use the rest for groceries. But he ends up going back to the rock house again and again until he uses up the whole two hundred. Once started into a freebase episode, people will use it until they drop. It generates a type of drug-seeking behavior previously unseen. It's more compelling than heroin." In California the rock houses seem to be controlled largely by street gangs. Law-enforcement officials worry that the rock-house phenomenon, like other trends in the drug culture, will move from West to East. According to Rawson, there have been un-

confirmed reports of rock houses operating in Arizona.

The problem of cocaine has attracted a substantial amount of professional attention in recent years. There have been clinical surveys. There has been laboratory research. There have been articles in law journals, learning on Capitol Hill, and commissions and task forces too numerous to cite. We know more today than we did a decade ago about cocaine specifically, about addiction generally, and about the baffling complexities of law enforcement. We know enough, perhaps, to agree that cocaine is a social ill that can be managed but one that cannot be easily cured. Enough evidence has accumulated to suggest where efforts to manage the problem are likely to go awry and where they may do some good.

The focus of the showpiece South Florida Task Force—interdiction—is extremely popular with legislators. Interdiction is "cleaner" than undercover work at home, and it is easier than trying to wean foreign economies from their dependence on sales of coca. Also, it makes use of alluring (albeit expensive) technology: radar aircraft, helicopters, and custom-built pursuit craft. Interdiction is highly visible, inspiring confidence that, yes, a war on drugs really is in progress. But Edward Jurith, staff counsel for the House Select Committee on Narcotics Abuse and Control, says, "The truth is, we're getting clobbered."

One clear consequence of interdiction has been simple diversion: smugglers alter their routes and landing spots to avoid areas that are "hot." In recent years, as security around south Florida began to tighten, much of the drug traffic shifted to the north and west. As Steven Wisotsky, a professor at the Nova Law Center, in Fort Lauderdale, puts it, "We've simply taken our garbage and dumped it in our neighbors' backyards." (The governors of Alabama, Louisiana, Mississippi, Florida, and Texas held an emergency meeting early last year to discuss the problem.)

Federal and state law-enforcement officials say that at the very least diversion disrupts established smuggling routes and distribution networks, leaving drug traffickers vulnerable. But the DEA's estimate that the quantity of cocaine finding its way into the United States has doubled since 1981 does not support that contention. Worldwide coca production is up. Brazil, Venezuela, and Ecuador have joined Peru, Colombia, and Bolivia as producers.

In order to understand interdiction's effect on the cocaine business, one should consider what has happened to the marijuana business. Before the interdiction effort, marijuana typically traveled in bales aboard slow, rusting freighters, called mother ships, or on lumbering, vintage aircraft. A ton of marijuana had the same market value as a kilogram of cocaine, but one was the size of a car, the other no bigger than a two-pound bag of sugar. Marijuana presented the easier target to law-enforcement officers. As a result, domestically grown marijuana, which had been much more expensive than imports, mainly because of higher labor costs, suddenly became competitive.

Today marijuana is probably the largest cash crop in the United States after corn; according to the National Organization for the Reform of Marijuana Laws, growing it is a $16.6 billion-a-year industry. Yet the market for marijuana seems to have remained stable. If, as this suggests, less marijuana is coming into the country, what has become of marijuana smugglers? In August of 1983 Frank Chellino, then a spokesman for the DEA and now the supervisor of DEA intelligence for Florida and the Caribbean, told a reporter for the *Miami Herald* that "we know that a number of individuals who were heavily involved in the growth of marijuana have severely curtailed their activities—probably beause of the task force—and have now switched to cocaine." Florida has the same mandatory prison sentence for trafficking in either marijuana or cocaine. A smuggler turned DEA informant, Luis Garcia, told me recently, "If you are going to get fifteen

years for doing one and fifteen years for doing the other, you're going to go for the coke. It's easier to handle, easier to fly, and easier to hide."

Interdiction has led law-enforcement officials into an unwitting symbiotic relationship with drug traffickers. The smugglers understand Washington's need to see a steadily rising number of arrests and confiscations. As a result, a smuggler sends into the country not less cocaine but more—divided among several boats, one of which the smuggler considers expendable. If the police capture the decoy, they get some cocaine, a boat, a crew, statistics, and arrests. These may or may not lead to convictions or information, however. Most captures at sea involve not the drug trade's linchpins but its lowliest laborers, who are generally too ignorant and fearful of reprisals to be of use. In any case, the other boats get through. Both sides are reasonably content, but only the smuggler has accomplished his purpose.

Even if interdiction did keep substantially more cocaine out of the country, no great change would occur in the market for it—which is ultimately what counts. Looking into this matter, Peter Reuter, an economist at the Rand Corporation, generously credited the current interdiction effort with stopping 20 percent of the cocaine headed for U.S. shores. He then calculated how the retail price of cocaine would change if 40 percent of the incoming drug were somehow seized. He concluded that the price for a kilogram would rise by a scant 3.4 percent—hardly enough to drive down demand. The reason the increase would be so modest has to do with cocaine's price structure. In addition to the costs incurred in transportation and distribution, middlemen and dealers take a huge profit. U.S. importers pay their suppliers roughly $50,000 for a kilogram of Colombian cocaine, which they in turn retail for upwards of $625,000. (The street value of a shipment of cocaine is the total that would have been paid to dealers if the shipment had been sold off by the gram.) If seizures really were running at 20 percent, as Reuter assumed for his model, an importer would have to buy 125 kilos from Colombia in order to get 100 kilos into the country. If seizures ran instead at 40 percent, the importer would have to buy 167 kilos. The additional 42 kilos would cost the importer $2.1 million, or just 3.4 percent of the retail value—not much of a difference.

Last July a spokesman for the Reagan Administration conceded that too much attention may have been focused on enforcement, at the expense of other drug-control efforts. Speaking before a Senate committee considering this nomination as head of the DEA, John C. Lawn, a former FBI agent and the DEA's acting administrator, testified that when he joined the DEA, in 1982, he believed that "with sufficient resources the drug problem could be addressed and solved with law enforcement alone." He had come to understand, however, that "the problem is greater than law enforcement is able to cope with." And Lawn regretted that Washington had focused on the supply side of the drug business. The real problem, he concluded, is demand.

Demand lies at the heart of the argument for the decriminalization of cocaine. The most articulate reasoning in support of that argument is found in a 120-page article by Steven Wisotsky, the Nova Law Center professor: "Exposing the War on Cocaine: The Futility and Destructiveness of Prohibition." *Wisconsin Law Review* published the article in 1983. Most people with an interest in the interdiction and control of cocaine are familiar with Wisotsky's work. His research is often praised even by those who are profoundly skeptical of the conclusions drawn from it.

The case that Wisotsky builds turns on the proposition that a "strongly inelastic demand always will support a black market." He points out that the demand for cocaine has been dominated by a core group of very heavy users. According to the National Narcotics Intelligence Consumers Commission, consisting of representatives of eleven federal agencies, as of 1981 about six percent of the nation's cocaine users were consuming about 60 percent of the cocaine entering the United States. These hard-core users were experiencing, on average, some 234 "abuses sessions" a year. They wanted cocaine badly, and they were willing to pay for it.

A gram of legal cocaine, pharmaceutically pure, costs less than two dollars. Wisotsky points out. Black-market cocaine, diluted with adulterants, costs as much as seven dollars a gram. It is this markup that draws smugglers, dealers, and other criminal elements into the cocaine trade. With them comes violence, corruption, tax evasion, property inflation, and the usual ugly manifestations of widespread social decay. As long as cocaine remains a black-market commodity, and as long as demand remains inelastic, traffic in the drug will be too profitable for some to resist.

The problem, Wisotsky writes, is not merely a domestic one. He worries about how the billions in profits from cocaine are being spent and what the implications might be for national security. The cocaine business has made multimillionaires of hundreds of criminals in Latin America and the Caribbean. In league with assorted guerrilla movements, or simply by throwing money around, many of these people have become sources of instability in their own countries. Some are virtual warlords. Reportedly, the M-19 Communist insurgents in Colombia and the Maoist Sendero Luminoso guerrillas in Peru are financed in part by the cocaine trade, as is the right-wing Cuban-exile group Omega-7. The bureaucracies and even the cabinets of some small island regimes are riddled with people involved in the drug trade.

Wisotsky worries that efforts by law-enforcement agencies and the military to crack down on cocaine and cocaine dealers might contribute to an erosion of American civil liberties: a more casual approach to wiretapping, search and seizure, the exclusive rule, and the basic rights of defendants. Although Wisotsky does not take the dangers of cocaine abuse lightly, he wonders whether our present policies might not prove ultimately to be even more pernicious. If cocaine were decriminalized, he argues, the black market in the drug, and the crime associated with it, would immediately disappear. The threats to national security and to the integrity of the Constitution would recede.

There are a number of objections to Wisotsky's position, the first of which he himself has raised: "It has no chance. Society isn't ready for it." Indeed, to mention the subject of drugs in a state legislature today is to invite a new round of repressive legislation. Not even the legalization of marijuana has a sizable political constituency. For this reason, Wisotsky now argues, in a book to be published this year, rather than change the laws governing cocaine we should simply enforce them more selectively.

Second, there is a precedent for decriminalization, and it is discouraging. The British have since the 1920s prescribed heroin for confessed addicts. This approach worked well enough as long as the number of heroin addicts remained small, but during the 1960s, when the number of addicts increased, it not only failed to deter the growth of a black market but led to notorious abuses. Some patients with prescriptions, it was learned, were selling their legal heroin to junkies. Others were supplementing their prescribed doses with heroin obtained on the black market. Today Britain has all but eliminated heroin-by-prescription.

Charles Rangel, a Democratic congressman from New York and the chairman of the House Select Committee on Narcotics Abuse and Control, dismisses the British experiment out of hand as "a remarkable failure." He believes that any attempt by the government to decriminalize and regulate the distribution of cocaine would raise practical questions that no one could answer. Should the drug be available to people under the age of eighteen? If not, wouldn't they perpetuate

the need for a black market? In what concentration should the drug be available? And in what form? Freebase and injectable solution, as well as powder? The problem, Rangel says, is that the black market will always offer choices that the larger society will not. And besides, he adds, there is the matter of principle: "It's pathetic when a great civilization and democracy reaches the point that it makes its citizens federally subsidized zombies."

From a legal standpoint, the decriminalization of cocaine would not be easy to achieve. No individual state can decriminalize the drug, because federal prohibitions exist, and they supersede state laws. Congress, in turn, cannot decriminalize it, because the United States is a party to the United Nations Single Convention on Narcotic Drugs. This is a treaty, and treaties supersede federal law. Under the Single Convention, adopted in 1961, signatory nations must regard the non-medical use of marijuana, cocaine, and opium derivatives as illegal. In order to decriminalize cocaine, the United States would have to withdraw from a treaty that it worked hard to bring about.

The most compelling argument against decriminalization is that it would almost certainly broaden the population of cocaine users. Significantly, the most-abused psychoactive substances in America today—alcohol, tobacco, and mood-altering drugs available over the counter (sleep inducers, for example) or by prescription—are all legal, though regulated to various degrees. If cocaine became legal, the crime and violence associated with it would probably decline. But deaths from overdoses would increase, as would seizures and other forms of physical trauma, automobile accidents, family troubles, and difficulties on the job. Carlton Turner, the President's adviser on drug-related issues, estimates that as many as 60 million Americans would become cocaine users if the drug were decriminalized. If 10 to 20 percent of these users became addicts (Mark Gold estimates that one in four would), then cocaine abuse would be a national scourge on the scale that alcoholism now is.

Short of decriminalizing cocaine, we might explore ways to blunt its negative physical effects. One is to create a replacement drug. To date an alcohol substitute has been the primary goal of researchers thinking along such lines. In small doses, alcohol relieves anxiety better than any other substance, but it also is addictive and highly corrosive to the user's system. Consequently, a "safe" alcohol or alcohol-like substance—one that retains alcohol's healthful qualities but lacks its dangerous ones—would be welcome. Theoretically, it might be possible to create a safe drug that somehow matched cocaine's performance in enhancing alertness, self-esteem, and sociability, without impairing judgment. In laboratory settings cocaine users have already shown that they can be fooled under certain circumstances by the local anesthetic lidocaine. But even if the development of a replacement for cocaine were socially desirable, which is by no means clear, it is not imminent. Nor is the history of replacement drugs encouraging. In the nineteenth century cocaine itself was recommended—by Sigmund Freud and others—as a non–habit-forming substitute for morphine.

A less problematical alternative to a replacement for cocaine is a drug to ease withdrawal. Research on one such drug has been conducted by Charles Dackis, of Fair Oaks Hospital. Theorizing that a lack of dopamine causes heavy users to crave cocaine, Dackis gave forty such users a prescription drug called bromocriptine, which does the work of dopamine in the brain without imitating dopamine's euphoric effects. (The drug is commercially available as a treatment for the symptoms of Parkinson's disease.) Subjects reported that their craving decreased sharply, and that they also experienced the other usual symptoms of withdrawal less intensely. Animal studies indicate that bromocriptine is not habit-forming. Dackis expects to make a full report later this year.

One hope for diminishing the demand for cocaine lies in education. Both in and out of school, drug-prevention programs aimed at young people are increasingly common across the country.

Educating children and teenagers about drugs is a well-intentioned idea, but no one really knows how workable it is. During Prohibition every state had educational programs designed to foster awareness of the dangers of alcohol. Yet alcohol remained popular. It's possible that drug education only stimulates curiosity rather than promotes self-control. Moreover, it may be difficult for teachers to commend permanent abstinence with respect to *some* psychoactive substances when their students know that society permits adults to engage in the use of others.

A report released in 1984 by the Rand Corporation suggests that anti-drug education will have the best chance of success if it employs techniques borrowed from anti-smoking campaigns for adolescents that are known to have worked. According to the report, these campaigns typically stress not the long-term health effects, which are likely to "seem uncertain and far in the future," but rather the short-term effects of smoking, "such as bad breath, discolored teeth, or increased carbon monoxide in the blood." The Rand analysts concluded, "Future efforts against adolescent drug use should give greater emphasis to prevention, and not continue to pin hopes largely on law enforcement." Their implicit conviction that adolescent experimentation with drugs cannot be stopped absolutely suggests that teachers should convey accurate information about which drugs and which methods of administration are most dangerous.

The Reagan Administration rhetorically favors drug education, but it has yet to devote much money to the effort. Indeed, the Department of Education's budget for programs to combat drug abuse has declined, from $14 million in 1981 to a paltry $2.9 million in 1985. Nevertheless, the Administration has managed to maintain a high profile when it comes to the perils of illegal drugs. For example, Nancy Reagan has made drug abuse her chief topic of concern; she served as the host of a television series *Chemical People*, that was intended to help promote an anti-drug atmosphere in the schools. And a year ago the Administration announced that it would be sponsoring anti-drug seminars featuring prominent athletes in 200 American cities. "Sports people are heroes to our young people," said William H. Webster, the director of the FBI. "I can't think of anyone better to get their attention." What impact such awareness campaigns have actually had is impossible to say. But the psychiatrist Robert Byck, among other researchers, has warned that using well-known personalities as "point men," particularly where cocaine is concerned, may serve subtly to glamorize the use of drugs. The cocaine scandals that have bedeviled baseball since last summer show that holding up athletes as models can easily backfire.

Prevention is the best approach to any public-health problem. But prevention cannot help the many hundreds of thousands who are already dependent on cocaine. These people constitute the core of the cocaine market. It is they who keep the producers, smugglers, and dealers in business, and it is they who thereby do the most damage to their communities, their families, and themselves.

One aspect of the drug wars on which Steven Wisotsky, who wrote the article advocating decriminalization, and Carlton Turner, the White House's adviser on drugs, might agree is the importance of the private sector in providing treatment for those who cannot cope with cocaine. Wisotsky considers the program of screening and follow-up care proposed for professional baseball players by Commissioner Peter Ueberroth a better solution than jail. Turner praises a number of corporations, including Greyhound, General Motors, U.S. Tobacco, Union Pacific, and Alcoa, that have set up treatment programs enabling drug users to get help but also keep their jobs. It may be that when professional inter-

vention is required, cocaine users have it slightly better than people with other drug habits. Cocaine abuse is far more a middle- and upper-class problem than heroin addiction ever was or will be. That simple fact creates a variety of financial incentives that result in superior care. "A heroin counselor is often an unlicensed, untrained ex-addict trying to help someone get a job," the psychiatrist Richard Rawson says. "Cocaine therapists typically are M.A.s or Ph.D.s who have a higher set of skills."

Rawson contends that after the initial trauma of withdrawal—usually about two weeks—85 to 90 percent of cocaine users can be treated on an outpatient basis. It often happens that patients, after passing through withdrawal, experience a "honeymoon" period of relief at being free of the drug. Afterward, however, they hit what Rawson calls a "wall of anhedonia." Still, those who continue with treatment through this stage generally manage to remain abstinent. Their chances improve if after detoxification they shun not only the drug but the life-style and acquaintances associated with it. Cocaine Anonymous and Narcotics Anonymous, therapeutic groups patterned after Alcoholics Anonymous, now have active chapters throughout the country.

Even when treatment does not succeed in keeping a patient permanently clean, it has an overall beneficial effect. "We have a definite indication that treatment does reduce cocaine use," Rawson says, "although we can't be sure yet whether the reduction is permanent." The majority of people with cocaine problems, unfortunately, never seek treatment. Many do not want to (and cannot be forced to). Many others do not know that treatment may be available. And many who want help can't find it. Federal subsidies for treatment programs, though never the prime source of funding for local drug-rehabilitation efforts, have been cut back in recent years; the cutbacks have taken their toll. The cocaine users who exist beyond the reach of therapy are to be found disproportionately among the ranks of the poor. Not everyone can afford a private clinic. Not everyone works for Alcoa or, for that matter, even has a job.

Public opinion seems to be united on the question of how society should deal with the vast army of the untreated and the untreatable. People are fed up with the crime and the urban squalor bred by drugs. They want users and dealers off the streets. "We have to start focusing on the users and make them pay the price, and we ought to have the death penalty for drug dealers," Carlton Turner told me recently. Last spring an editorial in *The New Republic* asserted that society had to choose between adopting "severe" mandatory penalties for drug possession and legalizing what are now controlled substances. In reality, the American public lacks the will, and their government the resources, to catch, try, and lock up any more than a tiny fraction of drug users.

One alternative to jail that has been proposed by various specialists in drug abuse, including Mark Gold, is the involuntary civil commitment of addicts to treatment facilities. All states make some provision for the involuntary commitment of people who exhibit psychotic behavior and who pose an immediate life-threatening danger to themselves or others. The third edition of the American Psychiatric Association's *Diagnostic and Statistical Manual*, whose taxonomy of psychiatric afflictions is used almost universally in commitment proceedings, makes reference to a number of drug-related disorders. Nevertheless, involuntary commitment on the grounds of drug dependency is rare. Many families and law-enforcement officials are unaware that this remedy exists. And as the laws are currently written, it could be prescribed unfairly.

Yet involuntary commitment does seem to work for one group of substance abusers—alcoholics. Over the past two decades, as the concept of alcoholism as a disease has gained acceptance, the national trend has been away from jailing alcoholics for an offense like public drunkenness. Most states now provide for the involuntary commitment of alcoholics, if only

for the purpose of detoxification. There is evidence to suggest that treatment even against a patient's will can be effective in the fight against alcoholism. The same seems to hold true for cocaine abuse.

In a landmark 1962 decision, Robinson *v.* California, the Supreme Court ruled that a person's status as a drug addict could not in itself be defined as a crime under the Constitution. However, the court upheld compulsory treatment for drug addicts on the grounds that treatment programs would advance legitimate state interests. A handful of states have enacted statutes that provide specifically for the involuntary commitment of addicts. Massachusetts had such a law until 1969, when it quietly expired. California has an addict-commitment law, but it is used strictly as a means of diverting people charged with or convicted of crimes out of the clogged criminal-justice system. Connecticut has a law allowing for the commitment of drug-dependent people who have not been charged with crimes. Poorly drafted, it has essentially gone unused.

Until recently Texas had a little-used law similar to the one in Connecticut. Last year, however, the state tight-ended up its statute. The principal architect of the new bill was Judge Patrick W. Ferchill, of Fort Worth. The motivation for the revision came not from cocaine, though more and more of it is being seen in Texas, but from legal substances called inhalants.

About a decade ago there was a flurry of national concern over juvenile glue-sniffing. In the Southwest the practice has never died out. Rather, it expanded to include spray paint, cleaning solvents, motor-fuel products, and a variety of other highly toxic substances. Thousands of youngsters, primarily poor Hispanics, have become addicted to inhalants. "Many of these people are married to their spray cans," Judge Ferchill says. "It's a hideous problem. The brain damage often is massive and permanent. They lose control of their speech, muscles, and kidneys. Some have to be diapered."

The amended law was passed last spring by the Texas legislature and took effect in September. It provides for the involuntary commitment of persons dependent on drugs or inhalants. Before a person can be committed, he must be given a jury trial (unless he waives this right); two psychiatrists must testify that his dependency requires treatment for his own welfare or the safety of others. The addict is given the benefit of legal counsel at every stage of the proceedings. "We don't want lay-down lawyers in this system," Ferchill says. "We want a fair, vigorous defense." If a person is committed, his term of involuntary treatment may not exceed six months. The judge or jury may find that treatment can be undertaken on an outpatient basis. If a person is hospitalized, it may be in either a public or a private institution, and the goal is to make the transition to outpatient care as quick as possible. The Texas statute applies only to those who have no criminal charges pending against them.

Two things make this approach appealing as a way of handling cocaine abusers. First, safeguards are built into the system to protect the rights both of the individual (to due process) and of society (to public safety). Second, the commitment option provides an alternative to involving the police. Mark Gold says, "We get a lot of calls at 1-800-COCAINE from people who say their son or husband weighs a hundred pounds, has lost his job, and is having seizures and automobile accidents. They don't know what to do." People are generally reluctant to initiate criminal proceedings against a relative, a friend, or a coworker. They might be more willing to testify at civil commitment hearings—provided that the treatment itself is genuine, the term of treatment no longer than necessary, and the place of treatment humane. It is essential, too, that laws sanctioning involuntary commitment be painstakingly crafted.

To Steven Wisotsky, involuntary commitment

smacked of "the Soviet asylum approach." He invokes the psychiatrist Thomas Szasz, who has objected to involuntary commitment for any reason on civil-liberties grounds. But a cocaine habit is not freedom; and when it has a destructive impact on the family, community, or workplace, attempting to cure it is in the spirit of civil liberties. John Stuart Mill, whose philosophy has helped to give that spirit definition, wrote, "The only purpose for which power can be rightfully exercised over any member of a civilized community, against his will, is to prevent harm to others. Surely the control of drug addiction is such a purpose.

Americans do not expect law-enforcement agencies to eradicate crime but merely hope that they will limit it as much as possible. No public official would ever promise to end rape, robbery, theft, or homicide. Yet politicians routinely vow to stop drugs cold, to sweep them from the streets and keep them from our children. In reality, law enforcement per se may have less control over drug trafficking than it has over other forms of crime. This is especially true in the case of cocaine trafficking. The drug is produced in remote regions of foreign countries where even local governments have little influence. It then enters the United States, in whose free society it is consumed more often than not by otherwise law-abiding people.

Because the traffic in cocaine is one of the most corrupting and corrosive forces in American society, Washington has an obligation to fight it. The Reagan Administration has tried to, mainly by jawboning the public and by attempting to intercept the drug before it hits the beach or the landing strip. But meanwhile, the government has virtually ignored the demand side of the cocaine traffic—the side that is somewhat more susceptible to government influence. It has invested a great deal of money in supply-side enforcement, and that, unfortunately, may very well have made the problem worse.

Analysis of Case Study No. 1

Based on the previous discussion of methods to define problems, how should we proceed to construct a definition of the problem suggested by the Lieber case study? Let us try the same methodology here: (1) gathering target data classifications and converting to performance measures where possible, (2) isolating the controlling and causal variables, and (3) analyzing stakeholder assumptions.

First, data need to be classified before the problem can be defined. Based on *induction* (reasoning from particular experiences to general conclusions: cycle hits bump and misfires; thus, bump causes misfire) and *deduction* (general knowledge to specific observation: cycle powered by battery; therefore, horn will not work if the battery is dead) (Pirsig, 1974, p. 92), we go through a process of refining data and problem statements or hypotheses until we are either satisfied or required to act by an imposed deadline (the dilemma faced by NASA policymakers in developing the space program). The classic scientific method asks us to define the problem first, come up with hypothetical causes, test the various hypotheses, and draw conclusions from the results. Note that almost paradoxically, we need some data before we can establish causation and even more for definition of the problem.

But the first step in classifying data is to develop inductive and deductive "hunches" or hypotheses that will be relevant to the problem and later its solution. Why? Because merely accumulating data would overwhelm us with "noise," for an analytic framework would be absent. Hunches aid in hypothesis development and need not be consistent with any framework or theory. But development of applied policy theory does demand a framework of tested hypotheses. Hence, eventually normative hunches and logical frameworks must merge if we are to develop applied theories linking observed facts about public policy behavior.

However we ultimately define the policy problem(s) of this case, the preliminary hypotheses or hunches must be related to (1) availability and use of cocaine, (2) the existence of a class of potential program beneficiaries, and (3) the demonstrated effects of current programs to reduce and eliminate drug abuse. We need data that can point to the intensity and severity of the apparent problem. During this phase, judgments will have to be made on essential versus nonessential data. Otherwise, the process would be inhibited by excessive data or system "noise." Though "noise" can serve a constructive role by changing views up to a certain threshold, beyond this point failure to screen for nonessential data can degenerate into uninformed arm-waving that paralyzes the decision process. Note that such distinctions about data relevance will also be based on hunches, past experience, comparative present experience, and probably political considerations (fear of retaliation for finding embarrassing facts on program performance). Remember that it is quite possible that the product of data analysis, controlled variables, and explicit stakeholder assumptions will lead to the conclusion that no actionable public policy problem exists.

First, then, what is the availability and use of cocaine? It must be pretty substantial to generate so many media stories, such intense public debate, and a program proposal of $1.7 billion! Table 2.1 indicated that reported use is up in two of three age groups. Lieber (1986, p. 40) suggests that in the last five years "availability and use of cocaine has risen sharply" and that cocaine abuse "has become a major public-health problem of major proportions." The first major comprehensive survey of drug abuse in three years, performed by the federal Alcohol, Drug Abuse and Mental Health Administration, indicates that "nearly 37 million Americans, about one of five people 12 years of age or older, used one or more illicit drugs in the last year" and "nearly 5.8 million people use cocaine at least monthly . . . a 38 percent increase in three years" (Brinkley, 1986a). Because public acceptance of drug use has declined over the last few years, federal officials believe these figures to be conservative—respondents probably lied to conform to this expectation.

Growing availability of cocaine is also suggested by data on price and seizures. Since the 1982 South Florida Drug Task Force began, cocaine dealers are paying 40 percent less for a kilogram of cocaine (Lieber, 1986, p. 40). Seizures, which are treated as a known fraction of total supplies of cocaine, have grown—from 6 tons in 1983 to 25 tons in 1985. Marijuana seizures are declining as a consequence and the price is increasing, reducing demand for marijuana and increasing it for cocaine—from 850 tons in 1983 to 750 tons in 1985 (Lieber, 1986, p. 40) and from $2,000 a pound in 1985 to $3,200 a pound in 1986 (Lindsey, 1986).

Further, data indicate the growing use of cocaine to be harmful to the public. Lieber notes that "the number of deaths reported to the Drug Abuse Warning Network in which cocaine was implicated increased by 324 percent —considerably faster than the reported number of deaths involving alcohol or other drugs" (Lieber, 1986, p. 43). In addition, the number of emergency-room visits linked to cocaine in 26 metropolitan hospitals has increased more than 300 percent—from 3,296 in 1981 to 9,946 in 1985 (Kerr, 1986b). Naturally, one needs to be skeptical of all data and ask the basic questions about the data's validity, reliability, and significance. The injury data, for example, need to be supplemented by other figures suggesting significant patterns of cocaine overdose and a linkage between cocaine drug abuse and crimes to person or property. That is, in 1984, cocaine was implicated in 604 deaths—third behind heroin and morphine (1,072 deaths) for a 324 percent increase. But automobiles result in many more deaths than this each year without anyone suggesting a $1.7 billion accident-prevention program. Hence, use data may be incomplete and inhibit problem definition.

In generating hypotheses on the availability of cocaine, policy analysts should also gather data on the effects of drug use. Cocaine possession, sale, and transport are all crimes and thus illegal activities. But does its use and abuse produce a "crime wave" beyond the fact of illegality injurious to people or property? Kerr (1986b) notes that in the first half of 1986, the police reported a sharp rise in murders, robberies, and other violent crimes in New York neighborhoods where "crack" (a highly potent cocaine derivative) use was widespread. Such "use impact" data are important in coming to grips with the perceived problem. Is cocaine abuse simply a moral problem? Or does it really cause violent crimes, loss of productivity, and deterioration of moral fiber as commonly suggested? More importantly, can education or enforcement make a significant difference to current behavior patterns? How will additional public expenditures surround the problem and reduce its impact on target groups?

Second, we need to know more about those who would benefit from elimination of this problem. Though part of the data will correspond to "stakeholder assumptions" below, the question is not unlike those related to drivers and seat belts, students and sex education, pilots and health-competence testing. Some of the program beneficiaries in each case tend to resist the program on the grounds that it can interfere with their freedom of movement. Would drug-abuse program beneficiaries want the problem eliminated? Just as a public problem may not exist when a subgroup of potential beneficiaries (zealots) clamor for action, so also a public problem can exist without beneficiary pressure for solution (such as in the case of an increase in babies born addicted to cocaine; Kerr, 1986b). Here, analysis must be carefully severed from actor pressures for solution or specific problem definition. Thus, policy analysts must attempt to view data trends in context (made possible by requiring the clash of stakeholder data and opinions in adversary policy proceedings such as budget hearings) before deciding on authorizations and appropriations.

The existence of a stable U.S. demand of 12 million drug users suggests that many would suffer short-term individual deprivation from a successful anti-cocaine policy. This "beneficiary" data indicate that the problem definition must include the larger dimension of the nation as beneficiary; that is, the problem of drug abuse is a "public bad" that must be countered by public policy for the benefit of long-term public interest. In short, beneficiaries are not hard to find for elimination of this problem, and this accounts for its appeal to many politicians.

Apparently cocaine is "among the most 'reinforcing' of drugs" (Lieber, 1986, p. 41). Hence, we would want to know just how addictive it is. Does it produce psychological dependence or physical addiction? Is the current abuse problem related to more efficient means of ingestion? Several inconclusive studies on the nature of addiction exist (Lieber, 1986, p. 41). But such knowledge may be less important (because similar questions exist for alcohol) than finding out about the correlates of abuse. One may be genetically or psychologically at-risk and still not consume excessive drugs because of peer group, family ties, or simply personal will power.

Historically, cocaine was considered a threat to society in the 1880s. But, by the end of World War II "cocaine was no longer a menace" (Lieber, 1986, p. 42). Why? Because the leaves were too bulky to transport, and major sources, namely Peru and Bolivia, lacked coca-refining capacity. Successful crackdown by police on amphetamine laboratories and trafficking networks later created a market for cocaine as a new stimulant, and it reappeared as a recreational drug in the late 1960s and early 1970s. More importantly, the methods of consumption changed. While Peruvian Indians have chewed coca leaves for 5,000 years with few ill effects and many health benefits, they deem snorting and intravenous use repulsive (Lieber, 1986, p. 41). Current cocaine-abuse problems stem from progression to intravenous injection, and smoking freebase from earlier snorting habits. What effect does cocaine price have on methods of consumption? Lieber notes (1986, p. 43) that California users can now buy $10 chunks of freebase at "rock houses," which, among other consequences, creates a market for cocaine among the very poor. Such questions lead to data on user level and method of consumption that are valuable in seeking a profile of the current drug user as intended beneficary. That is, can we change level of consumption and vary methods of use to reduce addiction? Or does increasing the price by reducing supply (from enforcement or even education) lead to market specialization for the poor with lower-quality but lower-priced cocaine? Data on potential beneficiary behavior can help give us such answers.

Third, we need to develop hypotheses and gather data on how related public programs have affected availability and use of cocaine. Four types of drug-enforcement programs (as opposed to education) are being implemented: those that target the cultivator (going to the source), those that target the U.S. importer (interdiction), those that target the U.S. dealers and profiteers, and those that target the users. Lieber suggests that the Reagan program has been mainly interdiction (1986, p. 39). More recent data indicate that the Reagan Administration intends to go to the source (Bolivia) and also target importers, dealers, and users (Anti-Drug Abuse Act of 1986). Have these tactics been effective? What does the data show? While the sight of U.S. jets and helicopters strafing crops in South America is impressive, it must not be forgotten that marijuana and cocaine grow extremely fast there—much faster than other cash crops tried for decades by the U.S. foreign aid program and that somehow have not generated sufficient incentive for sustained effort by local farmers. Eradication of foreign marijuana sources also increases U.S. prices, making U.S. growers (a $16.6-billion-per-year industry, second only to growing corn) happy in shifting the problem home.

In South America, paradoxically, drugs have provided enormous wealth not only for gangster families, the local military, and governments, but also to the poor. In Colombia, cocaine sales exceed those of coffee, the country's leading legal export. Similarly, Bolivia receives an estimated $600 million in repatriated earnings from coca sales, equaling the country's legal export revenues. For South American governments and their poor, "As murderous and corrupting as cocaine has become for them, its tainted profits also have kept some Andean economies from outright collapse" (Graham, 1987). According to a 1986 State Department report, "Bolivia's entire economic structure—labor, marketing, supply, and demand—is being distorted by growing reliance on coca.... The poor continue to migrate to key coca producing regions seeking ready work and cash" (Kline, 1987, p. 26).

In some remote villages on the Bolivian altiplano, nearly everyone has a VCR, and Mercedes automobiles can be found parked in front of mud and thatched huts. The U.S. foreign aid program, after spending billions of dollars, has been unable to accomplish for local people what the growing, marketing, and processing of drugs has accomplished—namely sustained incomes and employment, albeit in illicit activities. Some might even term this "economic development"! The United States will now spend billions of dollars in an apparent clash with our foreign aid program to "go to the source." For instance, the Anti-Drug Abuse Act of 1986 provides $55 million for aircraft to foreign governments and modifies the Foreign Assistance Act of 1961 "to allow U.S. drug agents to participate in foreign activities, including allowing officers to directly participate in foreign arrests" (*Drug Enforcement Report*, October 23, 1986a, p. 2). Clearly, more data are needed on the effects of this tactic before expenditures are increased. Policy analysts also need to question whether strengthening Latin American militaries via drug-enforcement funding may ultimately work against our historical goal of democratic development for that region.

Additionally, the Reagan Administration is now stressing interdiction. We have noted that more cocaine has been seized by these efforts. But more is coming in (Lieber, 1986, p. 40) on the heels of lower prices and greater demand. This has slowed the market for less dangerous drugs such as marijuana and raised the question of whether the interdiction strategy may by increasing the use of more dangerous and more easily concealable drugs such as cocaine. Policy-makers would need to know the importance of these trends (potential unanticipated effects) before defining the problem to be addressed by public programs.

Third, the Reagan Administration is enforcing laws against dealers and launderers in the U.S. The Anti-Drug Abuse Act of 1986, for example, provides for penalties for drug traffickers of 10 years to life without parole or pardon and established a new federal offense for "money laundering" (*Drug Enforcement Report*, October 23, 1986, p. 2).

Finally, the existing and proposed anti–drug-abuse programs have targeted users. Despite the recent realization that cocaine use is widespread, harsh penalties have existed in most states for some time. But a Florida law that provides a mandatory sentence for trafficking in either cocaine or marijuana ignores the differences in severity between the two drugs as well as potential for concealment (Lieber, 1986, p. 43). These and other excesses, such as federal laws against interstate shipment of roach clips ("drug paraphernalia") (*Drug Enforcement Report*, November 10, 1986b, p. 4) and public employee drug testing (beyond safety-related positions such as pilots and air traffic controllers), are the kinds of self-serving and misleading actions that are made possible by poor problem definition.

We have attempted to classify data on availability and use, on potential program beneficiaries and target groups, and, finally, on the effects of related public programs. Preliminary data on the extent of the problem, on who will benefit from its solution, and on effects of related public programs are essential before defining the present policy problem. The second step is to examine more thoroughly the nature of the cause of the problem. What factors trigger drug abuse, and which of these factors are actionable? In an earlier section we noted that if an event was a "substantial factor" in bringing a result about, we could consider it as major cause.

In classifying data on drug users, determinants of supply and demand, and the habits of potential beneficaries, we necessarily touched on the subject of causation. The "hunches" or hypotheses required at least some idea of how, for example, marijuana price increases stimulated substitution demand for cocaine. But we gathered data on factors affecting drug abuse with little consideration other than general knowledge. In the second stage, we attach resource constraints to problem definition by narrowing the causes.

It was noted previously that by using "hierarchy analysis" (Dunn, 1981, p. 124), we can distinguish three kinds of possible causes of a "problematic situation." First, "possible" causes range from proximate to remote. In the case of drug abuse, network television programs, rock music, movies, and genetic risk factors (Lieber, 1986, p. 41) would all fall into this category. If medical scientists could measure and predict genetic risk factor, they might be able to treat the most vulnerable cases and prevent future addicts. Similarly, poverty, broken families, and lack of education result from drug abuse; they can also contribute to its causes.

We have been discussing the possible causes of drug abuse rather loosely up to this point. This is the cab driver's view of an issue—the single-factor explanation of the rock music or television that leads to similarly fuzzy kinds of public responses (anticrack rallies and self-righteous media rhetoric), which then lead to "omnibus" programs that are both expensive and ill designed. Dealing with the "possible" causes leads one into analytic confusion, for practically anything can be related to a major ill-structured problem like drug abuse as a possible cause: civil liberties, foreign aid, athletic programs, safety-related jobs, enforcement contradictions, the limitations of training, and on and on.

For purposes of analytic sanity, then, we move to the "plausible" or probable causes or those based on research or experience that are believed to exert an important influence (substantial factors) on the problematic situation (Dunn, 1981, p. 125). Here we refer to cyclical trends in demand and supply (Table 2.1) that suggest either "leveling off" (Kerr, 1986b) or a "modest increase" (Brinkley, 1986a) in the number of people who use cocaine. Depending on the importance one attaches to either conclusion, the causes appear to be long-term rather than an immediate event generating new demand and supply.

Kerr (1986b) notes the likelihood that Congress responded to a "popular and seemingly one-sided" issue to avoid the risk of appearing insensitive before the public at election time (in November 1986). Despite conflicting evidence on cocaine's availability and use, the public perceived that policy efforts to stop cocaine were a failure. Thus, spurred on by the rhetoric of such figures as former Senator Paula Hawkins (R-Florida), and widespread television coverage of the drug-abuse issue, Congress promulgated the most far-reaching drug law ever passed. But the "plausible" causes—such as general public recognition of America's drug habit, and the heavy level of drug use that began in the 1960s and that took a heavy toll by the early 1980s (Kerr, 1986b)—are not really "actionable" causes. They are not as vague as "possible" causes, yet they fall into a similarly amorphous category of "unexpected explosion of concern" that almost could not be predicted at the time amidst the fever within Congress for balancing the federal budget.

In minutes, the Republican-controlled Senate endorsed the notion of exceeding the budget ceiling to pay $1.7 billion for the anti-drug measure. Though drug abuse has been a social problem for years, the Senate revealed a remarkable ability to "frighten itself with its own version of reality" (Greenhouse, 1986). This was partly due to the inability of policymakers to distinguish actionable from possible and plausible causes. However, it is conceivable that even by making such distinctions, legislators would fear that they had underestimated the frequent voter tendency to turn all problems into actionable ones!

Once we narrow the causes down to "actionable" ones, or those subject to control or manipulation by policymakers (Dunn, 1981, p. 125), the case for defining drug abuse broadly as a public problem becomes much more difficult. If the problem is simply drug supply, and "supply-siders" imagine its elimination via interdiction, this ignores the ability to replace destroyed sources rapidly. Drug demand may be so intense that such programs as interdiction and employee drug testing create new supplies of problems. For instance, Byrd Laboratories of Austin, Texas, now markets drug-free urine for $49.95 a bag! Some suggest that as drug tests become more widely used this will create a "flourishing black market in clean urine" (*New York Times*, November 29, 1986).

But if we remain oblivious of drug-abuse causation and likely unintended consequences of specific remedial programs, no definition of the problem would really be "actionable." For example, tough enforcement against suppliers can actually increase demand for more dangerous drugs. Education of users can produce curiosity (Lieber, 1986, p. 46) and, in the face of crack, new addicts. Decriminalization (Lieber, 1986, p. 45) can eliminate the black market and provide governmental revenues, but at a probable price of a broader base of cocaine users. "If cocaine became legal, the crime and violence associated with it would probably decline. But deaths from overdoses would increase, as would seizures, and other forms of physical trauma, automobile accidents, family troubles, and difficulties on the job" (Lieber, 1986, p. 45).

The one actionable cause of drug abuse, namely insufficient civil treatment of offenders (mostly voluntary), will receive $241 million from the Anti-Drug Abuse Act of 1986 in addition to the $576 million already appropriated in fiscal year 1987 (*Drug Enforcement Report*, October 23, 1986a, p. 3). Lieber correctly noted that federal subsidies for treatment programs had been cut back in recent years. But most states now provide for "involuntary commitment of alcoholics, if only for the purpose of detoxification" (Lieber, 1986, p. 47). Involuntary commitment of addicts using federal funding would seem to be an actionable cause, given the real limitations of the enforcement strategy in reducing the problem. Szasz (cited in Lieber, 1986, p. 48) opposes involuntary commitment on civil liberties grounds: "But a cocaine habit is not freedom; and when it has a destructive impact on the family, community or workplace, attempting to cure it is in the spirit of civil liberties." Put this way, the Reagan supply-side enforcement program would not be inconsistent with a broad perspective of civil liberties.

Additionally, treating drug abuse as a "supply-caused" problem leads to a simplistic enforcement emphasis and to such unproductive programs as public employee drug testing. Involuntary commitment of addicts should provide a procedure more consistent with due process than one that randomly sifts through the public sector for patriotic volunteers eager to urinate in a bottle. In short, it may be argued that absence of proper treatment is an actionable cause because addicts can be defined, while other users (voluntary treatment) might be coaxed into reasonable-consumption patterns. From the "demand-side" perspective, expected success of involuntary commitment and voluntary treatment programs would reduce demand, meaning more control over immediate or actionable variables, such as domestic supply and the direction of enforcement. Reduced expenditure needs for enforcement and international narcotics control would allow additional monies to be shifted to treatment, further reducing the actionable causes.

After valid and reliable data have been provided, and after actionable causes isolated (but before the problem can be authoritatively defined), the analyst needs to examine the assumptions of competing stakeholders. Throughout the first two stages, the analyst has probably already used them to gather data and outline probable causation. Data are provided selectively, for example, by a group representing one position on an issue (e.g., greater enforcement efforts). Naturally this needs to be recognized. But in contrast with those who caution against biased data, we suggest that the analyst actively encourage the generation of such data, for example, on general cocaine availability and use, determinants of abuse, and the results of related public programs. The active clash of competing figures can serve to generate criticism and mutual faultfinding in the highest of pluralist tradition. According to Mitroff and Emshoff (cited in Dunn, 1981, pp. 130, 131), "Conflict is needed to permit the existence of maximally opposing policies to ferret out and to challenge the underlying assumptions that each policy makes. Commitment on the other hand is also necessary if the proponents for each policy are to make the strongest possible case (not necessarily the best) for their respective points of view."

Only information provided through dynamic and creative conflict can provide policymakers with needed material for wise decisions. Built-in mechanisms to require information on actionable policy problems could avoid many problems of public policy-making. For example, the recent decision by President Reagan and a small clique of uninformed Executive Office advisers to provide 2,008 antitank missiles to Iran for at least $12 million suggests that improved information on the "causation" of the Iranian "problem" might have dissuaded them or others in this closed circle from such rash action. According to Senator Richard Lugar (R-Indiana), "Maybe what they need is a more generous supply of good ideas and a lively clash of intellect" (*Atlanta Constitution*, November 22, 1986). While "idiots don't listen," according to one reviewer, faith in human reason still requires that the results of stakeholder clashes on each issue be known in advance of the decision, not afterwards as in the Iranian case!

What are the stakeholder assumptions in the drug-abuse case and how might their "creative synthesis" (Dunn, 1981, p. 130) improve problem definition? The objective is to (1) identify stakeholders, (2) list their policy assumptions, and (3) systematically compare assumptions and counterassumptions (Dunn, 1981, p. 131). Given the information on stakeholders provided by Lieber (1986), this should not be difficult. The major stakeholders in this policy area are law enforcement officials, politicians, smugglers-launderers-traffickers, drug users, and public opinion (parents, family, law-and-order organizations, and civil rights groups). Each would define the drug-abuse problem differently based on selective interpretation of data.

The stakeholder assumptions are also predictable. Law enforcement officials largely favor tougher laws and more enforcement efforts through such programs as interdiction. Based on the proportion of funds devoted to enforcement in the Anti-Drug Abuse Act of 1986 ($1.04 billion out of $1.7 billion) (Brinkley, 1986b), it is clear that this stakeholder is the most powerful actor in the policy arena. However, judicial administrators need to be distinguished from enforcement advocates. While enforcement officials are generally in favor of tougher laws, more enforcement, and therefore more arrests and seizures, judicial officials are often at the other end. To some extent they view increased enforcement against cocaine as a threat to the case-processing capacity of the criminal justice system. For example, the new 1,000-member "anticrack" unit of the New York City Police Department has been very successful if measured by arrests for narcotics charges (3,706 arrests as of 1986), a 71 percent increase in felony indictments (5,000 in 1986 as opposed to only 3,106 in 1985). But this effort has taxed the police laboratory (which must return tests of seized narcotics to the grand jury), the plea-bargaining system (which forces earlier and shorter negotiated sentences), and the correctional system (overcrowding led to inmate riots in October 1986). Whether the system can keep up with the number of crack cases depends largely on whether crack use continues to grow. Unfortunately, the enforcement effort may have simply driven dealers "off the streets and into apartments," suggesting that the crack trade is either still growing or not leveling off (Kerr, 1986c).

Elected politicians comprise a group of stakeholders that often seek sophisticated, costly, and high-visibility solutions to complex social problems. In the case of cocaine, they often support the enforcers from fear of electoral retribution. While enforcement officials seek increases in arrests and amounts of drugs confiscated, politicians gauge their ultimate effectiveness in getting reelected. On the other hand, smugglers and traffickers would prefer less funds for enforcement and perhaps diversion of more funds to education for those "long-term attitudinal" changes that have little effect on current demand and supply. As noted by Lieber (1986, p. 43), smugglers understand enforcement activities so well that they want to give enforcers increased productivity (arrests and confiscations) by using decoy boats! This aids the enforcers and serves to increase smuggler profits as well.

Cocaine users fall into several categories—addicts, casual users, and apprentices. The addicts want less enforcement, lower prices, and will occasionally accept voluntary treatment as a solution to what they recognize as a social problem; casual users have slightly more elastic demand curves—if the price (financial and legal) increases too sharply, they shift back to alcohol and would also accept voluntary treatment in many cases; apprentices are even more tentative and could likely be coaxed out of greater demand by some combination of education and enforcement. As noted, education and treatment received the fewest funds in the Anti-Drug Abuse Act of 1986 ($660 million), indicating the differences in relative power shares among stakeholders.

The final group of stakeholders are the various subgroups known as the "public." Generally, they favor tougher enforcement despite rhetoric supporting treatment and education. Their stand has been toughened by media attention on drug abuse, the arrival of crack on the streets ("New Coke"), and evidence that cocaine use is spreading to the affluent population (in contrast with heroin, which affected mostly inner-city poor). The formation of their preferences for a get-tough policy coincided with recent congressional fear of opposing a popular and apparently one-sided issue: "Do we want drug abuse or not?" Though the public is divided into a variety of subgroups on this issue, most people appear to agree on tough enforcement, and this perception was enough to stimulate quick and decisive legislative action.

The key purpose of stakeholder analysis is to arrive at a "composite set of acceptable assumptions [which] can serve as a basis for the creation of a new conceptualization of the problem" (Dunn, 1981, p. 131). Much of the data suggests that with the exception of incumbent politicians up for reelection, most stakeholders seem willing to compromise on problem definition. What this means is that: (1) the problem has been defined in terms of hard-line enforcement, and (2) the basis for definition has been almost purely political, and not analytical. Even law enforcers recognize the need for selectivity in drafting and enforcing drug laws. Stepping up enforcement against marijuana traffic improves productivity figures on paper but encourages many casual users and apprentice users to shift into harder drugs with potentially permanent consequences. But to change laws or "soften" enforcement practices to, for instance, favor marijuana use could threaten political careers.

More importantly, in the case of complex ill-structured problems like drug abuse, a problem definition (objectives; measures of performance based on understanding of at least basic data: probable causation; and relevant stakeholder assumptions) should precede the legislative determination of authorizations and appropriations. If policy is determined by appropriations hearings, as noted, little analysis is likely to permeate policy-making (Goldwater, 1986;

Doyle and Hartle, 1986). Authorization hearings are the appropriate place for policy debates. But because of time limitations and the pressure for action (particularly salient here), data and assumptions are often ignored in the stampede for a law. What this suggests is that, absent a vehicle for conducting analysis to determine whether a problem exists, the problem is going to be created largely by uninformed politics. Because validating stakeholder assumptions must include politics, it cannot be imagined that policy analysis is purely technical or factual. But the politics should pertain to the weight of available data, causes, and assumptions—not simply personal agendas such as reelection at any cost!

To prevent policy-making without adequate information (it will always be incomplete but adequacy can be required), machinery needs to be in place that permits comparison of stakeholder assumptions and counterassumptions. Out of this dynamic tension, a problem definition can be forged that is related to the data. To some extent, "assumptional analysis" and creative use of conflict over decision premises are employed in policy brainstorming sessions by U.S. agencies such as DEA and FBI. But structural and procedural limitations often restrict immediate use of recently gained knowledge in the field. Additional data can provide further efforts to link data and assumptions for even better problem definitions. For example, how effective is the enforcement strategy in improving the lot of the target group (users)?

New York's "Rockefeller Law" was enacted in 1973 to get tough on drugs by sending sellers and users to prison for long terms. However, a 1977 evaluation found that the rigidities of the law (prohibition against plea-bargaining) actually worked against making it an effective deterrent (Lewis, 1986). There is no plea-bargaining restriction that hampers the New York "anticrack" unit. But owing to increased stress on the case-processing system, sentences are shorter. As noted, despite increases in productivity measures (arrests, indictments, confiscations), no evidence exists that shows the trade in or use of cocaine/crack has decreased. This is so even though enforcement against the cocaine industry means arresting a few traffickers of large organizations, while crack enforcement is directed against thousands of small-time entrepreneurs (Kerr, 1986c). Can the assumptions of enforcement advocates, namely that criminal law can solve this country's drug problem, be validated? If cocaine use is constant or rising in the face of already staggering expenditures on enforcement, how valid is the assumption that more funding is needed? Similar questions need to be raised on the assumptions of each group. While we cannot expect the "one best solution" to emerge in most cases, since partial solution of an interdependent problem may exacerbate component problems, the result should be a common set of accepted assumptions on analytical or political grounds, arrived at from reasoned debate among each stakeholder position.

What then is the definition of the drug-abuse policy problem? We have examined the data, sought control variables and causation, and juxtaposed stakeholder assumptions. We have followed numerous caveats, such as guarding against misconstruing the problem through careful data-gathering and use of controls. We now should be ready to offer a definition.

First, based on trends in availability and use, and preliminary evidence on health effects of cocaine/crack use, it can be argued that a policy problem exists in that a growing portion of the population is increasing its illegal use of a substance that directly or indirectly harms the user, user's family and friends, and the public at large in increased property/violent crimes. Even a demonstration that use was constant would, in the face of large enforcement efforts, suggest that a policy problem exists that targets the ultimate user as its beneficiary. One could feasibly swap definitions of problem severity here with data on use trends, and susceptibility of target groups to behavioral change by treatment, enforcement, and education. As indicated, a problem may not necessarily be a public problem and a "public" problem may not be "actionable." Problem definition is exacerbated by the addictive qualities of cocaine and the relative ease of degeneration from apprenticeship to casual user and then rapidly to addict.

Although a policy problem exists, it can also be argued that only part of it is "actionable" and even this part may not be definable so as to ensure substantial improvement in the lot of the target group. We have seen that possible causes of drug abuse include family breakdown and unemployment. Coupled with the technical potency of crack and ease of transport and sale of cocaine, enforcement to dent cocaine consumption might be possible only at a cost of hundreds of billions of dollars (the experience of the New York City anticrack unit might cast doubt on the assumption that it can be reduced at any cost!). Of course, at such a high cost it would become important to weigh such a public effort against other programs—social and defense—including reexamination of the efficacy of expenditures in these other areas if drug abuse became a national epidemic. Even plausible causes, such as cyclical trends in demand and supply, are longer term and hence riddled with potential errors of misconstruction and unanticipated consequences. To define a problem based on possible or plausible causes might be politically opportune, but empirically the potential for disaster is excessively high.

Hence, one possibility is that problem definition should be restricted to actionable causes to achieve the highest efficacy of public expenditures. In this case, assumptional analysis and data seem to suggest that drug abuse is more a problem of untreated abusers than selection of military hardware to interdict traffickers. Using the three-step process, see what other definitions you can generate and be prepared to justify them. The suggested problem-structuring process should serve to liberate policymakers (elected, appointed, or contracted) from their premises and enable one to focus on creative definitions of actionable causes in each case.

ADDITIONAL CASES

Students can apply the problem-structuring process described above to several other cases. However, the cases will not be reprinted and will require use of the library for materials. The first case is "Acid Rain" and requires reading the article in *Smithsonian* (November 1985, pp. 211–230) entitled "A Deathly Spell

Is Hovering Above the Black Forest," by Edwin Kiester, Jr. Additional data on causation and stakeholder assumptions can be found in the report entitled "Curbing Acid Rain: Cost, Budget and Coal-Market Effects," by the Congressional Budget Office (June 1986). The second case is the "Space Shuttle *Challenger* Accident." While many excellent articles have been written on this subject, and which provide insights into data, causation, and stakeholder assumptions, the most basic is the "Report of the Presidential Commission on the Space Shuttle *Challenger* Accident" (June 6, 1986), to be found in the Rogers Commission report (see References at the end of this chapter). A more critical case examination of the *Challenger* disaster can be found in Richard Cook, "The Rogers Commission Failed: Questions It Never Asked, Answers It Didn't Listen To," *The Washington Monthly*, November 1986, pp. 13–21.

REFERENCES

Atlanta Constitution. (1986, November 22). Testimony on Iran leaves lawmakers angrier than ever, p. 13A.

Brewer, Garry D., & deLeon, Peter. (1983). *The foundations of policy analysis.* Homewood, IL: Dorsey.

Baum, Dan. (1986, October 5). Police link doctors' suspensions to crime wave. *The Atlanta Constitution*, p. 1B.

Brinkley, Joel. (1986a, October 10). Drug use held mostly stable or lower. *The New York Times*, p. 10.

———. (1986b, November 2). Drug law raises more than hope: The turf battles are likely to reach new heights. *The New York Times*, p. 14.

———. (1986c, November 11). Key hospital accrediting agency to start weighing mortality rates. *The New York Times*, p. 1.

Cook, Richard. (1986, November). The Rogers Commission failed: Questions it never asked, answers it didn't listen to. *The Washington Monthly*, pp. 13–21.

Doyle, Denis P., & Hartle, Terry W. (1986, February). Student-aid muddle. *The Atlantic Monthly*, pp. 30–34.

Drabelle, Dennis. (1986, October). Review of *Wartime writings 1939–1944* by Antoine de Saint Exupery. *Smithsonian*, pp. 176, 177.

Drug Enforcement Report. (1986a, October 23). New York: Pace Publications.

———. (1986b, November 10). New York: Pace Publications.

Dunn, William N. (1981). *Public policy analysis: An introduction.* Englewood Cliffs, NJ: Prentice-Hall.

Goldwater, Barry. (1986, October 19). Why Congress needs a kick in the budget. *The Atlanta Constitution*, p. 20A.

Graham, Bradley. (1987, June 28). With each step forward, the U.S. loses ground in its war on cocaine: Paradox haunts antidrug compaign in South America. *The Washington Post*, p. 1.

Greenhouse, Linda. (1986, October 2). Drug war vs. budget deficit: The Senate blinked. *The New York Times*, p. 8.

Guess, George M. (1985, September/October). Role conflict in capital project implementation: The case of Dade County Metrorail. *Public Administration Review, 45*(5), 576–586.

Hayes, Robert M. (1986, November 27). The issue is housing. *The New York Times*, p. 16.

Hopkins, Sam. (1986, November 1). Bowers suggests making possession of small amount of pot a felony. *The Atlanta Constitution*, p. 1A.

Kerr, Peter. (1986a. September 17). Experts say some antidrug efforts by school harm more than help. *The New York Times*, p. 1.

———. (1986b, November 17). Anatomy of an issue: Drugs, the evidence, the reaction. *The New York Times*, p. 1.

———. (1986c, November 24). New York crack cases strain its justice system. *The New York Times*, p. 3.

Kline, David. (1987, May). Bolivia: How to lose a drug war. *The Atlantic Monthly, 259*(5), 22–27.

Lehan Edward A. (1984). *Budgetmaking: A workbook of public budgeting theory and practice.* Now York: St. Martin's Press.

Lewis, Anthony. (1986, September 29). The political narcotic. *The New York Times*, p. 22.

Lieber, James. (1986, January). Coping with cocaine. *The Atlantic Monthly*, pp. 39–48.

Lindsey, Robert. (1986, October 4). Marijuana drive reduces supplies and raises prices. *The New York Times*, p. 7.

Main, Thomas J. (1986, November 27). Hope for New York City's homeless? There is no quick fix. *The New York Times*, p. 11.

Mitroff, Ian I., & Emshoff, James R. (1979). On strategic assumption-making: A dialectical approach to policy and planning. *Academy of Management Review, 4*(1), 1–12.

Texan is selling drug-free urine to meet 'unanticipated demand'. (1986, November 29). *The New York Times*, p. 12.

Pirsig, Robert M. (1974). *Zen and the art of motorcycle maintenance: An inquiry into values.* New York: Bantam.

Prosser, William L. (1964). *Handbook of the law of torts.* St. Paul, MN: West Publishing.

Reich, Robert B. (1987, May). The rise of techno-nationalism. *The Atlantic Monthly*, pp. 62–69.

Rogers Commission. (1986, June 6). *Report of the Presidential Commission on the*

Space Shuttle Challenger Accident. Washington, DC: U.S. Government Printing Office.

Shell, Ellen Ruppel. (1986, August). Health: An endless debate. *The Atlantic Monthly*, pp. 26–31.

Shively, W. Phillips. (1974). *The craft of political research*: A primer. Englewood Cliffs, NJ: Prentice-Hall.

Wildavsky, Aaron. (1984). *The Politics of the budgetary process* (4th ed.). Boston: Little, Brown.

CHAPTER 3

Forecasting Policy Options

INTRODUCTION

We have seen that at some point in the process of acquiring data we should be able to decide if an actionable policy problem exists. The past behavior of target groups, historical causal forces, and the conflicting needs of stakeholders in the issue area all combine to suggest that a problem, ill-structured though actionable, exists for public policy. The conclusion that a problem does or does not exist is the product of the first part of the "diagnostic" phase of policy analysis.

The second part of the diagnostic phase seeks to uncover the future behavior of variables used to define the problem. Clearly, the two phases are related, for if preliminary data indicate that the "problem" will solve itself in the near future, additional diagnosis might not be warranted. Conceptually, we are still at the problem-definition phase. But because data forecasts and projections are necessary for determining costs and benefits of a problem solution, the subject should be treated separately as a bridge between initial problem definition (Chapter 2) and the problem-solution process (Chapters 4 through 6).

In this chapter, we focus on how policy problems will likely behave in the future. The development of reliable data forecasts will then give us a baseline from which to develop policy options. Just as an improperly defined problem (which should not be confused with an ill-structured one) can lead to costly and inefficient omnibus approaches (throwing dollars at the problem), so also the failure to establish how problem variables will behave in the future can result in public expenditures that could worsen the problem by failing to control for unanticipated consequences. If, based on past trends, drug abuse is a "problem," then setting out viable policy alternatives will depend on the accuracy of forecasts of how its various components will behave in the future. Being able to project trends accurately depends on experience (judgment), the accuracy of past data (time-series), and a thorough understanding of the determinants of hunger and homelessness (causal model). Based on the needs of real decision-makers faced with "messy" policy problems, this chapter will discuss: (1) the purposes of forecasting, (2) the kinds of forecasts commonly developed, and (3) useful techniques for forecasting data. This information will then be applied to the case study of a public-policy consultant forecasting the sales tax receipts required for the development of the budget for the Metropolitan Atlanta Rapid Transit Authority (MARTA).

PREDICTING THE FUTURE, CAUTIOUSLY

Before examining the range of techniques needed to predict the future, we need to know the objectives of forecasting. Usually the agency client (decision-maker) will want specifics, like an exact figure 20 years from now. For example: What will be our sales tax revenues in the year 2,000? How much oil will the United States be importing from the Persian Gulf states in 1990? Typically, the policy analyst will begin work by developing "projections" (or a range of forecasts) to avoid being pinned down on one figure (or forecast). "Forecasts" are single projections chosen from the process of developing a series of possible projections based on currently plausible assumptions. Policy analysts tend to avoid the term "prediction" because it implies "a statement of certainty about future events that obscures the conditional basis on which each of the projections, including the forecast, are based" (Klay, 1983, p. 289). Klay notes, for example, that the U.S. Bureau of the Census publishes several series of projections based on different assumptions about fertility, mortality, and migration "but it resists identifying any one of these projections as an official forecast" (Klay, 1983, p. 289).

What are the objectives of policy forecasting? Dunn (1981, p. 146) distinguishes between forecasts of existing and new policies, their contents, and stakeholders. Forecasts of new policy trends, where new government actions are taken often in response to market forces, tend to allow a wide range of assumptions and conclusions. For example, based on a price of $15 to $20 a barrel of oil, U.S. oil production declined 2 percent from the year previous while imports increased 8 percent in the same period, and these trends should continue until a stable $22 a barrel price is reached—the profitability point for drilling in the U.S. (Daniels, 1986). By contrast, forecasts of existing trends, where no new government actions are taken, such as revenue forecasting (no change in tax structure), typically require one figure, for example, a 2 percent increase in population or a 4 percent increase in revenues for 1987 to 1989. In the case below, MARTA requires exact knowledge of sales tax revenues for at least the next four years to avoid budget deficits or surpluses that would rouse the enmity of differing stakeholders: public unions, bond holders, the appointed MARTA board, riders that would face a fare increase, and bond-rating agencies such as Standard and Poor's. To recognize the gravity of revenue forecasting in the determination of policy, it should be noted that the fiscal year (FY) 1987 sales tax forecast of $155.8 million was high by $8.8 million. The resultant deficit had to be financed by a fare increase in June 1987 (Roughton, 1987). Depending on the patronage response, this policy move could either reduce deficits—or trigger larger ones in the future!

Finally, policy forecasts are also made of the contents of new policies and the behavior of policy stakeholders. Much of this is "judgmental" despite its often heavy quantitative foundation. For example, many policy analysts have attempted to forecast the political stability of different nations as a service to investors and other interested patrons. "Political risk analysis" is an effort to forecast the behavior of policy stakeholders by using such techniques as "political feasibilty assessment" of professors Coplin and O'Leary (*New York Times*, December 7, 1986) to be discussed below. Put simply, data are examined from multiple sources on a variety of structural and policy questions, and the country examined is given a rating from a panel of experts. The rating is then converted into an index or multiplier for forecasting existing trends into the future. Foreign investors then have an indicator of both the political and the economic and financial risk of success or failure. But in contrast with the slick "it depends" approach often proffered by new analysts and old pundits alike (the two-handed economist's "gift of maybe"), the emphasis in this chapter will be in developing a single figure.

Hence, the objectives of forecasting are a function of client needs, and these are often a product of whether the policy or program is old or new. We now turn to the basis (set of assumptions or data) for forecasting. Because a major purpose of this text is to provide a working knowledge of policy techniques and their bases, we will critically examine those techniques commonly used where elegance and sophistication are less important than providing a reasonably accurate answer in the least possible time with the minimum of resources required. The bases for policy projection are (1) judgmental, intuitive, or qualitative; (2) time-series trend extrapolation; and (3) causal or econometric modelling.

While important similarities and differences exist between the three approaches or bases, it should be stressed that in practice most policy analysts use some combination of all three. To cover oneself, it is always prudent to compare forecast results obtained from using each method if possible. Hence, professional forecasters such as Hammer, Siler, and George (see Case Study No. 2) employ multivariate recursive and nonrecursive (causal) models, linear and nonlinear extrapolative techniques, and judgment in order to overcome what are always weaknesses in the data and uncertainties about policymaker behavior. Policy analysts should recognize that revenue forecasting is not simply math and technique. Frequently, more depends on the administration of numbers and the institutional issues of accounting by the client. In the final analysis, forecasting policy options is really an exercise in explaining how people behave institutionally, a subject eminently suited for economic and public administration analysis!

JUDGMENTAL FORECASTING

The wise practitioner uses judgment to some extent in all forecasting. All forecasts involve some judgment. But judgment does not produce all forecasts. The terms "judgmental," "intuitive," "qualitative," and "subjective" are applied where "theory and/or empirical data are unavailable or inadequate"

(Dunn, 1981, p. 149) or where one finds "the failure to use the data in systematic, mathematical projections...(Toulmin and Wright, 1983, p. 221). In contrast with the use of deductive logic for causal models, and inductive logic for trend extrapolations, Dunn suggests that judgmental policy projections are based on "retroductive" logic. This is a "process of reasoning that begins with claims about the future and then works backward to the information and/or assumptions necessary to support [the] claims" (Dunn, 1981, p. 149).

Judgmental policy projections are used to a greater extent on the expenditure than on the revenue side of the budget. Data on the results of past program expenditures, reasons for failure to spend full budget authority (unobligated appropriations), and the rationale for future program changes are usually of questionable validity or reliability. This creates havoc for linear, nonlinear, and causal models, meaning a great deal of uncertainty must somehow be explained and controlled.

For example, the number of "homeless" people that would be eligible for program participation is a function of personal needs (it may be more feasible to use a nearby shelter than live in an apartment); the economy, meaning unemployment and consumer prices for housing and food (based on other "aboveground" or empirical and "underground" or emotional forecasts as well! (Silk, 1986); and other factors such as the local real estate market (affecting the construction and maintenance of single occupancy hotels or SROs). "The more uncertain the future chain of events, the more likely that judgmental forecasting will be the only basis for making expenditure projections" (Toulmin and Wright, 1983, p. 221). Put another way, it would be impossible to forecast the number of eligible homeless without program experience (expert judgment). The best policy analysts use their experience to judge the results of quantitative techniques. Reliance on method alone could produce numbers that, as one consultant put it, "could get us all fired!"

In most public-sector organizations, forecasts often boil down to expert judgments because they are the only ones who know their business. For instance, who is in a better position to describe present and future maintenance needs for a rail transit system than the crews in the maintenance department? Would the average budget or program analyst be likely to know the point at which "tunnel fan" operating efficiency would decline from absence of regular maintenance? Maintenance people can provide the best judgmental forecasts of such phenomena, and with improved data bases, they could probably provide both extrapolative and causal forecasts as well. The occasional scandal, where someone in this position exploits his or her technical knowledge to inflate budget requests, naturally generates suspicion of experts, resulting in elaborate attempts to control or at least counter their judgmental claims by detailed regulations and/or panels of other experts. The process of managing expert judgments can either produce better forecasts or, paradoxically, hamstring the experts, making it harder to manage effectively.

In many cases, good data may exist but uncertainty about the intervening variables demands explicit use of judgment. For example, in developing budget requests for the county budget office, departmental heads must use judgment to forecast even next year's costs of salary and fringe benefits (based on their more intimate knowledge of who is leaving in midyear and whether a new employee has decided to join the pension plan), supplies, and equipment. Departmental staff often know the probable effects of inflationary changes on particular line items, based on past actual changes in expenditures. Estimates from the budget staff are then challenged by other officials such as the assistant county manager and members of the county commission (who will usually compare them with private-sector forecasts). In short, the uncertainties of new program forecasting require "expert group consensus" (Toulmin and Wright, 1983, p. 223), such as the "Delphi technique" or the "bargaining approach" to stimulate a clash of projections that can lead to synthesis on a realistic forecast.

This approach is similar to "political risk analysis" where data producing conflicting projections on the future behavior of such variables as groups in conflict (unions, political parties), economic policies, exports, and debt management are hashed out among experts into one forecast. Obviously, this is a "workable" science rather than an exact one. For, as Dunn notes, the "method" does not ensure that assumptions are made explicit. That is, it is purely subjective ("facts" are also "values"). Further, expert judgmental forecasts for new programs or countries in volatile states of political conflict presume that "the positions of stakeholders are independent and that they occur at the same point in time. These assumptions are unrealistic, since they ignore processes of coalition formation over time and the fact that one stakeholder's position is frequently determined by changes in the position of another" (Dunn, 1981, p. 210). But with little else to rely on to forecast the future of policy expenditures, the analyst has little choice than to apply "expert group consensus" to existing data sources.

But most policies are driven by the budget cycle, which makes forecasting potentially more rigorous and successful. These programs, which seem immune from the political and economic vicissitudes that affect other programs, permit more systematic and quantitative treatment of data (meaning proportionately less judgment mixed into the final forecast). The fact that most governments budget their future annual resources "incrementally" from last year's base—under pressure from staff budgetary "guardians" who want to cut their requests, and to allow "spenders" to achieve no more than their "fair shares"—means that to a large extent, next year's appropriations will be around 5 percent to 15 percent of last year's on most line items.

Again, this underscores the unity of public budgeting and policy: Policy decisions are driven by the budget cycle and budgets require accurate revenue and expenditure forecasts. Such knowledge may please some forecasters (those that need to know budget authority), but usually not those who need to know actual outlays (some outlays may occur months or even years after obligations). Nevertheless, forecasters know that in most cases, barring unforeseen political changes, expenditures will change incrementally up or down for existing policies. As noted, this is probably not true for new programs or policies.

Governments need revenues to finance budgets, and budgets are the political expression of what policies are going to be next year (if one can sift through the accounting legerdemain and jargon to understand them!). Because revenues almost exclusively involve numbers, one would expect forecasters to have a field day, applying the highest-tech methods available with the most exacting results. Unfortunately, revenue projections often involve too many imprecise numbers. While expenditure forecasts are the aggregate of incremental changes in programs, revenue forecasts are the aggregate expression of interlocking economic variables. It is said that revenue forecasting is more risky, for, once made, it cannot be changed until next fiscal year (whereas programs can be cut or added during the year). That is, "revenue policy, in the short run, is a given fact rather than a variable, and the ensuing collections result from forces that are largely beyond the forecaster's control" (Klay, 1983, p. 289).

But revenue forecasting is made even more tenuous by its deceptive air of certainty. Economic forecasters, on which the accuracy of public revenue forecasting ultimately rests, overwhelm us daily with forecasts of consumer prices, growth, debt, inflation, and recession. These forecasts often represent clusters of micro-consensus, which, when magnified across institutions, such as Congressional Budget Office (CBO), U.S. Office of Management and Budget (OMB), Federal Reserve, and Salomon Brothers, can reveal substantial disagreement. For example, the "aboveground" forecast of slow but steady growth predicted for the United States in 1987 is "rational and based on what can be observed in the economic data, on consumer's behavior to date, on the lack of panic in the markets, and on the assumption that the Administration and the Federal Reserve will hold things together" (Silk, 1986).

Specifically, performance of the economy is said to be cyclical. Cycles are "caused by people and governments unknowingly acting in concert" (Kilborn, 1987). While cycle theory would predict economic expansion based on declining interest rates and dollar data, it hasn't happened. Why? One economist explains the death of the expansion cycle as "an accidental counterbalancing of developments in different sectors" (Kilborn, 1987). What this means is that econometric forecasters can understand cyclical patterns but cannot predict their timing. "The economy can go from one trough to another in less than a year, or it can take almost a decade or so" (Kilborn, 1987). This puts the policymaker in a precarious position. Although policy expenditures can technically be pared back if available revenues do not materialize, revenue projections are fixed and based on several levels of economic assumptions. If forecasters make a 1 percent error in a $5-billion projection, this amounts to $50 million that has to be found to finance programs, that could be added to the federal deficit, or that will simply result in fewer services produced by public agencies; for example, more homeless on the streets.

Hence, viewed as a strictly numbers-crunching activity, revenue projection is amenable to more sophisticated statistical techniques. But most ficsal forecasters would also admit that there are insufficient data points for taxation variables like income and employment. They would also note that hunches and judgment are liberally applied (subject always to expert consensus) to fill in the missing data and smooth out the curves. Perhaps the basic difference between expenditure (program and policy) and revenue (tax policy) projection is that judgment is applied at both the front end and the back end of the former, and only at the back end of the latter. Revenue forecasts are mostly technique and some judgment; expenditure forecasts are largely judgmental. Both types, when subject to the tests of professional group judgment, tend to project the future as "That period of time in which our affairs prosper, our friends are true and our happiness is assured" (Bierce, 1970, p. 247).

It should be noted before passing to the subject of *trend forecasting* that judgmental forecasts often include hard data. The "Accounting Identity-Based" technique (Toulmin and Wright, 1983, p. 224) or "Deterministic" approach (Schroeder, 1984, p. 272) forecasts revenues or expenditures by developing a multiplier (usually a ratio) to be attached to last year's base; for example, the price of a gallon of gasoline (rate) times the number of gallons of gasoline sold (base) should provide a multiplier from which to forecast accurately next year's tax receipts (if the price of gasoline behaves as estimated). The sum of the base and this rate then equals the forecast for the required period. For revenues, development of the "rate" often presumes knowledge of determinants of future revenue-producing behavior for each revenue source (sales; property and income taxes), such as consumer spending, migration, and inflation. Unless one employs trend or causal forecasting techniques to find the unknown at this point, use of a mathematical percentage for the rate then cloaks the essentially "judgmental" process in a scientific aura. For this reason, the Deterministic approach is included under judgmental approaches to forecasting rather than as a separate topic. The question begged by the Deterministic approach remains: How do you reliably estimate the rate which is to be added to the base?

The Deterministic approach is more commonly used for expenditure forecasting. Schroeder suggests that "Nearly all cities...use basically a deterministic method to forecast spending" (1984, p. 272). Again, the purpose is to develop a per capita cost multiplier for the base in order to relate inputs to planned outputs or expenditures (average cost of providing given levels of service). "In San Antonio, while the price assumptions are made centrally, departments are requested to produce documented projections of how many units of the several types of inputs will be required to produce services over the forecast period" (Schroeder, 1984, p. 272).

In practice, this means beginning at a micro-level of analysis or task within a cost center. For example, for the Bus Maintenance cost center of a transit agency, it can be calculated that below a certain level of inputs (pay hours), the ratio of bus miles to mechanical breakdowns decreases, which jeopardizes ridership, and by decreasing fare box coverage ratios, this decreases agency fiscal integrity and perhaps future bond ratings. Thus, using the Deterministic method, the percentage increase in pay hours required to maintain service levels (the per capita cost multiplier) could be added to last year's base as the forecast for the future. This method would combine empirical data on past expenditures with judgments on the relationships between service outputs and required new expenditures. Again, these are expert opinions, derived from experience and group bargaining on their validity.

TREND FORECASTING

"There's a strange rhythm to the Ripper murders. There are cyclical rhythms which control other things. There are rhythms which control the sun spots. Every 17 years a particular kind of locust swarms and flies. Every 14 years the price of nutmeg peaks then drops again. But in the Ripper murders, it is always 126 days between the first and second murder, but only 63 days between the second and last."

"Isn't it weird? I've heard of these rhythms. What causes them?"

"Ah, that is one of the mysteries of the universe!"

From: "Yours Truly, Jack the Ripper," an episode from Boris Karloff's *Thriller* series.

In contrast with judgmental forecasting, which is based largely on *post hoc* rationalizations of claims about the future founded on limited data, *trend forecasting* is based on inductive logic—reasoning from particular observations such as time-series data. Trend forecasting is usually based on some form of time-series analysis or numbers collected at multiple and chronological points in time. According to Dunn (1981, p. 151), the aim of time-series analysis is "to provide summary measures (averages) of the amount and rate of change in past and future years."

Trend or "extrapolative" forecasting can be accurate only where three assumptions hold: (1) past observed patterns will persist into the future, (2) past variations will recur regularly in the future, and (3) trends are measured validly and reliably. According to Schroeder (1984, p. 272) "Trend techniques extrapolate revenues or expenditures based purely on recent history. Most commonly, linear trends or linear growth rates are used as the underlying 'model.' Again, while relatively low-cost in terms of its data and computational costs, the approach is incapable of forecasting downturns if the past is characterized by continuous growth." But, as we shall see, this weakness also applies to nonlinear trend forecasting and causal models. The only difference is that in the latter case, we have more confidence in the techniques because they can ostensibly take account of a more dynamic reality.

Let us begin with a discussion of classical time-series analysis as the foundation for examination of more complex techniques of policy forecasting. Time-series data are affected by four components: (1) secular trends, (2) seasonal variations, (3) cyclical fluctuations, and (4) irregular movements. The effects of these components on forecasting accuracy may be demonstrated by a simple example. Recall from Chapter 2 that past data trends were important in establishing whether a drug-abuse policy problem existed. More sophisticated analysis requires an estimate of future data behavior, in this case cocaine usage. Looking at Figure 3.1, we see that the time-series variable cocaine use, on the Y-axis or ordinate, has been steadily growing for 12–17 and 26+ age groups from 1974 to 1985. During the same period, the 18–25 age group exhibited discontinuous use patterns. Similarly, it is evident from Figure 3.2 that cocaine-related emergency room visits from 1981 to 1985 (Brinkley, 1986) have increased at a relatively constant rate. The question is whether we can forecast future trends on the X-axis or abscissa from these data.

Simpler time-series techniques such as the classical time-series, visual estimation (also called the "black thread" technique), moving averages, exponential smoothing and regression analysis all rely on the assumption that the ordinate and abscissa move together (whether or not substantive or specious causality exists, for example, sun spots and changes in stock market prices). This depends on the degree of impact by the four components cited above. Where the other three components reveal irregular variation over time, other variables need to be included in a causal model to develop forecasts in which we can have greater confidence.

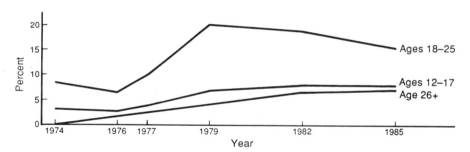

Figure 3.1. Trends in Cocaine Use 1974–1985

Source: National Institute on Drug Abuse

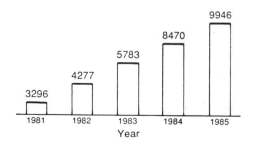

Figure 3.2. Cocaine-Related Emergency Room Visits

Source: National Institute on Drug Abuse

For example, the cocaine use for ages 26+ and 12–17 in Figure 3.1 as well as emergency room visits in Figure 3.2 seem to exhibit trends, or "smooth long-term growth or decline in time-series" (Dunn, 1981, p. 151). If so, one might have confidence in the results of averaging techniques to produce a forecast of future trends. There does not seem to be any "seasonal variation" (within a one-year period) or "cyclical fluctuation" (regular long-term changes that can alter trends). To forecast cycles, one must know how the many determinants of drug abuse—such as price, enforcement, user susceptibility—affect ultimate use, meaning a causal model.

Figure 3.1 also suggests that for the 18–25 age group, cocaine use exhibits "irregular movements." The curious shifts in use may be due in part to measurement problems, enforcement practices, social mores, or family structures. Whatever their causes, forecasting cyclical fluctuations or describing trends is made much more difficult. This underscores our earlier assertion that good data are essential both for defining a policy problem and analyzing policy options. Later shifts in trends that reveal irregular events to be regular cycles are important in redefining the problem, perhaps midway in the enforcement period.

Despite these caveats, forecasters often assume that trends will continue for the short term, and that changes in underlying variables, such as migration and birth rates affecting population trends, will "not change dramatically or unexpectedly over short periods of time" (Liner, 1983, p. 84). Given this relative freedom to engage in short-term trend forecasting, let us apply several simple techniques to the drug use data. Where application is made difficult by data limitations, we will employ alternative data for "whiskey excise taxes" in a small U.S. city. In our case study of MARTA below, we will supply some of the missing data by interpolation.

At the lowest level on any policy forecaster's scale of sophistication are averaging techniques, also called "moving average" (Toulmin and Wright, 1983, p. 226) or "proportionate-change" methods (Robin, Hildreth, and Miller, 1983, p. 35). These are basic and rudimentary time-series analysis methods that are widely used because of their simplicity and ease of calculation. Moving averages can be applied whenever it is necessary to make an estimate of a variable value for a short-term forecast of one to three time periods (months, years). "The concept of the moving average is based on the assumption that the past data observations reflect an underlying trend that can be determined, and that the averaging of these data will eliminate the randomness and seasonality in the data. The averaging of the data to develop a forecast value provides a 'smoothing' effect on the data" (Toulmin and Wright, 1983, p. 226). Averaging depends on the assumption that past patterns will continue and that "turning points" (irregular components) will not take place in the period to be forecast.

Suppose that we are asked to forecast cocaine use (Fig. 3.1) for users age 26 and older for 1986. We know from the difficulty of defining the problem in Chapter 2 that past trends are affected by both cyclical and irregular components

TABLE 3.1. **REPORTED USE AND PERCENTAGE CHANGE OF COCAINE USE, 1974–1986**

Year	Reported Use	Percentage Change
1974	0.0	
1976	0.6	60
1977	1.0	67
1979	2.0	100
1982	3.8	90
1985	4.2	11
1986	6.9	65

so that linear or nonlinear forecasting techniques may boil down to sophistic-ated guesswork or quantitative casuistry. Nevertheless, we need some kind of reading based on the usual caveats of uncertainly that apply to all forecasting efforts. Applying the averaging technique to Figure 3.1 data, we must find the percentage change in cocaine use for past years, average them, and multiply the average percentage change by the last year to obtain the forecast for the next year. (See Table 3.1.)

How did we calculate the percentage changes? First, we found the differ-ences in reported use between each year. The difference between 1976 and 1977 was 0.4 percentage points. To find the percentage change from 1976 to 1977, we divided 0.4 by the base year (0.6) and found it to be 0.666 or 67 per-cent. We then averaged the percentage changes by totaling the column and di-viding it by the number of changes (5). The average percentage change was found to be 65.6 percent. Because this will be our multiplier, we took the product of the last data year (1985) (4.2) and 0.656 and found the expected increase in use for 1986, or 2.75. Total reported percentage use for 1986 should then be 6.9 (4.2 + 2.7). Thus, by this method projected cocaine use for 1986 is based on a 65 percent increase over 1985.

The strength of this technique is also its telling weakness. It is based on straight projection of average past changes, which assumes that average dif-ferences between years will be a guide to next year. Specifically, as in regres-sion analysis to be discussed next, the averaging technique gives each data point the same weight in the analysis, "whereas, in actuality, the latest data may be of more importance because they may indicate the beginning of a new trend" (Toulmin and Wright, 1983, p. 234). Note that after increasing from 60 percent to 100 percent between 1974–1977 (Table 3.1) the percentage change dropped from 90 percent to 11 percent in the two most recent data years. Nevertheless, this method gives the 11 percent the same weight as 100 percent for forecasting purposes. What this means is that a "turning point" may have occurred in 1985 and that the 65 percent figure projected for 1986 may be too high.

Moving up the scale of time-series forecasting sophistication, better re-sults can be obtained by *regression analysis*. Though many refer to linear regression as "causal analysis" (Toulmin and Wright, 1983; Klay, 1983), we use the latter term in reference to deductive theory-based, usually econometric, analyses involving linear multiple-regressions and correlational analyses (Dunn, 1981, p. 150). All regression is "linear" in the sense that it is "curve fitting," and a straight line is one form of a curve.

The results of multiple and correlational analysis do not prove causation. For example, suppose one finds that a linear regression line closely links changes in food consumption (Y) with changes in family income (X). The data on the scattergram falls into a linear pattern with a beta 'b' slope or "regression coefficient" that tells us how much the dependent variable will change in 'a' or alpha for changes along that line. It could be concluded that higher food consumption depends on higher income, that higher income depends on higher food consumption, or that they are both influenced by some other factor(s). Because both X and Y increase together at a specific magnitude, any of these relationships could be supported (Schroeder, Sjoquist, and Stephan, 1986, p. 22). Causal models will be discussed in the next section.

Here we illustrate how regression analysis can aid forecasting. According to Dunn (1981, p. 154): "The most accurate technique for extrapolating linear trend is least-squares trend estimation, a procedure that permits mathematically precise estimates of future social status on the basis of observed values in a time series. While least squares regression is technically superior to the black-thread technique, it is based on the same assumptions of persistence, regularity and data reliability."

Policy analysis first needs to focus on the exploratory task of finding which variables are related to a given variable, such as population growth, per capita income, and consumer expenditure patterns in relation to sales tax collections. This gives us the "correlation coefficient" (a "descriptive statistic that measures the degree of linear association between two variables" denoted r; Schroeder et al., 1986; p. 25) for each pair of variables. The correlation coefficient only measures the degree of association. It says nothing about the reasons for the correlation, which may be: (1) cause and effect, (2) mutual causation, (3) both are related to a third variable, and (4) coincidence. However, the correlation coefficient (r, which ranges from -1.0 to $+1.0$, and indicates the direction of the relationship) and the coefficient of determination (R^2, which is an index of the amount of variation in the dependent variables explained by the independent variables) can supplement regression analysis and enable it to provide "much more information of direct relevance to policymakers than other forms of estimation" (Dunn, 1981, p. 195).

The analyst uses correlation coefficients to explore for the "significant variables" (Blalock, 1972, p. 361). After finding, for example, that per capita income growth (X, or the independent variable) and sales tax collections (Y, or the time-series variable) are positively correlated, (e.g., $r = 0.584$) one can then turn attention to "regression analysis in which we attempt to predict the exact value of one variable from the other" (Blalock, 1972, p. 361). Let us examine the regression technique more closely and indicate its strengths and

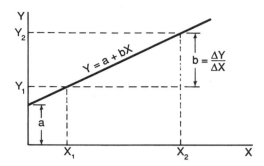

Figure 3.3. The Regression Equation

weaknesses for forecasting. According to Nachmias (1979, p. 113), "The objective of regression analysis is to formulate a function by which the researcher can predict or estimate the scores on a target variable from scores on independent variables."

From Figure 3.3, we note that each pair of X and Y values is a "coordinate" and where all coordinates fall on a straight line, the function relating X to Y is a linear function. The regression equation is: $Y = a + b (X)$. This suggests that Y is a linear function of X. The slope of the regression function (b) indicates how many units in Y are obtained for each unit change in X. The more rigorously we can estimate a regression line, the better chance of predictive accuracy for the future. The symbol (a) represents the point where the regression line crosses the Y axis (where X = O).

The regression equation hypothesizes tnat observed coordinates will fall along a straight line. But a regression line cannot minimize the distance between all observed points simultaneously. Thus, we need a means of averaging the distances to obtain the best-fitting line. "Goodness of fit" tests such as the coefficient of determination (R^2) (discussed in Chapter 2), indicate the strength and direction of the relationship between the variables. The most common form of regression analysis is "least-squares" regression, which focuses on the need to minimize errors (differences between observed and actual points due to randomness in behavior of other factors). By squaring errors, we eliminate the possibility that distances above and below the line would cancel. By not squaring errors, that is, by not using least squares, we could use several lines to minimize the sum of nonsquared errors (Schroeder et al., 1986, p. 20). "Thus, if we draw vertical lines from each of the points to the least-squares line, and if we square these distances and add, the resulting sum will be less than a comparable sum of squares from any other possible straight line" (Blalock, 1972, p. 371). According to Nachmias, "The least-squares method is a way for finding the one straight line that provides the best fit for an observed bivariate distribution." (1979, p. 114). Put more simply, the line will minimize the "residual" distance between the function line and any observed point on the scattergram. Simply averaging, as we did before, ignores the possibility that

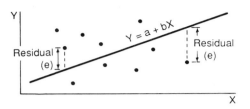

Figure 3.4. A Geometrical Interpretation of Residuals

several lines could "fit" if we ignore the need to minimize residual distances. (See Fig. 3.4.)

Let us now turn to an application of least-squares regression to extrapolate a trend from the data. Since the technique requires valid data, the cocaine-use data might be considered questionable. That is, the data are based on a sample of only 4,000 to 8,000 users (Kerr, 1986) to project the behavior of about 12 million admitted cocaine users. Let us therefore use whiskey excise-tax-collected receipts from a small city for five years to project collections for the next fiscal year. This is more realistic and useful for our case exercise below in that many commodity and excise tax projections must often be aggregated into one comprehensive sales tax revenue projection.

Based on the assumptions and formulae for least-squares regression, where a and b are calculated it is possible to estimate the Y variable (revenues, in this case) in the observed time series or in any projected time period. The calculations to project whiskey tax collected receipts in FY 1987 are illustrated in Table 3.2.

Calculating the trend values according to $Y = a + b(x)$, we now have enough data to calculate both *a* and *b*. The formula for *a* (also termed level in the central year) =

$$\frac{\Sigma Y}{N} \text{ or } \frac{489.1}{5} = 97.8 \quad \text{ and for b} = \frac{\Sigma(xY)}{\Sigma(x^2)} \text{ or } \frac{11.9}{10} = 1.19$$

With *a* and *b*, we can now compute the values for the trend line for each fiscal year in the past series and project the trend line for FYs 1986 and 1987 (Table 3.3).

We are now ready to graph the least-squares line (Fig. 3.5).

Two questions arise on the utility of the least-squares method now that we have our forecasts and have cashed our consulting checks. First, how confident can we be in the forecasted values? Second, how useful are linear methods such as least squares, when most ill-structured policy problems have data that are "often nonlinear, irregular, and discontinuous" (Dunn, 1981, p. 160)? The first question we will attempt to answer by using a method known as "percentage calculation of trend." The second question we will answer by changing the linear least-squares equation for secular trends to one suitable for nonlinear growth trends.

TABLE 3.2. **LEAST-SQUARES REGRESSION OF WHISKEY TAX COLLECTED RECEIPTS, 1982–1986**

Fiscal Year (X)	Collections (Y)	Coded Time Value (x)	Cross-Products (xY)	Years Squared (x²)
1982	$98,751	−2	−197.5	4
1983	95,075	−1	−95.0	1
1984	94,131	0	0	0
1985	97,794	+1	+97.7	1
1986	103,354	+2	+206.7	4
N = 5	$\Sigma Y = \$489,105$	$\Sigma x = 0$	$\Sigma(xY) = +11.9$	$\Sigma(x^2) = 10$

TABLE 3.3. **WHISKEY TAX RECEIPTS FORECAST FOR FYs 1986 AND 1987**

Fiscal Year	(a) Level in Central Year	+	(x) Numbers from Central Year		(b) Slope	=	Y Trend Line
1981	97.8	+	(−2	×	1.19)	=	95.4
1982	97.8		−1		1.19	=	96.6
1983	97.8		0		1.19	=	97.8
1984	97.8		+1		1.19	=	98.9
1985	97.8		+2		1.19	=	100.2
1986	97.8		+3		1.19	=	101.4
1987	97.8		+4		1.19	=	102.6

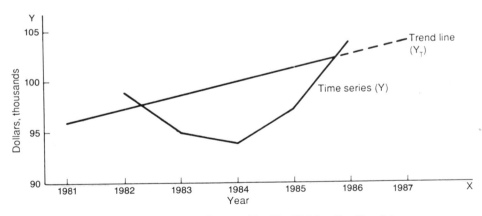

Figure 3.5. Plot of Least-Squares Line For Whiskey Tax Receipts

    To measure our confidence in the forecasts just obtained, we need to see how far past receipts data varied from the trend line. According to Liner (1983, p. 88): "Cyclical components will show up as high or low percentage of trend values during years of expansion and contraction. Major irregular components will show up as one-time deviations.... Confidence in the accuracy of the trend is gained if the percentage of trend values are close to 100%, and the assumption can be made that the variation in actual collections is due to the under-

TABLE 3.4. CALCULATION OF PERCENTAGE OF TREND

Fiscal Year	Actual Collections	Calculated Trend Value	% of Trend
1981	($98,751	95.4) × 100	= 103.5
1982	95,075	96.6 × 100	= 98.5
1983	94,131	97.8 × 100	= 96.2
1984	97,794	98.9 × 100	= 98.9
1985	103,354	100.2 × 100	= 103.1

lying trend. In contrast, if the percentage of trend values varies significantly above or below 100%, many other factors might account for the collections...." (See Table 3.4.)

The calculated percentages of trend values suggest that we should have a relatively high level of confidence in our forecasts, since the past has been largely unsullied by cycles or irregular (nonlinear) events. However, where past observations reveal a nonlinear pattern ("the amounts of change increase or decrease from one time period to the next"; Dunn, 1981, p. 158), other techniques must be used to forecast future time-series values.

While it can be said that, in general, public-expenditure trends vary with less regularity than revenues, exceptions exist that make it difficult to fit a curve or line to revenue data. Cycles, for example, are nonlinear fluctuations or, because segments of a cycle may be linear or curvilinear, occur with persistence and regularity. Growth or decline curves (S-shaped patterns) can occur between years, decades, or even longer periods. If we use a linear-regression equation for data (according to the scattergram) that appears to be increasing, our forecast will be off. For example, if the data suggest a growth curve, such as the periodic increases of $1,000 gaining compound annual interest in a bank account, a linear equation would produce a forecast appropriate only for constant increases, such as putting in $100 each year on a $1,000 account.

CAUSAL FORECASTING

We have seen that the analyst has a large bag of techniques to use for extrapolating linear and nonlinear trends from past data. But extrapolation has little to do with policy theory, other than in the exploratory phase of suggesting variables for possible correlation coefficients. Causal forecasting, by contrast, makes use of empirically testable laws or propositions that make predictions (Dunn, 1981, p. 148). As opposed to subjective, inductive, or retroductive logic, this approach is deductive, that is, reasoning from general statements and propositions to particular sets of information and claims. We recall that both deduction and induction are related in that deductive arguments are strengthened by empirical research, often turning the deductive statement into an inductive generalization. Deduction implies a "model" or systematic set of propositions that can be empirically affirmed or rejected.

Earlier we used the example of income and food purchases to illustrate regressions. On a more profound plane, the regression could serve as a test of the economic pricing theory that the quantity of a good that will be purchased by an individual depends on both income and the price of the product (Manning and Phelps, 1979, cited in Schroeder et al., 1986, p. 29). An empirical test verifies or rejects both the theoretical proposition and the statistical relationship. The purpose of using a model or theory is not simply elegance. According to Klay (1983, p. 299), for example, "The advantage of building formal revenue-forecasting models is that it forces the participants to think clearly about the relationships and assumptions which underlie their forecasts." The inductive methods applied so far do not require thinking about underlying causal relationships—only whether the curve or line fits the data.

Two kinds of causal models exist for revenue forecasting, which will be discussed here: (1) single-equation regression models that may have one or more explanatory variables, and (2) models that incorporate several regression equations (Klay, 1983, p. 299). Multiple regression models are useful for causal forecasting because "they more nearly approximate the real world situation in which several factors may influence and act on a dependent variable" (Toulmin and Wright, 1983, p. 233). An example of a single-equation multiple regression model is that developed for forecasting the City of Mobile's sales tax receipts (Fig. 3.6).

The regression equation on which this model is based ($Y = a + b_1 X_1 + b_2 X_2 + b_3 X_3$) states that, based on past relationships, the city's sales tax can be forecast by the sum of a constant (a, or the Y intercept) and three products. Put another way, there are three multiple, independent causes of Y. The regression coefficients in multiple regression are interpreted as "partial slopes" (Nachmias, 1979, p. 129). Partial slopes indicate how much change in Y is expected for each independent variable when all others are held statistically constant. Assuming no intercorrelation among independent variables, the regression coefficients will be the same as if the independent variables were

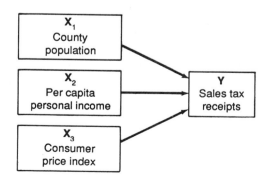

Figure 3.6. Single-Equation Multivariate Projection Model for Sales Tax Receipts

regressed one at a time with Y. As in bivariate regression, the intercept and regression coefficients are estimated by the last–squares method (Nachmias, 1979, p. 130). Since we are solving for three unknowns (a, b_1, and b_2), three equations must be solved by using the following least–squares formulas (which will again be used in our MARTA sales tax case below):

$$b_1 = \frac{(\Sigma\ x_1 y)\ (\Sigma\ x_2{}^2) - (\Sigma\ x_1 x_2)}{(\Sigma\ x_1{}^2)\ (\Sigma\ x_2{}^2) - (\Sigma\ x_1)}$$

$$b_2 = \frac{(\Sigma\ x_1{}^2)\ (\Sigma\ x_2 y) - (\Sigma\ x_1 x_2)}{(\Sigma\ x_1{}^2)\ (\Sigma\ x_2{}^2) - (\Sigma\ x_1 x)}$$

$$a = \frac{\Sigma\ Y - b_1\ \Sigma\ X_1 - b_2\ \Sigma\ X_2}{N}$$

Once the regression values are obtained, various measures of "goodness of fit" should be calculated as in the two-variable case. As noted, these measures enhance the utility of regression analysis by telling us the direction and strength of the relationships. More technically, goodness–of–fit tests indicate how close the regression line minimizes the sum of the squared error term (Schroeder et al., 1986, p. 26). For example, the difference between the actual and estimated value is "the error, also called the residual" and "these are analyzed through computation of a statistic such as the "standard error of the estimate" (or SEE) to develop judgment as to how well the model fits the past relationships" (Klay, 1983, p. 300).

The standard error of estimate would be 0, for example, where the regression line fit actual observations and the residual sum of squares are minimized (Nachmias, 1979, p. 116). The SEE must be first calculated in order to develop another measure of fit commonly used by policy analysts, which is called the "coefficient of determination" or R^2. This is a measure of "relative closeness" of the fit between the regression line and the data points, which, as indicated by the "R^2", is also the square of the correlation coefficient. In this case, "R" would be the multiple correlation coefficient (Blalock, 1972, p. 454). The R^2 measures variation in the dependent variable Y explicable by X_1, X_2, and X_3 as a percentage of total variation in Y (Nachmias, 1979, p. 133).

Finally, policy analysts can forecast by using causal models with several regression equations. Single-equation models assume that the value of each independent variable is determined independently of the dependent variable. So, for example, Mobile's sales tax receipts do not affect consumer personal income to the extent that they could contribute indirectly to the levels of receipts themselves, that is, the Laffer assumption that beyond a certain point tax incidence reduces propensity to save and invest, which also affects tax receipts (Browning and Browning, 1983, p. 440). But in reality, "some of the independent variables might be causes of others" (Nachmias, 1979, p. 145), meaning that we need to construct more complex multivariate models. Such models require development of equations for each dependent variable that include "disturbance terms" (Σ) allowing for the possibility that they are also independent variables (affected by exogenous forces, or variables not explicitly defined in the model). These equations are then solved simultaneously as simultaneous structural equations.

Structural-equation models can be "recursive" and "nonrecursive." Recursive models assume that the direction of influence from any variable does not feed back to it, meaning that each variable is an independent cause but can be influenced by prior variables. "Path coefficients" are often used in recursive models to measure the magnitude of linkage between two or more variables (Nachmias, 1979, p. 149). For example, Tompkins (1975, cited in Nachmias, 1979, pp. 154–156) found that ethnicity exerts a strong direct effect on welfare expenditures. But income levels also had a strong indirect effect via ethnicity and party competition. To derive forecasts of next year's welfare expenditures, it would be extremely useful to employ such a recursive model, assuming that it could be used *post hoc* to forecast past spending levels. However, in reality, variables often feed back into other variables. Welfare expenditures, for example, would also affect income, party competition, and even ethnicity (migration patterns). Nonrecursive models permit the use of both exogenous and endogenous variables via simultaneous equations (Nachmias, 1979, p. 156).

The use of causal modelling is more appropriate for advanced policy analysis, such as that conducted by the Congressional Budget Office or Brookings Institution. Because few expenditure and revenue forecasting assignments at the state or local levels of government would ever require techniques of such immense time, cost, and sophistication, let us end the presentation of such methods here and move on to a less complicated and more likely forecasting assignment. (Analysis of Case Study No. 2 follows on page 95.)

Case Study No. 2: Forecasting Marta Sales Tax Receipts

("Sales Tax Receipts Official Estimates," Richard J. McCrillis · Memorandum to Solbert L. Barth, Hammer · Siler · George · Associates, October 28, 1986)

Following, on pages 68–94:

In the Opinion of Bond Counsel based on existing statutes and other sources of law which they deem relevant and assuming continued compliance with certain covenants made by the Authority to satisfy pertinent requirements of the Tax Reform Act of 1986, interest on the Series H Bonds and on the Series I Bonds is exempt from all present Federal income taxes, except to the extent of the applicability of an alternative minimum tax and an environmental tax to certain corporations. See "Tax Exemption" herein. In the opinion of Bond Counsel such interest is exempt from all present taxation in the State of Georgia.

$170,000,000
Metropolitan Atlanta Rapid Transit Authority (Georgia)

Sales Tax Revenue Bonds
$ 50,000,000 Series H
$120,000,000 Series I

Dated November 1, 1986   **Due July 1, as shown below**

Principal and semi-annual interest (January 1 and July 1, first payment July 1, 1987 representing eight months' interest) are payable by check by The Citizens and Southern National Bank, Atlanta, Georgia, the Trustee. The Series H Bonds and the Series I Bonds are issuable as fully registered bonds in the denomination of $5,000 or any integral multiple thereof. The Series H Bonds and the Series I Bonds are subject to redemption prior to maturity as more fully set forth herein.

The Series H Bonds and the Series I Bonds are being issued for the purpose of financing costs of the construction and development of a rapid transit system.

The Series H Bonds and the Series I Bonds are payable from and secured by a pledge of and lien upon payments to be made to the Authority of receipts of a retail sales and use tax collected in Fulton and DeKalb Counties pursuant to a Rapid Transit Contract and Assistance Agreement. The Series H Bonds and the Series I Bonds do not constitute a debt of the State of Georgia or of any city or county thereof. The Authority has no taxing powers.

$26,685,000 Serial Bonds, Series H
$29,595,000 Serial Bonds, Series I

Year	Amount Series H	Amount Series I	Rate	Price or Yield	Year	Amount Series H	Amount Series I	Rate	Price or Yield
1987	$ 970,000	$2,130,000	4.20%	3.90%	1996	$1,575,000	$1,675,000	6.10%	100
1988	1,010,000	1,080,000	4.20%	100	1997	1,675,000	1,785,000	6.25%	100
1989	1,055,000	1,130,000	4.50%	100	1998	1,785,000	1,905,000	6.40%	100
1990	1,110,000	1,185,000	4.80%	100	1999	1,900,000	2,035,000	6.50%	6.55%
1991	1,170,000	1,250,000	5.10%	100	2000	2,030,000	2,170,000	6.70%	100
1992	1,240,000	1,320,000	5.40%	100	2001	2,170,000	2,315,000	6.80%	6.85%
1993	1,310,000	1,405,000	5.60%	100	2002	2,325,000	2,480,000	6.90%	6.95%
1994	1,390,000	1,490,000	5.80%	100	2003	2,490,000	2,660,000	7.00%	7.05%
1995	1,480,000	1,580,000	6.00%	100					

$ 8,605,000 7% Term Bonds, Series H due July 1, 2006 @ 99.00%
$ 9,190,000 7% Term Bonds, Series I due July 1, 2006 @ 99.00%

$14,710,000 7% Term Bonds, Series H due July 1, 2010 @ 98.125%
$81,215,000 7% Term Bonds, Series I due July 1, 2016 @ 98.125%

(Plus Accrued Interest)

The Series H Bonds and the Series I Bonds are offered subject to the approval of legality by Chapman and Cutler, Chicago, Illinois, and Atlanta, Georgia, Powell, Goldstein, Frazer & Murphy, Atlanta, Georgia, and Juanita Powell Baranco, Esq., Decatur, Georgia, Bond Counsel to the Authority. Certain legal matters will be passed upon for the Authority by its General Counsel, Kutak Rock & Campbell, Atlanta, Georgia. It is expected that the Series H Bonds and the Series I Bonds in definitive form will be available for delivery in New York, New York on or about December 4, 1986.

Shearson Lehman Brothers Inc.

Morgan Stanley & Co. Incorporated   ### The Robinson-Humphrey Company, Inc.

Advest, Inc.   **Outwater & Wells, Inc.**   **Mesirow & Company** Incorporated

Goldman, Sachs & Co.   ### Bear, Stearns & Co. Inc.   ### PaineWebber Incorporated

Prescott, Ball & Turben, Inc.   **Norris & Hirshberg, Inc.**   **Taylor Byrne Securities, Inc.**

Smith Barney, Harris Upham & Co. Incorporated

November 12, 1986

ACTUAL AND ESTIMATED RECEIPTS FROM SALES
TAX BY FISCAL YEAR, 1973–86 AND 1986–2014
(Dollars in Thousands)

Fiscal Year Ending June 30.	Actual Authority Receipts	Fiscal Year Ending June 30.	Estimated Authority Receipts	Fiscal Year Ending June 30.	Estimated Authority Receipts
1973........	$ 43,820(1)	1987.......	$154,818	2001.......	$348,030
1974........	50,501	1988.......	164,183	2002.......	363,767
1975........	50,946	1989.......	174,643	2003.......	380,468
1976........	52,819	1990.......	187,256	2004.......	397,642
1977........	57,933	1991.......	205,580	2005.......	415,298
1978........	66,120	1992.......	220,145	2006.......	433,552
1979........	75,472	1993.......	233,523	2007.......	452,420
1980........	88,342(2)	1994.......	247,045	2008.......	471,885
1981........	99,836	1995.......	260,676	2009.......	492,012
1982........	104,685	1996.......	274,512	2010.......	512,786
1983........	112,008	1997.......	288,547	2011.......	533,123
1984........	123,407	1998.......	302,769	2012.......	554,023(4)
1985........	134,902	1999.......	317,520	2013.......	287,760(5)
1986........	147,149(3)	2000.......	333,202	2014.......	299,236

(1) July 1, 1972 through June 30, 1973 was the first full fiscal year of Sales Tax receipts.
(2) Figure reflects 12 payments in fiscal year 1980, although 13 payments were actually made.
(3) Figure reflects first full year of exemption of prescription drugs from the Sales Tax.
(4) Sales Tax levy reduced to 1/2 of 1% from 1% on July 1, 2012.
(5) First full fiscal year of Sales Tax levy at 1/2 of 1%.

Sources: Actual—Georgia Department of Revenue
          Estimated—Hammer, Siler, George Associates

---------------- ɧ ----------------

HAMMER · SILER · GEORGE · ASSOCIATES

ECONOMIC AND DEVELOPMENT CONSULTANTS

October 28, 1986

Mr. Solbert L. Barth
Assistant General Manager
  for Finance
Metropolitan Atlanta Rapid Transit Authority
401 West Peachtree Street - Suite 2200
Atlanta, Georgia 30365

Dear Mr. Barth:

In accordance with your instructions we have prepared a report as a basis for evaluating sales tax receipt income to the Authority. This report reflects the actual sales tax receipts to MARTA through fiscal year 1986 and also includes information regarding factors which influence our economic projections and estimates of sales tax receipts.

Since our report to the Authority in 1985, inflation rates have decreased substantially. Growth in real income has been revised downward, reflecting trends in recent years. On the other hand, population growth has been greater than expected and the populations of both Fulton and DeKalb Counties are expected to increase at a faster rate than previously forecast. These revisions have caused us to adjust previous projections of sales tax revenues through the 1980's and 1990's. Our estimates of sales tax receipts to MARTA are somewhat higher than those forecast in earlier reports.

We believe it reasonable to use a level of less than four percent in the 1990's as an inflation rate for planning purposes. For the rest of the 1980's inflation rates have been also refined to reflect recent trends. The historically high rates experienced in the 1970's are not expected to continue.

Projections of MARTA sales tax receipts are inflation rate sensitive. An increase or decrease in the assumed inflation rate used in arriving at

Atlanta   •   Denver   •   Silver Spring   •   Washington

1422 West Peachtree Street • Suite 520 • Atlanta, Georgia • 30309 • 404/876-9962

the projections of sales tax receipts could materially affect such projections over the forecast period.

Methodology

The projections of MARTA sales and use tax receipts were derived chiefly from estimates of retail trade sales developed in terms of constant dollars. These data were converted to current dollars through the use of adjustment factors based on estimates of changes in consumer prices. Our analysis involved estimates of past trends and projections of several economic indicators. At various stages each of these factors was checked for reasonableness.

The terms "Atlanta MSA", "Metropolitan Atlanta", "MSA", and "Atlanta" as used herein refer to the 18-county Atlanta Metropolitan Statistical Area. As a result of this revised definition by the U.S. Census, the basis for our analysis has changed. All data in this report addresses the 18-county region. Consequently, some data, even for past years, is not directly comparable.

A brief outline of the methods and relationships utilized follows.

- Non-farm wage and salary employment estimates were formulated by applying employment participation rates to projections of the metropolitan population at rates consistent with past trends.

- Population estimates for the Atlanta MSA were refined by using employment projections based upon changes in employment participation rates. These participation rates, in turn, reflect the ratio of Atlanta employment rates to the rates for the nation.

- To provide the basis for estimates of retail sales in Metropolitan Atlanta, total personal income of residents of the MSA was calculated from estimates of Georgia income.

- Retail sales and taxable sales for Metropolitan Atlanta were calculated from estimates of total personal income based on past trends and projections in the relationships of the two.

- Retail sales, which account for about two-thirds of taxable sales upon which MARTA's one percent local option tax is based, were used in projecting taxable sales in Fulton and DeKalb Counties.

- The Fulton County and DeKalb County share of Metropolitan Atlanta taxable sales was projected to decline from its level of 62.5 percent in 1985 and an estimated 50.9 percent for 2000 to 38.0 percent in 2014.

- MARTA tax receipts, which are collected in Fulton and DeKalb Counties under a one percent levy, were calculated from taxable sales as defined by the state under its sales and use tax.

- All estimates pertaining to the above methodology were for calendar years, except for population and employment projections, which were based on mid calendar year data and annual averages, respectively.

- Fiscal year estimates of MARTA sales and use tax receipts for fiscal years ending June 30 were calculated from calendar year estimates.

- Conversions of income into current dollar estimates were calculated with allowances for inflation and changes in the Implicit Price Deflator for Personal Consumption Expenditures as defined by the U.S. Department of Commerce. Inflation is estimated to average 3.6 percent between 1986 and 1991 and 3.25 percent thereafter to 2014.

Basic Assumptions

In addition to the aforementioned methods and relationships utilized, the following basic assumptions were used in the development of our projections.

- Employment and economic recovery from the recession of the early 1980's was much stronger than anticipated, with the major rebound in 1984 continuing into 1985 and 1986, albeit at a slower pace.

- Atlanta's relative economic position -- in the nation and the southeastern region -- will continue the trend established during the first part of the 1980's.

- No significant changes will be made in Fulton County and DeKalb County boundaries or changes in types of governments of incorporated and unincorporated areas of the two counties.

- Several regional shopping centers are planned for the metro-politan area in the near future. One mall will be built in North Fulton County, another in southeast DeKalb County, and a third mall in Douglas County. All three malls should be opening in the early 1990's; one possibly by 1989.

- No significant changes will be made in the state sales and use tax coverage or termination dates. Current estimates take into account the exemption of prescription drugs authorized by the last General Assembly.

- Imposition of an additional local option sales tax in any of the metropolitan counties will not significantly affect retail shopping patterns or the amount of MARTA sales and use tax receipts.

Primary Economic Factors

The following discussion traces in more detail the analysis of primary economic factors leading to projections of sales and use tax receipts. These factors include: 1) employment, 2) population, 3) income, 4) retail sales, and 5) taxable sales.

Employment Trends and Projections

The 18-county Atlanta Metropolitan Statistical Area (MSA) constitutes the largest employment center in the Southeast. In 1984 Atlanta outranked the second largest employment center, Miami-Hialeah, by 486,000 employees. Employment in the Atlanta MSA currently accounts for over 50 percent of all Georgia employment and 11.2 percent of all southeastern employment (Georgia and its five bordering states are defined as the Southeast for the purposes of this report).

Between 1978 and August 1986 Atlanta's employment increased at a compound rate of 4.7 percent annually. During this period of time 413,500 new workers were added to the Atlanta employment base.

Unemployment in Atlanta remains low when compared to the state and the nation as a whole. U.S. Department of Labor's latest statistics indicate the unemployment rate in Atlanta as of August 1986 was 4.8 percent, while the unemployment rate in Georgia was 5.9 percent, and the U.S. was 6.8 percent for the same period.

Table 1. TRENDS IN NON-FARM WAGE AND SALARY EMPLOYMENT,
ATLANTA MSA, 1978-1985

	Average Annual Employment	Annual Change		Unemployment Rate
		Number	Percent	
1978	922,400	-	-	5.5%
1979	974,600	52,200	5.7%	4.7%
1980	1,004,700	30,100	3.1%	5.6%
1981	1,032,100	27,400	2.7%	5.4%
1982	1,044,700	12,600	1.2%	6.4%
1983	1,096,000	51,300	4.9%	6.5%
1984	1,193,500	97,500	8.9%	4.8%
1985	1,271,500	78,000	6.5%	5.0%
August 1986	1,335,900	51,700	4.0% 1/	4.8%

1/ From August of previous year.

Source: U. S. Department of Labor and Georgia Department of Labor.

Atlanta MSA employment increased by 97,500 workers in 1984 and 78,000 in 1985. This was the largest single year growth in employment recorded in the metropolitan area. Atlanta's economy is expected to cool off in the latter portion of the 1980's, reflecting a slowdown in the national economy. However, new jobs will still be added at a rate of over 45,000 per year through 1990. By 1990 Atlanta's total employment is forecast to reach 1.5 million , 2.1 million by the turn of the century, and 2.8 million by 2014.

Table 2. FORECAST CIVILIAN NON-FARM WAGE AND SALARY EMPLOYMENT,
          ATLANTA MSA, 1978-1985 AND 1990-2014

	Number of Employees	Annual Average Change	
		Number	Percent
Actual			
1978	922,400	-	-
1982	1,044,700	30,575	3.2%
1985	1,271,500	75,600	6.8%
Projections			
1990	1,498,500	45,400	3.3%
1995	1,771,300	54,560	3.4%
2000	2,051,800	56,100	3.0%
2005	2,368,800	63,400	2.9%
2010	2,650,500	56,340	2.3%
2014	2,837,800	46,825	1.7%

Source: Georgia Department of Labor; 1985-90 forecasts by Georgia
         State Economic Forecasting Center; 1990-2014 forecasts by
         Hammer, Siler, George Associates.

Atlanta's economic base is well balanced between manufacturing, wholesale and retail trade, personal and professional services, and government. Atlanta is the regional headquarters for most major firms serving the Southeast. As the state capital of Georgia, Atlanta's state government employment lends stability to the economy. Atlanta is now one of the three largest convention center cities in the country, adding another important dimension to the local economy.

Because of Atlanta's explosive commercial and residential growth, the construction sector has experienced the largest employment gains in recent years. While growth in the private sector is expected to moderate over the next several years before picking up again, major public highway and rapid transit construction is still underway.

Table 3.   NON-FARM EMPLOYMENT, BY MAJOR INDUSTRIAL
GROUP, ATLANTA MSA, 1983-AUGUST 1986

	Number of Employees		Periodic Change		1986 Percent
	1983	Aug. 1986	Number	Percent	Distribution
Mining	1,000	1,600	600	60.0%	0.1%
Contract Construction	51,700	88,800	37,100	71.8%	6.6
Manufacturing	160,500	182,600	22,100	13.8%	13.7
T.C.U. 1/	93,900	107,400	13,500	14.4%	8.0
Wholesale Trade	112,200	138,200	26,000	23.2%	10.3
Retail Trade	193,500	247,400	53,900	27.9%	18.5
F.I.R.E. 2/	77,100	94,200	17,100	22.2%	7.1
Services	234,700	298,300	63,600	27.1%	22.3
Federal Government	34,700	38,400	3,700	10.7%	2.9
State and Local Govt.	136,700	139,000	2,300	1.7%	10.4
Total Employment	1,096,000	1,335,900	239,900	21.9%	100.0%

1/ Transportation, Communications, and Utilities.
2/ Finance, Insurance, and Real Estate.

Note: Benchmark revisions prevent meaningful comparisons with pre-1983
employment data.

Source: U. S. Department of Labor and Georgia Department of Labor.

Within the 18-county Atlanta MSA 63.8 percent of all employment was
located in Fulton and DeKalb Counties in 1985.   This represents a decline
from 68.2 percent in 1978.   However, part of that slip in market share was
due to the transfer of 10,000 jobs at the Atlanta Hartsfield Airport from
Fulton County to Clayton County, where the airport terminal was moved in
September 1981.

Employment in Fulton and DeKalb Counties has increased at a compound
annual rate of 3.7 percent between 1978 and 1985.

In the two-county area the greatest gains have been made in construction and services employment, followed by finance, insurance, and real
estate.   Much of this growth can be related to the rapid pace of office
space absorption in the Buckhead area of Fulton County and the Perimeter
Center area of DeKalb County.

Wholesale and retail trade also showed significant growth over the 1978-1984 period. Manufacturing showed a modest gain over the same time period in the two counties. Land within the two counties has become too expensive for most manufacturing concerns.

Table 4.   NON-FARM WAGE AND SALARY EMPLOYMENT, BY MAJOR INDUSTRIAL GROUP, FULTON AND DEKALB COUNTIES COMBINED, 1978-1985

	Number of Employees		Periodic Change		1985 Percent Distribution
	1978	1985	Number	Percent	
Mining	500	600	100	20.0%	0.1%
Contract Const.	24,000	39,400	15,400	64.2%	4.9
Manufacturing	85,800	88,700	2,900	3.4%	10.9
T.C.U. 1/	53,900	70,600	16,700	31.0%	8.7
Wholesale Trade	71,000	95,800	24,800	34.9%	11.8
Retail Trade	115,900	138,000	22,100	19.1%	17.0
F.I.R.E. 2/	49,800	69,300	19,500	39.2%	8.5
Services	123,700	198,100	74,400	60.1%	24.4
Government	104,300	111,200	6,900	6.6%	13.7
Total Employment	628,900	811,700	182,800	29.1%	100.0%

1/ Transportation, Communications, and Utilities.
2/ Finance, Insurance, and Real Estate.

Source: U.S. Department of Labor and Georgia Department of Labor.

Table 5.   TRENDS AND FORECASTS, NON-FARM WAGE AND
           SALARY EMPLOYMENT, FULTON AND DEKALB
           COUNTIES COMBINED, 1978-2014

	Two-County Total	Percent of Atlanta MSA
Actual		
1978	628,900	68.2%
1980	687,600	68.4%
1985	811,700	63.8%
Projections		
1990	936,600	62.5%
1995	1,080,500	61.0%
2000	1,220,800	59.5%
2005	1,190,000	58.0%
2010	1,497,500	56.5%
2014	1,560,800	55.0%

Source: Georgia Department of Labor; forecasts
          by Hammer, Siler, George Associates.

Population Trends and Projections

The population of Metropolitan Atlanta gained nearly 454,000 new persons between 1970 and 1980 -- an increase of 27 percent. Much of Georgia's population growth is focused in Atlanta. In 1970, 36.7 percent of Georgia's population lived in Atlanta, and by 1980, 39.1 percent lived in Atlanta.

Over the past six years Atlanta's population growth has been even more remarkable. The average annual population gain has been over 70,000 persons. Metropolitan Atlanta's population as of mid 1986 is estimated at 2,578,000.

While the rate of growth of Atlanta's population is expected to slow somewhat over the coming decades, the average annual gain will be about 90,000 persons between 1986 and 2000 and 108,000 per year between 2000 and 2014. By 1990 the Atlanta population is expected to reach 2.9 million, 3.8 million by the turn of the century, and 5.3 million by 2014.

Fulton and DeKalb Counties gained over 52,000 in population over the decade of the 1970's, with population losses in Fulton County being more than offset by gains in DeKalb County. Since the 1980 Census, population growth in both Fulton and DeKalb Counties has been exceptionally strong. This is particularly true in Fulton County, where the City of Atlanta has reversed a long-term decline in population and is actually showing slight gains. These events have caused recently-made population projections to understate growth over the near and mid term in the two-county area.

Fulton and DeKalb Counties are expected to gain almost 33,000 residents by 1990 (over 1986) and reach 1.4 million by 2000, and 1.7 million by 2014. Development is expected to take place mostly in previously underdeveloped north and south Fulton County and as urban infill housing continues within the City of Atlanta. Growth in DeKalb County will slow somewhat compared to the 1970's and early 1980's primarily due to a shortage of prime developable land. Most of the new residential development will take place in southeast DeKalb County.

Together, Fulton and DeKalb Counties are expected to decline in share of metropolitan area population as suburban residential trends continue. In 1970 they contained 60.6 percent of metropolitan area population and by 1980 had declined to 50.2 percent, and 45.2 percent by 1986. By 2000 this proportion can be expected to decline to 37.3 percent and 32.3 percent by 2014.

Table 6. POPULATION TRENDS AND PROJECTIONS, FULTON AND DEKALB COUNTIES AND ATLANTA MSA, 1970-1980 AND 1986-2014

	Atlanta MSA	Fulton County	DeKalb County	Combined Two Counties Number	Combined Two Counties Percent of MSA
Trends					
1970	1,684,200	605,210	415,387	1,020,597	60.6%
1980	2,138,231	589,904	483,024	1,072,928	50.2%
Estimate					
1986	2,578,000	642,700	522,800	1,165,500	45.2%
Projections					
1990	2,939,000	684,800	555,500	1,240,300	42.2%
1995	3,381,000	746,700	597,300	1,344,000	39.8%
2000	3,834,400	800,200	630,000	1,430,200	37.3%
2005	4,349,700	872,600	671,700	1,544,300	35.5%
2010	4,892,500	942,000	707,200	1,649,200	33.7%
2014	5,346,200	994,800	730,600	1,725,400	32.3%

Source: 1970 and 1980 Census; Atlanta Regional Commission; Georgia State Office of Planning and Budget; and Hammer, Siler, George Associates.

Personal Income Trends and Projections

Total personal income as defined by the U.S. Bureau of Economic Analysis is a key factor for analysis of retail trade, taxable sales, and sales and use tax receipts. Income projections for the 18-county Atlanta MSA, in constant 1986 dollars, provide the foundation for future estimates of sales and use tax receipts. Projected personal income of the residents of Fulton and DeKalb Counties is developed from an analysis of past relationships with respect to the total personal income of all Atlanta MSA residents and overall trends in the United States economy.

Table 7.   TRENDS IN TOTAL PERSONAL INCOME,
ATLANTA MSA, 1969-1986

Year	Current Dollars (000)	Constant 1986 Dollars 1/ (000)	Annual Average Real Growth
1969	$ 6,357,000	$16,898,700	-
1980	$21,905,300	$28,757,200	5.0%
1981	$24,711,500	$29,951,700	4.2%
1982	$26,611,000	$30,389,800	1.5%
1983	$29,712,300	$32,657,800	7.5%
1984	$33,695,000	$35,596,400	9.0%
1985	$37,482,600	$38,270,100	7.5%
1986e	$40,617,000	$40,617,000	6.1%

e = estimated

1/ Conversion to constant dollars based upon changes
in the implicit price deflator for personal
consumption expenditures as published by the U.S.
Department of Commerce, Bureau of Economic Analysis.

Source: U.S. Department of Commerce; Georgia State
Forecasting Center; and Hammer, Siler, George
Associates.

Per capita income is derived by dividing total personal income by
total population. Per capita income of Atlanta MSA residents increased
from $3,845 in 1969 to $15,755 in 1986. Atlanta per capita incomes are
estimated by Hammer, Siler, George Associates to be about nine percent
higher than the $14,461 per capita income estimated for the United States
as a whole. Annual compound growth in per capita incomes averaged 9.3
percent per year during the 1969-1980 period and grew at 7.5 percent
between 1980 and 1986.

However, income growth in real terms was much lower. When per capita
incomes are converted to constant 1986 dollars, a procedure which allows
comparison of "real growth" and actual change in spending power, per
capita income growth in the Atlanta MSA only averaged 2.5 percent, com-
pounded annually, between 1969 and 1980. Between 1980 and 1986 real

growth in Metropolitan Atlanta was 2.8 percent. Of course, the same devaluing effects of inflation were experienced all over the country.

Table 8.   TRENDS IN PER CAPITA PERSONAL INCOME, ATLANTA MSA, 1969-1986

| | Per Capita Income | | Annual Compound Rate of Change | |
	Current Dollars	Constant 1986 Dollars	Current Dollars	Constant 1986 Dollars
1969	$ 3,845	$10,220	-	-
1980	$10,192	$13,380	9.3%	2.5%
1981	$11,230	$13,612	10.2%	1.7%
1982	$11,847	$13,529	5.5%	0.6%
1983	$12,882	$14,159	8.7%	4.7%
1984	$14,133	$14,930	9.7%	5.4%
1985	$15,108	$15,425	6.9%	3.3%
1986e	$15,755	$15,755	4.3%	2.1%

e = estimate

Source: Total Personal Income as defined by U.S. Department of Commerce.

Per capita income projections for the Atlanta MSA are based on historical and forecast relationships with U.S. per capita incomes for the nation, as projected by the Bureau of Economic Analysis, U.S. Department of Commerce. Forecasts are presented in terms of 1986 constant dollars.

Atlanta MSA per capita income is projected to rise from $15,755 in 1986 to $20,199 by 2000 and $23,807 in 2014. This represents a real increase in spending power of 1.49 percent per year. For the United States as a whole, per capita incomes are projected to increase by 1.30 percent per year over the same 28-year period.

Per capita income in Fulton and DeKalb Counties is projected to increase from $16,523 in 1986 to $23,588 in 2014, a real increase of 1.28 percent per year. Per capita incomes in Fulton and DeKalb Counties have traditionally been higher than those in the MSA as a whole. They will continue to be higher but are not expected to continue increasing at rates experienced in the past.

Total personal income in the Atlanta MSA is forecast to increase from $40.6 billion in 1986 to $127.3 billion in 2014; this represents a compound annual increase of 4.16 percent. Fulton County and DeKalb County total personal income is decreasing as a percent of MSA total personal income primarily because of lower population growth in these counties. Change in total personal income reflects change in both numbers of residents and in their incomes. Total personal income in the two-county area should reach $22.1 billion by 1990, $29.5 billion by 2000, and $40.7 billion by 2014.

Analysis of personal income provides the base for estimates of retail trade in Fulton and DeKalb Counties. Because of the inflow of customers from surrounding counties, the share of metropolitan retail sales held by the two counties is substantially larger than the share of personal income.

Table 9.   TRENDS AND FORECASTS, PER CAPITA AND TOTAL PERSONAL INCOME, ATLANTA MSA AND FULTON AND DEKALB COUNTIES, 1969-2014
(constant 1986 dollars)

| | Per Capita Income | | | Total Personal Income (000) | | |
| | | Fulton & DeKalb | | | Fulton & DeKalb | |
	Atlanta MSA	Amount	Percent of MSA	Atlanta MSA	Amount	Percent of MSA
Past Trends						
1969	$10,220	$11,071	108.3%	$ 16,898,700	$11,321,600	67.0%
1980	$13,380	$14,164	105.9%	$ 28,757,200	$15,206,800	52.9%
1983	$14,159	$14,885	105.1%	$ 32,657,800	$16,446,700	50.4%
Estimate						
1986	$15,755	$16,523	104.9%	$ 40,617,000	$19,257,000	47.4%
Forecasts						
1990	$17,129	$17,826	104.1%	$ 50,341,000	$22,109,000	43.9%
1995	$18,954	$19,531	103.0%	$ 64,084,000	$26,249,000	41.0%
2000	$20,199	$20,606	102.0%	$ 77,450,000	$29,470,000	38.1%
2005	$21,425	$21,633	101.0%	$ 93,194,000	$33,408,000	35.8%
2010	$22,718	$22,701	99.9%	$111,147,000	$37,438,000	33.7%
2014	$23,807	$23,588	99.1%	$127,275,000	$40,699,000	32.0%

Note: Metro and county level data has been adjusted to revised state estimates released by U.S. Department of Commerce in August 1986.

Source: U. S. Department of Commerce, Bureau of Economic Analysis; and Hammer, Siler, George Associates.

Retail Sales Trends and Projections

Retail sales in the 18-county Atlanta MSA almost increased fourfold between 1972 and 1985 -- from $4.7 billion to $17.4 billion over the last 13 years. Sales in Fulton County increased by $3.8 billion over the same period, while DeKalb County retail sales increased by $3.9 billion. While the two-county area's market share declined between 1972 and 1982, it increased between 1982 and 1985 as new retail strip and specialty centers were built in both counties. Nearly two-thirds of the retail purchases in the metropolitan area are made in Fulton and DeKalb Counties.

Table 10. RETAIL SALES TRENDS, ATLANTA MSA AND
FULTON AND DEKALB COUNTIES, 1972-1985
(millions)

	Atlanta MSA	Fulton County	DeKalb County	Fulton & DeKalb Amount	Fulton & DeKalb Percent of MSA
1972	$ 4,675	$2,098	$1,071	$ 3,169	67.8%
1977	$ 7,085	$2,517	$1,810	$ 4,327	61.1%
1982	$11,707	$3,589	$3,050	$ 6,638	56.7%
1985	$17,419	$5,939	$4,953	$10,892	62.5%

Note: 1972 retail sales adjusted to exclude sales tax for comparative
purposes.

Source: 1972, 1977, and 1982 Census of Retail Trade; "Survey of Buying
Power"; Sales & Marketing Management.

Forecasts of Metropolitan Atlanta MSA retail sales are based on
forecasts of total personal income and are expressed in terms of constant
1986 dollars. Retail sales as a percent of resident total personal income
declined from 47.9 percent in 1977 to 45.0 percent in 1985.

The long-term trend is for retail sales to get a declining share of
personal income as consumers spend increasing amounts on recreation,
travel, personal and professional services, and medical care. Retail
sales as a percent of total personal income is expected to decline to 44.8
percent by 1990, 42.8 percent by 2000, and 35.6 percent by 2014.

Table 11. TRENDS AND FORECASTS OF RETAIL SALES,
ATLANTA MSA, 1977-2014
(millions of 1986 constant dollars)

	Total Personal Income	Retail Sales as Percent of Personal Income	Total Retail Sales
Trends			
1977	$24,042	47.9%	$11,514
1985	$38,270	45.0%	$17,230
Forecasts			
1990	$ 50,341	44.8%	$22,528
1995	$ 64,084	43.8%	$28,037
2000	$ 77,045	42.8%	$33,110
2005	$ 93,194	41.7%	$38,908
2010	$111,147	40.7%	$45,292
2014	$127,275	39.9%	$50,846

Source: 1982 Census of Retail Trade; U. S. Department of Commerce;
"Survey of Buying Power"; Sales & Marketing Management; and
Hammer, Siler, George Associates.

Taxable Sales Trends and Projections

The basis for MARTA's sales and use tax receipts is a local option one percent levy against taxable sales in each jurisdiction, as determined by the State of Georgia. Taxable sales include retail store sales (about two-thirds of the total) and receipts of certain service establishments such as hotels and motels, amusement parks and automobile dealers, and repair establishments. The state's use tax relates directly to taxable purchases by Georgia firms from suppliers outside the state. While not reported separately by the state, the use tax represents about 10 percent of total taxable sales (statewide).

The ratio of taxable sales to total retail sales historically has exhibited a close relationship. This relationship has recently been changed by the exemption of prescription drugs from sales tax beginning in 1985. However, in total, changes in state laws on taxable items have resulted in a decline in revenues of only one to two percent over the past decade. No major changes in state law are expected over the forecast period.

In 1985 the ratio was 149.9 percent taxable sales to total retail sales. The ratio is expected to decline to 148.6 percent in 1987 because of the loss of prescription drugs and is expected to remain at that ratio over the forecast period.

Taxable sales are projected to increase from $16.3 billion in 1985 to $25.0 billion by 2000, and $28.7 billion by 2014, as shown in the table following.

Table 12. TRENDS AND FORECAST, TAXABLE SALES,
ATLANTA MSA, 1972-2014
(000,000 dollars)

	Total Retail Sales	Taxable Sales 1/	Taxable Sales as Percent of Total Retail Sales
Past Trends (current dollars)			
1972	$ 4,675	$ 6,646	142.2%
1977	$ 7,095	$10,513	148.2%
1982	$11,707	$18,110	154.7%
1985	$17,419	$26,115	149.9%
Forecast (constant 1986 dollars)			
1990	$22,528	$33,477	148.6%
1995	$28,037	$41,663	148.6%
2000	$33,110	$49,201	148.6%
2005	$38,908	$57,817	148.6%
2010	$45,292	$67,304	148.6%
2014	$50,846	$75,557	148.6%

1/ Based on sales and use tax receipts.

Source: Georgia Department of Revenue (unpublished data); forecasts by
Hammer, Siler, George Associates.

Fulton and DeKalb County Taxable Sales. Historically, Fulton and
DeKalb Counties have captured a larger portion of total taxable sales than
of retail sales because of the greater concentration of service establishments in these counties. However, Fulton and DeKalb Counties' share of
retail sales and taxable sales in Metropolitan Atlanta has been declining
and can be expected to continue to decline further in the future as
suburbanization outside the urban counties continues at a faster rate of
growth than development within. Fulton County's share of taxable sales
has declined from 54.1 percent in 1972 to 38.5 percent in 1985. This
decline will continue but at a slower rate over the forecast period.

DeKalb County's share of taxable sales increased from 19.9 percent in 1972 to 25.1 percent in 1982, but has since declined to 24.0 percent in 1985. The principal reason for the decline is the opening of a regional retail mall and a large number of small shopping centers in neighboring Gwinnett County. Also, DeKalb County is not growing as fast as it has in the past. DeKalb's share of metropolitan taxable sales is expected to decline over the forecast period.

Despite a declining market share, Fulton and DeKalb Counties taxable sales should increase significantly over the next 28 years -- from $16.3 billion in 1985 to $19.4 billion by 1990, $24.0 billion by 2000 and $28.7 billion in 2014 (in constant 1986 dollars).

Table 13.   FULTON COUNTY AND DEKALB COUNTY
TAXABLE SALES, 1972-2014
(000,000 dollars)

	Atlanta MSA	Fulton County as Percent of MSA	DeKalb County as Percent of MSA	Fulton & DeKalb Amount	Percent of MSA
Past Trends (current dollars)					
1972	$ 6,646	54.1%	19.9%	$ 4,915	74.0%
1977	$10,513	44.9%	24.3%	$ 7,275	69.2%
1982	$18,110	41.4%	25.1%	$12,043	66.5%
1985	$26,115	38.5%	24.0%	$16,324	62.5%
Forecasts (constant 1986 dollars)					
1990	$33,477	35.9%	22.0%	$19,383	57.9%
1995	$41,663	33.5%	21.7%	$22,984	55.2%
2000	$49,201	30.3%	20.6%	$25,037	50.9%
2005	$57,817	27.4%	18.6%	$26,594	46.0%
2010	$67,304	24.8%	16.8%	$27,984	41.6%
2014	$75,557	22.8%	15.2%	$28,738	38.0%

Source: Georgia Department of Revenue; and Hammer, Siler, George Associates.

Sales and Use Tax Receipts

The sales and use tax is the major single source of state income, accounting for 37.3 percent of total state tax revenues. Georgia sales and use tax revenues in FY 1985 totaled $1.63 billion. Nearly one-third of all state sales and use tax collections are received from Fulton and DeKalb Counties.

In fiscal year 1985 retail trade categories accounted for 67.5 percent of all state sales and use tax receipts, providing the primary base of estimating future collections. Service activities, principally hotel accommodations and amusement and sports events, account for another 6.6 percent of collections; utilities sales account for 13.9 percent. Together, these three general types of sales and use tax receipts account for 88 percent of the totals.

Fulton and DeKalb Counties, with their concentration of population, employment, entertainment, convention, and sports events, will continue, in our opinion, to provide a substantial portion of sales and use tax receipts to the state, despite the effect of additions of shopping centers outside the two counties or the gains in manufacturing activity in distant counties. We expect the two-county share, however, to become smaller, while increasing in dollar volume.

As noted above, sales and use tax receipts are derived primarily from retail trade transactions but also include receipts of such service establishments as hotels and motels, amusement parks, and automobile repair facilities that are not counted as part of retail trade for census purposes.

Although the Fulton County and DeKalb County shares of retail sales will decline, the two counties should maintain their share of sales and use tax receipts from the non-retail items such as hotel and motel rooms, utility services and fuels, and charges for admission to places of amusement or sports.

Estimated MARTA Sales and Use Tax Receipts

Analyses of the factors influencing taxable sales were undertaken with data for calendar years. In Table 14, following, the net sales taxes received by MARTA from the local option MARTA tax collected in Fulton and DeKalb Counties are presented for fiscal years ending on June 30 of each year. These estimates are shown in current dollars, so that the effects of inflation and real growth in the local economy are reflected in the estimated payments to MARTA.

They represent "net" sales tax received that excludes adjustments for vendors compensation paid, penalty and interest payment, refunds, returned checks, overpayments, underpayments, plus a one percent collection fee kept by the State of Georgia.

The percent of taxable sales actually received by MARTA from the one percent local option tax has ranged from .85 percent to .94 percent and averaged .88 percent between 1973 and 1986. Last year the ratio was .87 percent. A ratio of .875 percent was used in the following forecasts of fiscal year payments to MARTA.

Table 14. RECEIPTS FROM LOCAL OPTION MARTA TAX,
BY FISCAL YEARS 1972-2014
(current dollars)

Fiscal Year (ending June 30)	Payments to MARTA 2/	Percent Change Over Previous Year
Actual		
1972	$ 2,574,057	N.A.
1973	$ 43,820,106	N.A.
1974	$ 50,501,404	15.25%
1975	$ 50,945,695	0.88%
1976	$ 52,818,991	3.68%
1977	$ 57,932,506	9.68%
1978	$ 66,120,022	14.13%
1979	$ 75,472,385	14.14%
1980	$ 95,119,599 3/	26.03%
1981	$ 99,836,249	4.96%
1982	$104,684,840	4.86%
1983	$112,007,047	6.99%
1984	$123,406,620	10.18%
1985	$134,901,631	9.31%
1986	$147,148,816	9.08%
Forecast		
1987	$154,818,000	5.21%
1988	$164,183,000	6.05%
1989	$174,643,000	6.37%
1990	$187,256,000	7.22%
1991	$205,580,000	9.79%
1992	$220,145,000	7.08%
1993	$233,523,000	6.08%
1994	$247,045,000	5.79%
1995	$260,676,000	5.52%
1996	$274,512,000	5.31%
1997	$288,547,000	5.11%
1998	$302,769,000	4.93%
1999	$317,520,000	4.87%
2000	$333,202,000	4.94%
2001	$348,030,000	4.45%
2002	$363,767,000	4.52%
2003	$380,468,000	4.59%
2004	$397,642,000	4.51%
2005	$415,298,000	4.44%
2006	$433,552,000	4.40%
2007	$452,420,000	4.35%
2008	$471,885,000	4.30%
2009	$492,012,000	4.27%
2010	$512,786,000	4.22%
2011	$533,123,000	3.97%
2012	$554,023,000	3.92%
2013 1/	$287,760,000	-48.06%
2014	$299,236,000	3.99%

1/ One percent tax levy drops to one-half percent June 30, 2012.
2/ Actual payments fiscal 1972 through 1986. Forecasts made with
MARTA receipts from one percent levy from fiscal 1986 through
fiscal 2012 and a one-half of a one percent levy for fiscal 2013
and thereafter. For purposes of this analysis, it can be assumed
that amounts to be received by MARTA in each bond year ending
July 1 would be the same as amounts received for the corresponding
fiscal year ending on the immediately preceding June 30.
3/ Figure reflects 12 payments in fiscal year 1980, although 13 payments
were actually made.

Source: Metropolitan Atlanta Rapid Transit Authority; and Hammer,
Siler, George Associates.

Conclusion

This report has been prepared for inclusion in the Official Statement of the Metropolitan Atlanta Rapid Transit Authority relating to its proposed Sales Tax Revenue Bonds, Series H and Series I, and has our approval for inclusion therein.

The assumptions included in this report are based upon information obtained from the Georgia Department of Revenue in the case of historical sales and use tax collections and from the Metropolitan Atlanta Rapid Transit Authority in the case of local option sales tax receipts from the State of Georgia. Hammer, Siler, George Associates expresses no opinion as to and has made no independent investigation concerning the accuracy or completeness of the information obtained from the sources cited above or other sources referenced in tabular material in the report. The assumptions may be affected favorably or unfavorably by future events and, therefore, the actual results that will be achieved during the projection period may vary from the projections contained in the report and such variations may be material.

Sincerely,

J. D. Wingfield, Jr.
Senior Vice President

JDW,Jr:al

METROPOLITAN ATLANTA RAPID TRANSIT AUTHORITY
ADOPTED OPERATING BUDGET FY87
SUMMARY OF TRANSIT SUBSIDY

	Actual FY84	Actual FY85	Actual FY86	Adopted FY87
Expenditures				
Bus Operations	$72,811,411	$78,357,496	$81,713,722	$84,014,005
Rail Operations	23,935,103	29,847,302	37,516,896	44,679,832
Prior Year Deficits	—	—	—	—
Operations Planning & Marketing	2,677,361	3,672,254	3,888,448	4,407,322
	$99,423,875	$111,877,052	$123,119,066	$133,101,159
Revenues				
Transit Related	($36,597,658)	($39,788,920)	($45,089,274)	($44,669,626)
Federal Operating Assistance	(6,983,563)	(10,934,505)	(7,115,679)	(6,472,422)
Sales Tax Required	$55,842,654	$61,153,627	$70,914,113	$81,959,111
Prior Years Carry-Over Applied				($4,040,611)
FY87 Sales Tax Applied				$77,918,500
Sales Tax Receipts	$123,406,622	$134,901,631	$147,148,822	$155,837,000
Percent of Sales Tax Required Subsidy	45.3%	45.3%	48.2%	52.6%
Funds Eligible for Future Operating Subsidy	$5,860,657	$6,297,189	$2,660,298	—0—

**Analysis of
Case Study
No. 2**

For our second case study, we are asked as consultants to forecast sales tax receipts for a transit authority for the next two years. How typical is this kind of activity for policy analysts? Given the relative stability of tax rates and the fact that interval-level data exist for both tax receipts and its causes, such as income and taxable sales, one might expect this to be either a narrow, technocractic, and perhaps trivial kind of policy exercise—in contrast with meaty policy-option issues like defense, poverty, and environmental affairs. Sales tax forecasting may not be messy enough. In fact, revenue forecasting is plagued with many of the same kinds of uncertainties as expenditure forecasting, proving that the availability of numbers does not cure every disease.

More importantly, revenue forecasting permits less room for error. While expenditures (outlays) can be varied throughout the year by supplemental appropriations, rescissions, deferrals, earmarks, and decisions not to obligate, revenue decisions are usually made only once each year. Although it is true that revenue estimates are updated monthly and this can affect expenditures, the structure (relative contribution of each tax) and incidence (politics of who pays) of state and local revenue sources are normally locked in at the beginning of the fiscal year. Further, in contrast with federal budgeting, MARTA expenses are mostly fixed and thus easier to project than revenues!

At the state and local levels, budgets must be developed on the basis of revenue availability. For example, MARTA, is especially dependent on sales tax receipts for its operations. The MARTA Act of 1965 (amended in 1983) provided for a 1 percent sales tax to be levied by the two member counties. The proceeds of the tax are used for bond debt service and operating costs. However, the act provides that no more than 50 percent of the sales tax proceeds can be applied to subsidy of operating costs. Where sales tax receipts are too low (either because expenses increase or forecasts were too low), MARTA must carry over prior reserves to make up the difference. As indicated in the case study (Adopted Operating Budget FY87), because expenses were higher than expected for FY 1987, MARTA had to carry over $4 million to cover the sales tax subsidy rate of 52.6 percent. Should such carryover reserves be insufficient, MARTA would have to consider fare increases or service decreases—both highly unpopular political decisions. Hence, the need for an accurate sales tax forecast—riders, bondholders, board members, labor unions, bond-rating agencies such as Standard and Poors, and senior management all rely on this for planning next year's activities.

Special fund, autonomous transit authorities (also called public enterprises) such as MARTA depend on accurate sales tax forecasts, and the range of available forecasts from consultants and in-house experts varies widely. Some forecasters (often in-house) hide a growth premise in their calculations in the belief that they will receive more money to pay for capital projects. Others without latent political premises simply lack appropriate methodological skills and the knowledge of how to deal with data that are often missing or incomplete. This exercise aims at the second category of analysts. Sales-tax-revenue forecasting is an appropriately messy but actionable policy problem because one must make decisions on which variables to include and how to measure them. Forecasters have varied widely as to these choices, meaning that their results have also varied widely.

Suppose you are a consultant for Hammer, Siler, and George Associates (HSGA) and are asked to develop a multiyear forecast of FY 1987–1990 sales tax receipts? (Schroeder and Bahl classify three- to five-year forecasts as "multiyear"; 1984, p. 7). Despite the elastic disclaimer on A-24 that "The assumptions may be affected favorably or unfavorably by future events and, therefore, the actual results that will be achieved during the projection period may vary from the projections contained in the report...," it should be noted that this company is the "official" and in fact the most accurate forecaster (to date) of MARTA sales tax receipts projections with actual receipts. This is indicated in Table 3.5 by a comparison of receipts projections with actual receipts. Though an exact receipts figure is essential, the most important figure for projection purposes is the growth rate. From 1983 to 1986, HSGA projected growth rates conservatively in all years except 1984, a year of rapid expected economic growth.

Accordingly, their forecasts are found in the "Official Statement" (issued by the authority at the time of bond sale to provide information on financial condition and security pledged for securities being offered, to enable investors to judge the quality of securities being offered) reproduced here as Case Study No. 2. This case study challenges us to supply the missing data and to apply the appropriate techniques in an attempt to replicate HSGA answers. We are just as interested in "right answers" as we are in your ability to substantiate the use of your methods, and to explain your answer.

To demonstrate knowledge of the use of policy-forecasting techniques, one should be able to answer two questions related to the case study. First, one needs to know which variables determine sales tax receipts. As noted, correlation analysis serves the purpose of finding the "significant" variables. Because most sales tax forecasters use roughly the same variables to link "retail trade sales in constant dollars" (HSGA, A-2) to sales tax receipts with varying degrees of success, we will eliminate this step and assume we have the variables. According to HSGA, five factors affect them: (1) employment, (2) population, (3) income, (4) retail sales, and (5) taxable sales (A-4).

The analyst should apply a range of techniques relating these variables to

TABLE 3.5. COMPARISON OF SALES TAX RECEIPTS PROJECTIONS ($ MILLIONS)

| Actuals | % | Series D | | Series E | |
		Year	$	%	$	%
112.0	6.99	1983	111.3	6.3	—	—
123.4	10.18	1984	121.6	10.5	119.1	6.36
134.9	9.31	1985	130.6	7.4	128.1	7.53
147.1	9.08	1986	140.4	7.4	138.1	7.78

Source: Memo from R.J. McCrillis to S.L. Barth, "Sales Tax Receipts 'Official' Estimates," November 4, 1986, Atlanta: MARTA

sales tax yields (receipts) before judging the accuracy of the forecast. Here we need an appropriate "function" such as linear least-squares regression or even simply averaging to predict future receipts from the independent variables. Note that the function may also be obtained from guesstimates and hunches as well as multivariate regressions, and they may be just as accurate. The best analyst will combine critical use of the most sophisticated techniques with hunches based on experience.

Unfortunately, sufficient data on our variables for regression purposes cannot be feasibly obtained. For example, income and sales data are about a year old. Such data lag can affect forecasting where "turning points" start to develop and current data are unavailable to note them. The experience of HSGA suggests that the key is the behavior of variables over the last six months, which means that forecasting from the last several years with interpolated data into the future will to some extent be blind. Further, some of the data includes benchmarks for the national and state levels but not for counties or localities. This means that sales and income must be estimated by extrapolation from national data and available local data. Dallas, for example, forecasts its sales tax receipts from trends in the Dallas consumer price index and population (Klay, 1983, p. 305).

Additionally, forecasting accuracy can be weakened by the existence of county revenue competition. As in many U.S. metropolitan areas composed of multiple counties, Atlanta contains counties in competition with each other for sales tax revenues (namely Fulton County and DeKalb County). This complicates the projection process in that fiscal decisions of each county may be based on what it perceives the other is doing, such as provision of incentives for regional shopping malls. Unfortunately, no consistently accurate methodology exists to project the results of "zero-sum games" into the future.

More importantly, in order for regression analysis to be of any value, according to Toulmin and Wright (1983, p. 234), "the data must contain sufficient observations so that a statistical relationship can be established clearly. This means that for most practical purposes at least 20 or more data points (that is, observations) should be available." Other than the dependent variable, namely sales tax receipts, all independent variables contain fewer than 10 observations. This means that we need to use some technique to "estimate missing data" such as interpolation or extrapolation (Simon, 1978, p. 251). Also, because regression techniques treat all data equally, we may want to "shed" earlier data and emphasize more recent trends. This will be illustrated below.

Additionally, many of the independent variables relate to each other (the intercorrelation or "multicollinearity" problem) and to other exogenous variables. While population and sales do not correlate highly, income and retail sales do (A-16). Also, taxable sales and retail sales exhibit a close relationship (A-18). Where correlation coefficients of all independent variables explain only slightly more than partial correlations of each independent variable, the multicollinearity problem exists (Toulmin and Wright, 1983, p. 234). According to

Nachmias (1979, p. 134), "The problem can be remedied to some extent by combining highly correlated independent variables into a single variable (for example, an index) or by eliminating all but one of the highly correlated independent variables." The related problem of serial correlation or "autocorrelation" is discussed in Chapter 2.

Beyond multicollinearity is the problem of exogenous variables determining the values of the endogenous variables. For instance, the value of the dollar and level of inflation both affect the propensity of the public to consume certain durable and nondurable items, which would then affect sales tax receipts. This means that often inflation alone is a major determinant of the actual dollar amount of retail sales and sales tax receipts. As noted, the technical solution to such a problem is development of a nonrecursive model. But the costs of such an effort may not be worth the increases (if any) in forecast accuracy. Faced with this dilemma, the analyst may simply average each time-series variable until a reasonable line or curve develops.

The second question we need to answer is what technique(s) should be employed to obtain an accurate forecast? Different techniques will produce different forecasts. To some extent, selection is determined by the quality of the data. Where good interval-level data exist and one can presume that past trends should continue for the short term, one should develop as elegant a model as time and resources permit. Let us then compare the results we obtain by using: (1) simply averaging and exponential smoothing, and (2) a "soft" causal approach that combines interpolated data and linear least squares, with those obtained by HSGA.

The least-cost method, as noted, is to simply average past data for fiscal years using such techniques as the "proportionate change" method. We know from the case study official statement (OS) and A-23 that we have more data points (14) for receipts (collections paid to MARTA by the state from the two counties) than any of the other variables. We therefore begin our quest for the ultimate forecast by averaging this data and forecasting receipts for 1987 and 1988. As indicated, we first need to calculate the percentage change in receipts between fiscal years (see Table 3.6).

Using the same procedure for FYs 1988–1990, we forecast:

                    FY 1988 $177,499
                    FY 1989 $195,000
                    FY 1990 $214,227

Note that the proportionate-change method requires the assumption that FY 1987–1990 increases will increase at a constant 9.86 percent rate as this is the average of the previous fiscal years. As indicated in Figure 3.7, this forecast is substantially higher than that developed by HSGA. Should we want to stick with this method, it may be improved by exponential smoothing, using "alpha weights" to rectify the difference. As noted by Toulmin and Wright (1983, pp. 227–228), where considerable randomness in actual observations is expected, one should use a higher alpha factor. However, comparing HSGA forecasts with those just obtained, it is evident that the percentage difference is

TABLE 3.6. **TIME-SERIES TREND ANALYSIS: PROPORTIONATE
CHANGE METHOD**

Fiscal Year	Payments to MARTA ($000)	% Change
1973	$43,820	
1974	50,501	15.25
1975	50,946	0.88
1976	52,819	3.67
1977	57,933	9.68
1978	66,120	14.13
1979	75,472	14.14
1980	88,342	17.05
1981	99,836	13.01
1982	104,685	4.86
1983	112,008	7.00
1984	123,407	10.18
1985	134,902	9.31
1986	147,149	9.08

$\dfrac{128.24}{13} = 9.86$ FY 1987 = 0.0986 × 147,149 = $14,420 + 147,149 = $161,569.

not constant but increasing (FY 1987, 4.36%; FY 1988, 8.10%; FY 1989, 11.66%, and FY 1990, 14.40%). To increase accuracy, alpha weights would have to be varied each year to match this curvilinear pattern.

Let us then move to an application of a "soft causal" approach to see if our accuracy can be improved. Though this is hardly state-of-the-art, it should enable us to get closer to HSGA results. More sophisticated forecasters, such as the Georgia State Department of Revenue and Taxation, use recursive multivariate models with complex vectors on a year-round basis to project and track sales tax receipts. Such econometric forecasters rely more on method than judgment and claim to produce sophisticated, highly accurate results.

These models are so sensitive that where monthly forecasts diverge slightly from actuals, potential residual error correlation analysis (autocorrelation) begins immediately. According to Schroeder et al., (1986, p. 75): "Autocorrelation can be caused by several factors, including omission of an important explanatory variable or the use of an incorrect functional form. It may also simply be due to the tendency of effects to persist over time or for dependent variables to behave cyclically." The most common technique for determining whether autocorrelation exists is the Durbin–Watson coefficient, which is "used to test the null hypothesis that successive error terms are not correlated" (Schroeder et al., 1986, p. 75). If autocorrelation exists, forecasters can then transform the variables through use of generalized least-squares regression (Schroeder et al., 1986, p. 75).

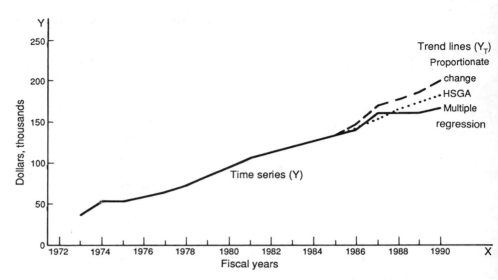

Figure 3.7. Comparison of Averaging and Least-Squares Forecasts With HSGA Results

However, at the introductory level, we need an approach that is more accurate than simple averaging but not as costly and time-consuming as recursive model-building. If that is our objective, given the sales tax problem we need to perform three prior tasks. First, we need to improve the data for key variables by some technique of interpolation (Simon, 1978, p. 251). Often sales tax receipts can be extrapolated as growth rates or ratios from some combination of population and income data. Because taxable sales are largely a function of income, however, we may be able to do the forecast off of income growth or a ratio of taxable sales to income. But population, taxable sales, and personal income variables contain only three or four data points. We need more data points, especially for recent years. Additionally, the client (MARTA) needs sales tax data for fiscal years as it budgets on this basis. However, 90 percent of base data, such as income, sales, population, and employment, is calculated on a calendar year basis. To be precise, we would have to convert calendar year data to fiscal year data.

Second, we need to take a more deductive or econometric approach to the determination of sales tax receipts. So far, our calculations have assumed that time alone causes changes in sales tax receipts, which is a questionable methodological approach. As noted, HSGA suggests that five variables determine receipts. But they also suggest that taxable sales and per capita income may be the key variables. Because we have our best data for employment (1979–1986), we can use that variable to interpolate data points for the others. Employment data, of course, attempt to get at the rate of labor force participation, and the data offer a picture of the resident population that make purchases. Retail and taxable sales data are closely related to total personal income (population × per capita income). Hence, we need data for these two key variables before we can forecast with greater accuracy.

Third, we should use a method such as exponential smoothing or ordinary least squares (OLS) regression for each variable. Use of such simpler techniques before applying multivariate regressions recognizes that the future may not be like the past and that old data should not be accorded the same weight as more recent data. This probably means that we must apply some exponential smoothing to the least-squares results as well. A ratio of taxable sales to income should give us the basis for extrapolating sales tax receipts.

Let us first attempt to supply missing data points for our key variables. (See Table 3.7.) Employment data (A-5) indicate a decline in annual growth from 1978 to 1982, rapid growth between 1983 and 1985, and reduced growth from 1986 onward. As noted by HSGA, "Atlanta's economy is expected to cool off in the latter portion of the 1980s, reflecting a slowdown in the national economy" (A-5). Given the direct or indirect relationships among population, income, employment, and taxable sales rates, we should be able to use these growth rates for our other variables with some confidence.

A forecast of greater accuracy would include the effects of legislative changes, county competitive positions in relation to other metro counties, sales to nonresidents, service sector growth (one-third of taxable sales), the use tax (utilities and manufacturing activities), and the changing retail structure (mail orders and other resident expenditure patterns). As noted, the $8.8 million forecasting difference for FY 1987 was largely due to the assumption (apparently erroneous) that the utility and manufacturing component (whose sales taxes fluctuate widely month to month) would cancel out and grow at the same rate as the rest of retail sales. For our less ambitious purposes in this text, it is important to recognize that the policy analyst must trade the cost of developing totally comprehensive multivariate models with the time necessary to do so and the potential gains in forecasting accuracy. To date, models of lesser sophistication had served client purposes admirably.

Using the interpolated data (Table 3.7), let us try forecasting receipts first with the ratio of income to sales, then with a regression coefficient(s) of forecasted income and sales using a multiple-regression model (Fig. 3.8). If either of these two methods approximates that obtained by HSGA, we have accomplished our purposes. Whether or not we obtain close results, for consistency they should be compared with those obtained by more complex techniques, such as multivariate regression, which we shall perform below.

Since a "turning point" seems to have begun in 1984–1985 (based on shifts in all variables listed in Table 3.7), we probably should use the ratio of the last two years. The average ratio of taxable sales to income for 1985 and 1986 (Table 3.7) is 16.67/18.78 or 8/9 = 0.88. Using this ratio, then, simply the 4.0 percent growth rate interpolated from the 1985–1986 population growth rate, we see that the first projections are uniformly high, the latter much closer, but still higher than the population growth rate. Compared to the HSGA forecast, then, the average population growth rate for the last two years serves as our

TABLE 3.7. **INTERPOLATING DATA WITH EMPLOYMENT VARIABLE**

Year	'77	'78	'79	'80	'81	'82	'83	'84	'85	'86
Employment	—	—	5.7	3.1	2.7	1.2	4.9	8.9	6.5	4.0
Population	—	—	—	1.07	1.08	1.08	1.11	1.14	1.15	1.16
Per Capita Income	—	—	—	15.20	15.60	16.00	16.44	17.37	18.30	19.25
Taxable Sales	7.27	8.27	9.7	10.0	11.0	12.04	13.0	15.30	16.35	17.00

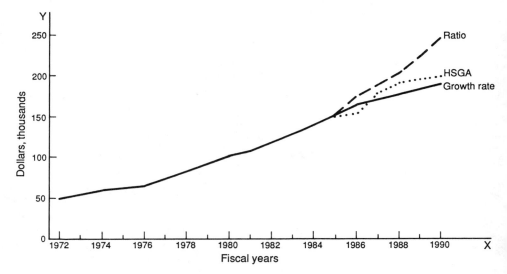

Figure 3.8. Forecast Using Ratio of Income to Taxable Sales

TABLE 3.8. **RATIO AND GROWTH RATE PROJECTIONS vs. HSGA RESULTS**

Year	Ratio of Sales: Income	1985–1986 Population	HSGA
1987	(0.88 × 147.1 = 160.0)	(0.52 × 147.1 = 154.7)	154.8
1988	200.8	162.7	164.1
1989	217.6	171.1	174.6
1990	236.7	180.0	187.2

best predictor function to this point (Table 3.8). Naturally, this may or may not approximate the real-world behavior of sales tax receipts.

Let us now try a multiple-regression model using taxable sales and income as independent variables to see if their regression coefficients with the dependent variable, namely sales tax receipts, can improve on what we have obtained so far. We are justified in using a linear multiple-regression model because taxable sales, per capita income, and sales tax receipts seem to exhibit linear growth patterns (even though their rates vary). Multiple regression allows us to develop partial slopes of taxable sales to receipts and per capita income to receipts. This method allows us to estimate the effect of changes in per capita income on changes in sales tax receipts, taking into account (or holding constant) the effects of taxable sales. Conversely, income could be held constant and the effects of taxable sales on receipts examined. Using the multiple-regression equation, we can then select the highest regression coefficient as multiplier for forecasting purposes. The model can be described as:

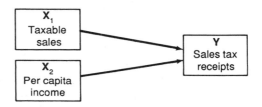

The predicted equation would be:

$$y = a + b_1X_1 + b_2X_2$$

Using real and interpolated data from 1979–1986, we can estimate the intercept (a) and regression coefficients for both independent variables. The data are presented in Table 3.9. Using these data and the multiple-regression formula provided, perform the simple mathematics necessary to obtain the multiplier. Assuming that multicollinearity (intercorrelated independent variables) has been remedied, use the variable explaining the greatest variation in sales tax receipts as your multiplier. In this case, since per capita income explains 0.032 and taxable sales only 0.026, let us try 0.32 as the multiplier to see if HSGA estimates can be replicated.

TABLE 3.9. CALCULATIONS FOR MULTIVARIATE LEAST-SQUARES FORECAST

Y	X^1	X^2	Y^2	$X_1{}^2$	$X_2{}^2$	X_1Y	X_2Y	X_1X_2
95.11	10.0	15.20	9044.01	100	231	951.1	1445.6	152
99.83	11.0	15.60	9960.04	121	231	1098.1	1557.3	171.6
104.83	12.04	16.00	10941.16	144	256	1260.3	1673.6	192
112.00	13.00	16.44	12544.0	169	268.9	1456.0	1836.8	213.7
123.40	15.30	17.37	15227.56	234	299.2	1888.0	2143.45	260.5
134.90	16.35	18.30	18198.0	265.6	334.8	2205.6	2468.6	298.2
147.14	17.00	19.25	21638.4	289	370.5	2501.3	2832.4	327.2
817.21	94.69	118.16	97553.17	1322.6	1991.4	11360.4	13957.75	1615.2

Using Nachmias' formulae (1979, pp. 130, 131), we obtain the following:

$$\Sigma X_1^2 = \Sigma X_1^2 - \frac{(\Sigma X_1)^2}{N} = 1322.6 - \frac{1747684}{7} = 248346.5$$

$$\Sigma X_2^2 = \Sigma X_2^2 - \frac{(\Sigma X_2)^2}{N} = 1991.4 - \frac{4012009}{7} = 571152.7$$

$$\Sigma X_1 X_2 = \Sigma X_1 X_2 - \frac{(\Sigma X_1)(\Sigma X_2)}{N} = 1615.2 - \frac{(94.6)(118)}{7} = 20.5$$

$$\Sigma X_1 Y = \Sigma X_1 Y - \frac{(\Sigma X_1)(\Sigma Y)}{N} = 11360.4 - \frac{(94.6)(817)}{7} = 318.8$$

$$\Sigma X_2 Y = \Sigma X_2 Y - \frac{\Sigma(X_2)(\Sigma Y)}{N} = 13957.8 - \frac{(118)(817)}{7} = 185.5$$

$$b_1 = \frac{(\Sigma X_1 Y)(\Sigma X_2^2) - (\Sigma X_1 X_2)(\Sigma X_2 Y)}{(\Sigma X_1^2)(\Sigma X_2^2) - (\Sigma X_1 X^2)^2}$$

$$= \frac{(318.8)(571152.7) - (20.5)(185.5)}{(248346.5)(571152.7) - (20.5)^2} = .026$$

$$b_2 = \frac{(\Sigma X_1^2)(\Sigma X_2 Y) - (\Sigma X_1 X_2)(\Sigma X_1 Y)}{(\Sigma X_1^2)(\Sigma X_2^2) - (\Sigma X_1 X_2)^2}$$

$$= \frac{(45,800,000) - (6535.4) = 45,793,465}{14,800,000,000} = .032$$

$$a = \frac{\Sigma Y - b_1 \Sigma X_1 - b_2 \Sigma X_2}{N} = \frac{817 - 94.7 - 118}{7} = 86.33$$

y = 86.3 + .026 (TAXABLE SALES) + .032
(PER CAPITA INCOME)

y = 86.4

Thus, we obtain: $y = 86.3 + 0.026 X_1 + 0.032 X_2$. Based on a comparable model used by Schroeder et al. (1986, p. 31), this means that for a \$1.00 increase in per capita income, we can expect a 3.2-cent increase in sales tax receipts. Using 0.032 as our multiplier, we can forecast receipts as in Table 3.10.

From the growing difference between multivariate and HSGA numbers, it is evident that the equation is taking us in a linear path away from what HSGA predicts as the future. Based on a comparison of the growth rate and multiple-regression techniques, one could conclude that either methodological elegance does not always purchase forecasting relevance, or that mistaken as-

TABLE 3.10. **MULTIVARIATE FORECAST VERSUS HSGA RESULTS ($000)**

Year	Multivariate	HSGA	Difference ($ millions)
1987	151.8	154.8	3.0
1988	158.5	164.1	5.6
1989	165.5	174.6	9.1
1990	172.8	187.2	14.4

sumptions about the behavior of determinants (utility and manufacturing sales contributions to the use tax) lead to inaccurate forecasts. The HSGA forecast for FY 1987 was $8.8 million high, meaning that forecasts for the later years (A-23) must also be off. HSGA must now reexamine its data assumptions and rework its figures using methods screened by experience.

CONCLUSION

Policymakers would like to control the consequences of public expenditures consistent with programmatic objectives. Techniques for forecasting alternative policy consequences can serve policy objectives by providing advance notice on design, redesign, and implementation. But even with the best of past data, most feasible techniques presume the future will look something like the past. So, even with the best sales tax receipts forecasts, MARTA policy-makers cannot be certain that they can avoid raising fares or cutting back services to cover revenue shortfalls. Even more sophisticated econometric models can only describe such phenomena as the cyclical patterns of the economy. Because they cannot usually predict cyclical timing (Kilborn, 1987), policy-makers cannot know with precision how to manipulate governmental power over, for example, spending, taxation, and interest rates to ensure efficient and effective policies.

Hence, the quest continues for the genie of forecasting certainty. In this chapter we noted several basic techniques that can be applied to both interpolated and valid-reliable data to provide forecasts. At the most basic level, we can average time-series data to develop trends by such techniques as proportionate change. More sophisticated extrapolative and causal techniques employ bivariate or multivariate least-squares regression equations to try to fit the data (explain the variation and residual variation in the target variable). Where the techniques do not seem to fit, as in our sales tax problem, we can employ a more basic averaging-ratio method with exponential smoothing, or move to nonlinear regression.

REFERENCES

Bierce, Ambrose. (1970). The Devil's Dictionary. In *The collected writings of Ambrose Bierce*. New York: Citadel.

Blalock, Hubert M. (1972). *Social statistics*. New York, McGraw-Hill.

Brinkley, Joel. (1986, October 10). Drug use held mostly stable or lower. *The New York Times*, p. 10.

Browning, Edgar K., & Browning, Jacqueline M. (1983). *Public finance and the price system* (2nd ed.). New York: Macmillan.

Coplin, William D. & O'Leary, Michael K. (1976, Winter). Teaching political strategy skills with 'The Prince.' *Policy Analysis*, *2*(1), 144–160.

Daniels, Lee A. (1986, December 11). U.S. oil output is declining. *The New York Times*, p. 15.

Dunn, William N. (1981). *Public policy analysis: An introduction*. Englewood Cliffs, NJ: Prentice-Hall.

Kerr, Peter. (1986, November 17). Anatomy of an issue: Drugs, the evidence, the reaction. *The New York Times*, p. 1.

Kilborn, Peter T. (1987, January 11). The business cycle rolls over and plays dead. *The New York Times*, p. 6F.

Klay, William Earle. (1983). Revenue forecasting: An administrative perspective. In Jack Rabin and Thomas D. Lynch (Eds.), *Handbook on public budgeting and financial management* (pp. 287–317). New York: Marcel Dekker.

Liner, Charles D. (1983). Projecting local government revenue. In Jack Rabin, W. Bartley Hildreth, and Gerald J. Miller (Eds.), *Budget management: A reader in local government financial management* (pp. 83–92). Athens: University of Georgia Press.

Manning, W.G., & Phelps, C.E. (1979). The demand for dental care. *Bell Journal of Economics*, *10*, 503–525.

Metropolitan Atlanta Rapid Transit Authority. (1986, November 1). *Sales Tax Revenue Bonds, Series H and I Official Statement*.

McCrillis, Richard J. (1986, November 4). Memorandum to Solbert L. Barth, "Sales Tax Receipts 'Official' Estimates." Atlantia: MARTA.

Nachmias, David. (1979). *Public policy evaluation: Approaches and methods*. New York: St. Martin's Press.

The New York Times. Two Syracuse teachers rank political climate in 85 nations. (1986, December 7), p. 14.

Rabin, Jack, Hildreth, W. Bartley, & Miller, Gerald J. (Eds.). Public budgeting laboratory: Workbook and data sourcebook. (1983). Athens: University of Georgia Press.

Rabin, Jack W. & Lynch, Thomas D. (Eds.). (1983). *Handbook on public budgeting and financial management*. New York: Marcel Dekker.

Roughton, Bert. (1987, June 23). MARTA fare to be $0.75 this sunday. *The Atlanta Constitution*, p. 12A.

Schroeder, Larry D. (1984). Multi-year forecasting in san antonio. In Carol W. Lewis & A. Grayson Walker (Eds.). *Casebook in public budgeting and financial management*, pp. 268–300. Englewood Cliffs, NJ: Prentice Hall.

Schroeder, Larry D., & Bahl, Roy. (1984, Spring). The role of multi-year forecasting in the annual budgeting process for local governments. *Public Budgeting and Finance*, 4(1), 3–14.

Schroeder, Larry, Sjoquist, David L., & Stephan, Paula E. (1986). *Understanding regression analysis: An introductory guide.* (Sage Paper No. 57) Beverly Hills, CA: Sage.

Silk, Leonard. (1986, December 10). A season of Cassandras. *The New York Times*, p. 32.

Simon, Julian L. (1978). *Basic research methods in social science: The art of empirical investigation* (2nd ed.). New York: Random House.

Tompkins, Gary L. (1975, May). A causal model of state welfare expenditures. *Journal of Politics*, 37, 392–416.

Toulmin, Llewwllyn M., & Wright, Glendal E. (1983). Expenditure forecasting. In Jack Rabin & Thomas D. Lynch. (Eds.), *Handbook on public budgeting and financial management* (pp. 209–287). New York: Marcel Dekker.

CHAPTER 4

Pricing and Public Policy: The Case of Hospitals

INTRODUCTION

In this chapter we move from the diagnostic phase of public-policy analysis—problem definition and projection of trends—to the analytic phase. We are now concerned with developing the tools and methodology needed to evaluate alternative policy options. This chapter will focus on the determination of prices and their relationship to public-policy goals. How prices are set in the private sector is often of concern to public decision-makers and regulatory agencies. The issues of hospital pricing and cost allocation are part of a larger set of policy issues involving both efficiency in the allocation of society's scarce resources and questions of the proper distribution of income among individuals in the society. In the next chapter the relationship between costs and output will be examined. Producing goods and services at minimum cost has always been a major concern of private firms in competitive markets. As the case in the next chapter illustrates, confronting the difficult issues of how to measure public and private services and relating this output to the costs of production have become increasingly important problems for public-policy analysis. The final chapter will focus on benefit-cost analysis and the problems involved in trying to place a value on the output of public programs. The quantitative techniques used in these chapters will draw upon the basic microeconomic analysis of market operation and its impact upon the consumers and producers in the economy. However, the economic analysis will be related to the political environment, for both of these are crucial elements of overall public-policy analysis.

Pricing is the key element in an economic system based on the marketplace. Prices are the factors that help determine the answers to the fundamental resource allocation questions that all economies face: (1) *What* goods and services should be produced from the vast range of available inputs? (2) *How* should these goods and services be produced if more than one method of production is feasible? (3) How should the output of the economy be *distributed* among the individuals in the society? Because society has values about how these questions are answered, government policymakers may want to influence either the process by which prices are established or the final prices themselves. For example, some prices such as those for agricultural output or the wages paid for low-skill jobs may be considered to be "too low." Thus, legislators have enacted both price-support and minimum-wage programs. When prices are thought to be "too high," various forms of price controls have been implemented. These would include rent controls passed by various city councils and the general controls temporarily enacted under the Nixon Administration's Economic Stablization Program in the early 1970s.

Government decision-makers influence prices when they regulate business activity. Some of this regulation results from concern over the acquisition of market or monopoly power by firms, which allows companies to charge prices that are substantially higher than the cost of production. In the case of regulated electric or gas utilities, a governmental commission or agency explicitly determines how prices are set in relation to costs. Other regulation arises because businesses may not always consider the full costs of production when determining prices. Pollution occurs when companies use the air or water for waste disposal without recognizing that they may be imposing costs on other groups of individuals. Finally, certain services such as national defense are provided by government because they will not be provided in the marketplace. In these cases, the government must explicitly decide on a tax-price to cover the costs of production. Any form of taxation will cause a burden on consumers and will influence the prices established in the private marketplace.

The prices of health-related goods and services and the resulting expenditures are matters of great importance in current public policy, for health spending in the United States reached $425 billion in 1985, a figure that was up 8.9 percent from the previous year. These expenditures amounted to $1,721 per person. Fifty-nine percent of these expenditures were derived from the private sector, largely from private health insurance and from consumers and their families. The remaining 41 percent was funded from government programs, primarily the Medicare and Medicaid programs. National health expenditures have grown from about 6 percent of the country's gross national product (GNP) in 1965 to 10.7 percent of GNP in 1985 (Waldo, Levit, and Lazenby, 1986, p. 1). Almost one-half of the money spent on health in 1985 was used to purchase hospital and nursing home services. Hospital expenditures totalled $167 billion in that year.

These aggregate figures illustrate both the impact that health and hospital expenditures have on the economy and the extensive involvement of the government in the health sector. This government involvement raises several important public-policy questions: What role should the government play in the provision of health and hospital care and what is the impact of this involvement on consumers and producers of hospital services? More specifically, who should be responsible for hospital bad debts and care of the indigent? How should these financial burdens be allocated among hospitals, private insurers, and the government? The various stakeholders in this policy arena have defined these issues as key public-policy problems. To answer these questions we need to know what factors affect the determination of hospital prices and how these prices influence consumer behavior. The rationales for government involvement in an economy based largely on private market activity must also be analyzed. These questions will be discussed in relation to the specific case for this chapter, "Hospital Cost Shifting," by Paul B. Ginsburg and Frank A. Sloan. This case study focuses on how hospitals shift costs among different groups of insured patients and between insured and uninsured patients. (Analysis begins on page 121.)

Case Study No. 3
Hospital Cost Shifting

(Paul B. Ginsburg and Frank A. Sloan, "Hospital Cost Shifting."
The New England Journal of Medicine, 310, pp. 893–898, April 5, 1984)

Recently, the Health Insurance Association of America (HIAA), which is the trade association for commercial health insurers, has mounted a campaign to call attention to what it perceives as "cost shifting" in payment for hospital care.[1] Specifically, HIAA claims that insurers that pay hospitals through methods other than the payment of charges—such as Medicare, Medicaid, and some Blue Cross plans—pay less than the cost of treating their beneficiaries and that, as a result, charge-paying patients (or their insurers) must pay more. It estimates the cost shift for 1981 to have been about $4.8 billion.

HIAA fears a marked increase in the magnitude of this phenomenon as a result of recent legislation. It is estimated that the Tax Equity and Fiscal Responsibility Act of 1982 (TEFRA) and the Social Security Amendments of 1983, which established a prospective-payment system for Medicare, will reduce federal payments to hospitals by $6.8 billion over the fiscal period 1983 to 1985, as compared with what they would have been under previous policies (U.S.

From the Congressional Budget Office, U.S. Congress, and from the Department of Economics and the Institute for Public Policy Studies, Vanderbilt University, Nashville, Tenn. Address reprint requests to Dr. Ginsburg at the Congressional Budget Office, House Annex #2, Rm. 419, Washington, DC 20515.

Supported in part by a grant (#1-R03-HS04665-01-HCT) to Dr. Sloan from the National Center for Health Services Research, U.S. Department of Health and Human Services.

The opinions and conclusions expressed herein are solely those of the authors and should not be construed as representing the opinions or policy of the National Center for Health Services Research, the Congressional Budget Office, or Vanderbilt University.

Congressional Budget Office: unpublished data). Hospitals may reduce costs in order to adjust to lower payments, but they will also probably make up some of the shortfall by raising charges to private patients.

Even though third-party payment is pervasive, some hospitals cannot raise charges without losing a substantial number of private patients. As a result, some hospitals, especially those serving large numbers of low-income patients, find their financial viability threatened by the policies that are followed by insurers that reimburse through methods other than by paying charges.[2]

This paper analyzes the issue of cost shifting, though it uses the less value-laden term "payment differentials" to refer to this phenomenon. We begin with a discussion of the sources of payment differentials. We then give estimates of the magnitude of such differentials, discuss whether they are justified, and assess their effects on hospitals, insurers, and the public at large. In the final section we consider three policy options to deal with some of the sources of the problem.

Sources of Payment Differentials

Differences in the amounts paid for hospital care by different patients are not a new phenomenon. Historically, an important proportion of patients received charity care, paid for principally by philanthropy.[3] With the advent of Medicare and Medicaid and the growth of private insurance, the proportion of charity patients declined, but so did philanthropic subsidies. The payment policies of insurers became critical to the financing of care for the indigent.

Insurers pay hospitals in one of three ways. Some simply pay the hospital's charges. Others, with more market power, either reimburse what they determine to be the hospital's legitimate incurred costs (this group includes many Blue Cross plans, Medicare until recently, and many Medicaid programs) or specify in advance the amounts they will pay (e.g., Medicare's new prospective-payment system).

Three aspects of the policies of insurers that pay on a cost or prospective basis are responsible for most payment differentials: limitations in the cost-finding accounting systems that are used to allocate costs among different groups of patients; costs of hospital activities that are not directly attributable to the care of paying patients, such as charity care and unfunded research; and prudent purchasing policies of insurers.

Cost Finding

Cost-finding systems attempt to determine the proportions of hospital costs that are attributable to each insurer, but the extensive resources required for detailed allocations limit the accuracy of the process. For example, Medicare for many years added an 8½ percent nursing differential to its reimbursements for routine costs, on the presumption that elderly patients required more nursing time per hospital day than others. The absence of research supporting the differential, however, contributed to its recent elimination in the context of budget stringency.[4] Another example is Medicare reimbursement for malpractice premiums. Analysis of patterns of malpractice awards led Medicare to conclude that payment of a proportional share of premiums constituted overpayment. Other difficult cost-allocation issues involve differences in the ease of collection of amounts due from patients, in promptness of payment by patients, and in the level of amenities—for example, telephones and television sets—paid for by the insurer.

Most payment differentials arising from inaccuracies in cost-finding systems are difficult to identify. Hospitals have substantial latitude in the degree of sophistication with which they allocate costs.[5] This means that when a finer breakdown would increase reimbursement from

cost payers, a hospital can employ it, whereas if the opposite is the case, a cruder breakdown can be used. Such discretion in accounting has tended to raise the level of reimbursements from Medicare and Medicaid.

Hospital Activities Not Directly Related to the Care of Paying Patients

Policies governing reimbursement of the costs of hospital activities that are not directly attributable to the care of paying patients account for a larger share of payment differentials. Hospitals' provision of care to patients who are unable to pay their bills is generally recognized as a community responsibility. In 1981, charity care and bad debts accounted for 5.2 percent of hospital billings (Morrisey M: personal communication). Cost payers usually contribute to the cost of such uncompensated care only to the extent that their own beneficiaries do not pay the part of their bill that they are obligated to cost-share.

In contrast to their policies on charity care and bad debts, however, cost-paying insurers include medical education as a reimbursable expense; thus, medical education has tended so far not to lead to payment differentials. Yet, there is some question about whether patients should continue to pay for this expense. Indeed, the issue may arise soon, as some insurers initiate "preferred-provider" plans that steer patients toward hospitals not burdened with the cost of medical education. Research based on regression analysis has indicated that, despite the services provided by residents, teaching results in slightly higher costs.[6]

Prudent Purchasing

Insurers that pay costs have considered it a responsibility to their policyholders (or taxpayers, in the case of Medicare and Medicaid) to pay only those costs that are "reasonable." Medicare's "Section 223" limits, for example—part of the Social Security Amendments of 1972 (P.L. 92–603)—implemented the legislative requirement that Medicare not pay more than the costs of efficient provision of care. These reimbursements evolved into Medicare's prospective-payments system, which carries prudent purchasing policies a giant step further. Some Blue Cross plans use a similar rationale for reimbursement limits or set rates prospectively.

Policies setting reimbursements for capital costs also reflect prudent purchaser considerations. Medicare and Medicaid, for example, do not pay a return on equity to not-for-profit hospitals, because some of the equity is donated. But philanthropy and government grants have become a less important source of funds for hospital investment.[7] Not-for-profit as well as investor-owned hospitals must now compete for funds in capital markets with other industries. Payment for depreciation on the basis of historical costs does not cover the replacement costs of capital facilities during a period of rising inflation. To the extent that hospitals consider such payments from cost-payers inadequate and are successful in recovering higher capital reimbursements in their charges, payment differentials arise.

Magnitude of Payment Differentials

Measurement of payment differentials is necessarily imprecise. Although actual reimbursements by insurers can be measured with some accuracy, assigning costs to various classes of patients is more difficult. The only practical way to do this for the hospital industry as a whole is to assume that the ratio of costs to billed charges (but not reimbursements) is uniform from one insurer to another. On the basis of this assumption, payment differentials are measured by comparing the ratio of reimbursements to billed charges from each insurer.

Estimates for a Recent Year

Use of this method and of 1981 data from the American Hospital Association annual survey makes it evident that substantial payment differentials exist (Table 1). Although the average

TABLE 1. **PERCENTAGE OF HOSPITAL CHARGES PAID BY REVENUE SOURCE, 1981.***

Source	Percentage Distribution of Gross Charges by Source (A)	Payments as a Percentage of Charges (B)
Medicare	37	80
Medicaid	10	79
Blue Cross	18	85
Commercial	19	89
Self-pay	8	72
Other	8	80
All	100	82

* Data are derived from unpublished tabulations from the 1982 American Hospital Association annual survey. The percentages in Column B may be slightly inaccurate because revenue received by the hospital directly from patients may appear in a category other than the major source of payment. It is possible to compare column B percentages for Blue Cross with data obtained directly from Blue Cross plans rather than from hospitals. For 1979, the most recent year for which a comparison can be made, the correlation between the two sets of numbers is 0.88.[8] In any case, it is doubtful that the percentages could be inaccurate enough to change the rank-ordering.

ratio of reimbursements to charges was 82 percent, commercial insurers had an 89 percent average, whereas the average for Medicare and Medicaid was 80 percent. Blue Cross had a ratio that was lower than that of the commercial insurers but higher than the average. Unfortunately, the Blue Cross figure masks the distinction between charge-paying plans, whose experience is closer to that of the commercial insurers, and cost-paying plans, which have ratios closer to that of Medicare.[8]

Trends in Differentials

Payment differentials appear to have grown over time. It is difficult to construct a version of Table 1 for earlier years, but Medicare program data indicate that nonrecoverable charges as a percentage of billed charges increased from 14 percent in 1975[9] to 23 percent in 1981 (Lazenby H: personal communication). Although some people have attributed much of this increased payment differential to Medicare cost-containment policies, this is an unlikely explanation. The greatest change in Medicare reimbursement policies during this period was the implementation and progressive tightening of the Section 223 reimbursement limits. But these limits reduced Medicare reimbursements by only 0.6 percent in 1981 (U.S. Department of Health and Human Services: unpublished data).

Increased amounts of charity care and bad debts can lead to larger payment differentials, but they probably do not explain the trend either. Although bad debts have increased recently as a result of high unemployment and reductions in Medicaid eligibility, their level as a proportion of billed charges was probably stable during the period in question.

A more likely explanation is that hospitals (not-for-profit hospitals and others) raised charges faster than costs increased. Hospitals have seen donated capital, both private and public, become scarcer, and they have become much more dependent on debt and equity financing. Capital reimbursement based on historical costs became less adequate for replacement needs as the inflation rate increased during the 1970s. According to a number of measures of financial status, hospitals were, if anything, better off in 1981 than in 1977.[10] Data from the American Hospital Association's annual survey indicate that community hospitals' net revenue margins increased from 0.7 percent in 1975 to 3.6 percent in 1981.[11,12]

Are Payment Differentials Justified?

Many of the vigorous arguments for and against the appropriateness of payment differentials have over-simplified the issues. Consider bad-debt and charity care, for example. Medicare, Medicaid, and some Blue Cross plans have claimed that they should be responsible only for the bad debts that are attributable to the persons they insure. That argument may be particularly cogent in the case of Medicare and Medicaid,

which have relieved hospitals of a large burden of uncompensated care. Although this is plausible, the same logic would suggest that charge-paying insurers should not be responsible for bad debts either, since the largest part of bad debts is for the care of uninsured patients. If indigent patients are to be cared for without additional public subsidies, all privately insured patients may be expected to share the cost. The implications of options that would require privately insured patients to support care for the indigent are discussed below.

Another controversy concerns markups of charges over costs that yield a surplus to the hospital. Cost payers argue that, since they explicitly reimburse for capital costs, they should not contribute to the surpluses of hospitals. This assumes that capital reimbursements are adequate. Yet insurers face a dilemma, in that more generous payment for capital will undoubtedly increase hospital investment in plant and equipment, which will in turn further boost hospital operating costs.[13]

With respect to both bad debts and capital reimbursement, the payment-differential controversy represents only a small part of policy questions that are much broader. The issue of coverage of bad debts leads to the questions: What kind of access to hospital care should low-income uninsured persons who are not eligible for Medicaid have? and Who should pay for it? The capital-reimbursement issue stems from concerns that neither market forces nor regulation adequately restrains resource use in hospitals at present and that either increased price competition or government intervention is needed. Changes in policies affecting payment differentials would not get to the heart of either matter.

Another argument concerns whether differences in administrative costs incurred by hospitals dealing with various insurers justify payment differentials. Blue Cross plans, for example, have long claimed that hospitals have realized administrative savings through their payment policies. To the extent that administrative savings are realized, a discount based on them would be justified. Singling out particular elements of cost, for special focus, such as administration or nursing care, can be misleading, however. Although some identified costs may be lower for treating patients of certain insurers, relative total costs may be quite different because of some offsetting cost elements that have not been identified and analyzed. In fact, a recent national study shows that a hospital's mix of patients according to payer has no influence on total hospital expense per diem.[14]

The argument that is most difficult to resolve concerns payment differentials that result when an insurer or government agency sets hospital rates prospectively. As long as prospective payment results in cost reduction of the same percentage as the reduction in payments, then such policies do not affect payment differentials. But this is not likely to be the case.[8] When prospective payment applies only to a single payer, hospital incentives may not be altered sufficiently to achieve cost reduction in line with the reduction in revenue, and the payment differential may widen, especially if charge payers are excluded.[8]

Effects of Policies Leading to Payment Differentials

Policies leading to payment differentials have effects on resource allocation in the hospital industry, competition among health insurers, and the distribution of the burden of financing hospital care for the elderly and the poor.

Hospital Resource Allocation
Since the level of reimbursements affects operating surpluses, policies resulting in low reimbursement levels may reduce the volume of capital investment in the industry. Hospitals may not only have less retained money with which to finance capital projects, but their access to debt may be reduced by their having

less cash flow to cover the required payments.

Reduced access to capital funds affects individual hospitals very unevenly, however. The greater the percentage of patients not covered by insurers that pay charges, the greater the impact. The impact is particularly large for hospitals with large numbers of indigent patients who are not eligible for Medicare or Medicaid. These hospitals often also have relatively high percentages of patients covered by Medicare and Medicaid, which will not reimburse for bad debts or charity care. Thus, hospitals with the largest indigent-care burdens to shift have the fewest charge-paying patients on whom to shift these burdens. Indeed, such hospitals may face threats to their financial viability in the short run through inadequate cash flow, as well as in the long run through limited access to capital funds.

Insurer Competition
Payment differentials affect competition in some areas between Blue Cross plans and commercial insurers. In areas where Blue Cross plans reimburse on the basis of costs or set rates prospectively, the wider the payment differential, the greater their advantages over charge-paying commercial insurers. A continued widening of differentials could have either of two effects. Commercial insurers could cease doing business in the area, or they could innovate, as for example with preferred-provider plans. By steering policy-holders to low-priced hospitals, commercial insurers could offset at least some of the Blue Cross plans' competitive advantage.

Financing Medicare and Medicaid
The impact of reimbursement policies on the financing of Medicare and Medicaid is difficult to evaluate. In one sense, these programs have reduced payment differentials by providing insurance for large numbers of indigent patients. In another sense, by paying less than other payers, Medicare and Medicaid have shifted some responsibility from the taxpayers to those paying private insurance premiums and hospital

charges directly. Taxes reduced as a consequence of savings to the Medicare and Medicaid programs are a combination of payroll taxes (Medicare) and federal, state, and local general revenues (Medicaid). Most private health insurance is obtained through employment, and almost all employers currently offer some coverage. A substantial part of any increase in premiums will ultimately be borne by employees in the form of reduced wage rates and other fringe benefits.[15] Those who bear the burden of payroll taxes overlap substantially with those who ultimately pay private health-insurance premiums. A recent study concludes that higher premiums are a more regressive means of financing than a payroll tax.[16]

Policy Options

A number of policy options are available to alter payment differentials and their effects. They include direct subsidies to hospitals to cover the cost of uncompensated care, use of state-level commissions to set hospital rates, and an antitrust exemption to permit commercial insurers to negotiate as a group with hospitals. Although increased competition in the market for health services might resolve some of the problems arising from policies that lead to payment differentials, that is a potential solution only for the long run. National health insurance is another option, but because of substantial budget deficits both current and projected, few of its advocates are actively pressing for it.

Grants to Hospitals for Bad Debts and Charity Care

Public funds could be granted to hospitals that are in financial distress as a result of delivering large amounts of uncompensated care. In order to distinguish this option from a program of national health insurance for hospital services, the subsidy would have to be carefully limited, being based on factors other than the number of patients unable to pay their bills.

Subsidies could be granted only to hospitals meeting rigid criteria for both financial distress and the provision of care for large numbers of indigent patients lacking health insurance. Incentives could be used to encourage recipient hospitals to make cost-effective efforts to collect bad debts. Annual appropriations for such subsidies could be varied according to economic conditions influencing the magnitude of demands for uncompensated care.

In view of the large budget deficits facing all levels of governments, revenue increases to fund these subsidies might be incorporated in legislation implementing this option. One source could be a tax on employer-provided private health-insurance premiums. Alternatively, outlays for Medicare could be reduced—for example, by increasing beneficiary cost sharing—but the projections of deficits for the Medicare trust funds are so alarming that any savings in this area may be needed to maintain solvency in the program and thus may not be available to fund new programs.[17]

A grants program would increase access to care for low-income persons but would cost less than other programs with this aim, because only hospitals with large burdens of uncompensated care would receive assistance. With the care of indigent patients less likely to put a hospital out of business, hospitals would turn away fewer patients for lack of insurance coverage. With certain hospitals protected from bankruptcy, access for other users of these hospitals would also be protected. The limitation of subsidies to hospitals that were disproportionately affected by the provision of uncompensated care would avoid a costly entitlement to hospitals for reimbursement of the costs of all care provided to indigent patients.

This option may be a more efficient way to finance care for the indigent than current cross-subsidy arrangements. In theory, explicit taxes are preferable to implicit cross-subsidies. Many would consider it a step toward fairness to reduce the part of payment differentials that reflects uneven distribution of the burden of uncompensated care among insurers.

A disadvantage of the option would be the difficulty of isolating the effects of serving indigent patients in causing financial distress in a particular hospital from other causes, such as poor management. Overcapacity in an area could be frozen in, and some inefficient hospitals sustained.

The option would not solve the entire payment-differential problem, either. The cost of uncompensated care at hospitals that were not financially distressed would not be affected nor would other sources of payment differentials.

An alternative to a direct hospital subsidy is a public catastrophic-illness insurance plan that would reduce the level of bad debts attributable to costly illness. An advantage of a catastrophic-illness plan is that it is patient-specific, which obviates the need to judge which hospitals require a direct subsidy, but the wider coverage would imply much larger government outlays. Evidence is beginning to accumulate that high-cost illness is responsible for an appreciable part of the total expenditure of hospital care,[18-20] and whether or not a patient has full coverage for such illness may have an important effect on how much is spent on treatment. Also, states might curb benefits for hospital care under Medicaid further if a federal catastrophic-illness program would pick up the tab. A direct subsidy of certain financially distressed hospitals would be much cheaper.

All-Payer Hospital Rate Setting
Problems caused by insurers' policies that lead to payment differentials could be resolved by "all-payer" hospital rate setting. Agencies in Maryland and New Jersey, and more recently in New York and Massachusetts, set hospital rates for all payers and make explicit public decisions concerning payment differentials.

When rate-setting agencies have authority over all payers, explicit decisions may be made on each of the cost-allocation issues examined

in this paper. For example, a specific allowance for uncompensated care can be built into each hospital's rate and thus allocated proportionately to all insurers. Similarly, capital reimbursement can be handled by deciding on the appropriate amount for each hospital and then allocating responsibility for it to different insurers.

Many factors are involved in the decision to adopt an all-payer system—among them cost containment, payment differentials, and the financing of care for indigent patients. The research literature shows conclusively that rate setting has reduced hospital expenditures.[21,22] Another advantage of all-payer systems is the framework they provide for dealing with price differentials among payers and hospitals.

On the other hand, the process of setting rates globally can be a very cumbersome one because of the lack of consensus concerning what is an equitable rate structure. Also, the prospects for competitive alternatives are reduced. These alternatives, such as patient cost sharing, preferred-provider organizations, and health-maintenance organizations, provide incentives to reduce the volume of services as well as the price, but at the risk of some reductions in access for the disadvantaged.

Antitrust Exemption
Commercial insurers contend that the small market share of each individual company prevents them from employing prospective reimbursement or using other methods to negotiate a discount with hospitals. They claim that if they were permitted to negotiate jointly with other commercial insurers, they could reduce their competitive disadvantage while increasing pressure on hospitals to contain costs.

With an antitrust exemption, commercial insurers would be able to negotiate a lower rate with hospitals, especially if they were willing to require beneficiaries to pay a substantial amount of coinsurance if they used hospitals that had failed to reach agreement with them.

Although collective negotiating by commercial insurers could narrow payment differentials, other problems could surface. Commercial insurers and Blue Cross plans could wind up competing vigorously with one another on the basis of how little they could pay hospitals. In that case, no payers would cover the costs of serving the indigent or provide sufficient capital reimbursement so that hospitals could finance the replacement of plant and equipment. Indeed, an antitrust exemption could produce the spectacle of hospitals, which usually oppose rate setting today, lobbying for it in order to protect themselves from the market power of payers.

Conclusion

The issue of payment differentials or "cost shifting" is a complex one to analyze and a difficult one to resolve. Its resolution may not be found in specific changes in reimbursement policies but rather in dealing with broad policy issues, such as whether to use greater reliance on market forces or increased regulation to constrain the growth of medical-care costs and the extent to which indigent patients who are not eligible for Medicare and Medicaid are to be served and how such care should be financed.

We are indebted to Gerard Anderson of Johns Hopkins University, Edmund Becker of the American Hospital Association, Thomas Buchberger of the Congressional Budget Office, Robert Derzon of Lewin and Associates, Nancy Gordon of the Congressional Budget Office, and Irwin Wolkstein of Health Policy Alternatives, Inc., for their helpful comments on earlier versions of this paper.

References

1. Hospital cost shifting: the hidden tax. Washington D.C.: Health Insurance Association of America, 1982.
2. Hadley J, Mullner R, Feder J. The financially distressed hospital. N Engl J Med 1982; 307: 1283–7.
3. Stevens R. "A poor sort of memory": voluntary hospitals and government before the depression. Milbank Mem Fund Q 1982; 60:551–84.
4. Do aged medicare patients receive more costly routine nursing services? evidence inconclusive. Report of the General Accounting Office to the Congress of the United States, January 20, 1982.
5. Danzon PM. Hospital "profits": the effects of reimbursement policies. J Health Econ 1982; 1:29–52.
6. Sloan FA, Feldman R, Steinwald B. Effects of teaching on hospital costs. J Health Econ 1983; 2:1–28.
7. Mullner R, Matthews D, Byre C, Kubal J. Funding aspects of construction in U.S. hospitals (1973–1979). Hosp Financ Manage 1981; 35 (11):31–4.
8. Adamache K, Sloan FA. Competition between nonprofit and for profit health insurers. J Health Econ 1983; 2:225–43.
9. Helbing C. Ten years of short stay hospital utilization and cost under Medicare, 1967–1976. Baltimore: Health Care Financing Administration. (DHHS publication no. (HCFA) 03053).
10. Cleverly WO. Hospital industry analysis report, 1981. Washington D.C.: Health Care Financial Management Association, 1982.
11. American Hospital Association. Hospital statistics. Chicago: American Hospital Association, 1976.
12. Idem. Hospital statistics. Chicago: American Hospital Association, 1982.
13. Bentkover JD, Sloan FA. Hospital capital and operating costs. Adv Health Econ Health Serv Res (in press).
14. Sloan FA, Becker ER. Cross-subsidies and payment for hospital care. J Health Polit Policy Law 1984; 8:660–85.
15. Hamermesh DS. New estimates of the incidence of the payroll tax. South Econ J 1979; 45:1208–19.
16. Meyer JA. Passing the health care buck: who pays the hidden cost? Washington D.C.: American Enterprise Institute, 1983.
17. Ginsburg PB. Prospects for Medicare's hospital insurance trust fund. Health Affairs 1983; 2: 102–12.
18. Congressional Budget Office. Catastrophic medical expense: patterns in the non-elderly, non-poor population. Washington, D.C.: Gov-

ernment Printing Office, December 1982.

19. Schroeder SA, Showstack JA, Roberts HE. Frequency and clinical description of high-cost patients in 17 acute-care hospitals. N Engl J Med 1979, 300:1306–9.

20. Zook CJ, Moore FD. High-cost users of medical care. N Engl J Med 1980; 302:996–1002.

21. Coelen C, Sullivan D. An analysis of the effects of prospective reimbursement programs on hospital expenditures. Health Care Financ Rev 1981; 2(3):1–40.

22. Sloan FA. Rate regulation as a strategy for hospital cost control: evidence from the last decade. Milbank Mem Fund Q 1983; 61:195–221.

As noted in the opening of the case study, the Health Insurance Association of America (HIAA), a trade association for commercial insurers, has recently alleged that certain insurers and private-paying patients are bearing an unfair share of hospital charges because other payers such as the government Medicare and Medicaid programs and certain Blue Cross plans are paying less than the cost of treating their beneficiaries. HIAA fears that this situation will grow worse given the changes in government reimbursement policies under the Tax Equity and Fiscal Responsibility Act of 1982 (TEFRA) and the Social Security Amendments of 1983. These changes include the establishment of diagnostic-related groups (DRGs) under which hospitals are reimbursed a fixed amount for patients in each group. If a hospital can provide services for less than the reimbursed amount, it earns a profit on that patient. Otherwise, it loses money.

These reimbursement changes raise public-policy questions about who will pay for hospital care in this country, whether the reimbursement which hospitals receive is sufficient to cover all of their current costs of operation and expected future capital costs, and what will happen to those individuals who are not able to afford private insurance and who are not covered by government programs. As Ginsburg and Sloan note at the conclusion of their article, the answers to these questions "may not be found in specific changes in reimbursement policies but rather in dealing with broad policy issues, such as whether to use greater reliance on market forces or increased regulation to constrain the growth of medical-care costs and the extent to which indigent patients who are not eligible for Medicare and Medicaid are to be served and how such care should be financed." These broad policy issues will be discussed in the next section and then related to the specifics of the case.

Unique Characteristic of the Health Care Sector. To understand the policy issues raised in the Ginsburg and Sloan article, it is necessary to first ask why third-party payers—both private and public—are involved with medical care, and more precisely hospital services, and what impact this reimbursement has on both producer and consumer decisions. The opening statements in the case study show the potential conflict among the various interested parties in the hospital sector—commercial insurers, Blue Cross, the federal government through its Medicare and Medicaid programs, those individuals who choose to pay their own hospital bills, and indigent people who cannot afford private health insurance, who may or may not be covered by government programs, and who have medical needs that may not be met. What are the differing interests of these groups and why is there potential conflict among them?

To answer these questions we need to determine whether or not health-related goods and services are similar to other goods and services that are typically bought and sold in the marketplace. Apples and oranges are often used as examples of these types of goods. These goods are divisible into small units so that the consumer is able to make marginal decisions (to purchase three apples versus four apples or two oranges versus three oranges). Thus, the concept of equating marginal benefit to price is applicable. It is argued in microeconomics that the price a consumer is willing to pay for a product is related to the marginal or additional benefit that he or she derives from that output, not to the total benefit derived. The price that a consumer is willing to pay for an apple is related to the valuation the consumer places on the additional apple, not to the total valuation of all apples consumed. This marginal-total distinction explains why consumers typically will pay less for water, which is necessary to sustain life, than for diamonds, which most people would consider a luxury. Because water is plentiful, the valuation of the additional unit is low whereas it is high for the first diamond.

Consumers also have well-defined tastes and preferences for apples and oranges. Individuals can easily evaluate the quality of these goods. They have a good idea of the satisfaction or benefit they will derive from the product. Moreover, if an incorrect decision is made (too many apples are purchased or some of them are rotten), the consequences of this mistake are not serious. Apples (or oranges) can be thrown away without a great loss of satisfaction or income. A person can use the information gained from this incorrect decision the next time apples or oranges are purchased in the market.

On the supply side, conditions are also favorable to competitive market allocation. Apples and oranges are fruits that can be produced with a relatively small scale of production. There are not huge capital requirements that could act as a barrier to entry and restrict the mobility of resources into or out of apple (or orange) production. (Contrast this situation with that of an automobile assembly line.) Thus, competition among a large number of apple producers, for example, is viable. While an individual producer might have some control over the price of apples, the major forces determining prices will be market forces—the number of apple producers, the weather, expectations about future prices, etc. Apples are relatively homogeneous products within categories so that determining their quality is not difficult. Information about agricultural products is widely available and is quickly reflected in their prices. Thus, shifts in market demand and supply result in new equilibrium prices, which then perform their allocating and rationing function. The many apple and orange producers are in direct competition with each other so that they must try to maximize profits to survive in the marketplace. Lack of profitability drives individual producers out of the market. Competition gives producers the incentive to try to minimize the costs of producing their output. It also results in the equality of prices (reflective of people's marginal benefits) and the marginal cost (the additional cost) of producing output. This condition represents economic efficiency in the allocation of society's resources.

Economic efficiency can be explained as follows. Suppose the price of a product ($5.00) is less than the marginal cost ($10.00) of producing that unit of output. In this case the valuation that people place on that output, their marginal benefit, is $5.00. However, it costs society $10.00 to produce that unit of output. Thus, $10.00 worth of resources are being used to produce a product for which people are willing to pay only $5.00. This outcome means that an inefficiently large amount of this output is being produced. Society would be better off devoting less resources to the production of this product and more resources to producing other goods and services. On the other hand, if the price of a product ($10.00) is greater than its marginal cost ($5.00), then the valuation that people place on the output is greater than what it costs the economy to produce it. Society would be better off producing more units of this output. A price greater than marginal cost represents an inefficiently small amount of output. Thus, economic efficiency is achieved when the prices of products are exactly equal to their marginal costs of production.

Finally, society does not attach major significance to income distribution issues in the apple market. Not consuming apples is usually attributed to taste and preference and not to a lack of income. There is no legislation demanding that "every individual be able to consume apples regardless of his or her income," that is, that apple consumption be made a "right" similar to the right to vote. Thus, society is content to use the market mechanism to determine the allocation and distribution of apples.

Many of these conditions obviously do not hold when we examine products in the health care sector. First, there is the problem of uncertainty and the lack of information for consumer decision making. Consumers do not receive satisfaction or utility from the purchase of medical services in the same way as from the purchase of apples. Medical or health services are typically consumed in order to avoid an undesirable condition—being sick. Thus, good health is the final output desired. Medical goods and services are purchased as a means of obtaining the final output. Of course, good health may also be achieved without the purchase of medical inputs. Thus, there is likely to be substantial ignorance surrounding the consumption of medical services. Consumers may not be easily able to evaluate different types of medical treatment or to determine whether they are "worth the price" (equating marginal benefits and price). In some cases, no one—consumers, doctors, and other medical professionals alike—may have good knowledge about the effectiveness of various medical procedures. Even if individuals were provided more information from research studies about the risks of surgical procedures or the side effects of drugs, it is not clear that they could correctly evaluate that information to improve their decision making.

Since the conditions for rational consumer decision making do not exist in many health-related areas, physicians make decisions for consumers. It is often said that the physician acts as the agent for the consumer. Indeed, society makes it impossible for individuals to make certain medical decisions on their own—admission into the hospital, the purchase of prescription drugs, etc. If the doctor is truly acting as the agent for the consumer, he or she would make the same decisions as the consumer would make if the latter had the complete and correct information to do so. However, a potential conflict arises in the fee-for-service form of medical care production that is typical in the United States. Because physicians benefit financially from the consumption of many medical services, they may have the incentive to increase or induce demand for these services. Whether or not physician-induced demand exists is an empirical question that is difficult to answer (Feldstein, 1983, pp. 181–188). However, the role of the physician is extremely important in the health care sector, and it has a major impact on the behavior of hospitals.

Uncertainty also affects consumer decision making. Although the incidence of different illnesses can be predicted for large groups in the population, a given individual does not know when he or she is going to become ill or how much it will cost to become well again. Thus, individuals (particularly if they are adverse to risk) have an incentive to purchase health insurance. The widespread use of health insurance, however, has an impact on medical care costs and prices. Much of this influence relates to the existence of moral hazard—an insured individual is likely to take less precautions in maintaining his or her own health and to use more medical services if he or she does not have to pay the full market price for these services. Consider the demand and marginal cost curves shown in Figure 4.1. The demand curve shows the relationship between the price of the medical service and the quantity demanded or utilized. The price is reflective of an individual's marginal benefit while the marginal cost curve shows the additional cost of producing an additional unit of output. Marginal cost has been drawn as a horizontal line for simplification. Thus, marginal costs remain constant as the output of the medical service is increased. If price P_1 equal to marginal cost was charged for this service, individuals would demand quantity Q_1 of the output. This would be the efficient level of output where marginal benefits equal marginal costs.

Suppose the individual purchases a health insurance policy that reduces to zero the price of medical services available to that person. Given his or her downward sloping demand curve, the person will increase his or her quantity demanded of the service to Q_2, where the price equals the marginal benefit equals zero. Although the individual's marginal benefit of the unit Q_2 is zero, the marginal cost of producing that unit is positive. Thus, the individual is consuming an inefficiently large amount of medical services. Marginal cost exceeds marginal benefit for all units of output between Q_1 and Q_2. Furthermore, even though the individual is not directly paying the price for those units of output, someone does have to pay the cost of producing them. These cost are spread to other individuals in the economy and are also reflected in the premiums charged for insurance. Health insurance lowers the price and increases the quantity demanded of medical services for an individual. However, it increases the overall demand for medical services for society as a whole, which increases the costs and prices in this sector of the economy. Insured consumers also do not have as much incentive to shop around for the lowest-cost medical services. Their demand is said to be *inelastic*, which means that they will not decrease their quantity of medical services utilized very much in response to price increases (or more precisely, the percentage change in quantity demanded will be less than the percentage change in price). This behavior, combined with the lack of information on relative costs and prices, decreases the incentives for minimizing the costs of producing medical services. Doctors also have fewer incentives to limit the number of treatments and procedures recommended if they know that consumers are not paying the full cost of pro-

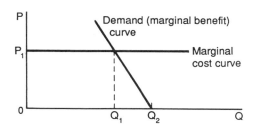

Figure 4.1. The Existence of Moral Hazard

ducing those services. This health insurance effect is also combined with the fear of malpractice on the part of the physician. Thus, the widespread existence of health insurance is a major contributor to the rapid increase in health care costs in this country.

The inefficiencies in the medical marketplace arising from health insurance combine with equity issues to place even further pressure on health-related costs and prices. Society *is* concerned about people's access to medical care. That is why congress passed the Medicare and Medicaid programs in the 1960s to provide health insurance for the aged and disabled and for certain categories of low-income individuals. In 1985, $71 billion or 19 percent of all personal health care expenditures was spent under the Medicare program. The proportion of spending attributable to Medicare has increased slowly but steadily since the program's inception in 1966. Expenditures from the Medicaid program totalled an additional $40 billion in 1985 (Waldo and others, 1986). Although access to medical services has been increased under both of these programs, it has long been recognized that both programs have contributed greatly to health care and hospital cost inflation given the increases in demand for medical services arising under these programs and given the method of reimbursement under these programs. Until 1983, Medicare reimbursement of hospitals was essentially done on a cost basis. This procedure gave hospitals little incentive to search for the least-costly methods of producing services.

Cost reimbursement and the demand increases from third-party payment combined with the other special characteristics of hospital behavior have been interrelated factors resulting in hospital cost inflation. These special characteristics relate to the overall goals and objectives of hospitals. Specifically, the hospital sector in this country has been dominated by the nonprofit form of organization for most of this century. Of the more than 7,000 hospitals registered with the American Hospital Association in 1977, only 11 percent were organized on a for-profit basis. This represented a decline from 56 percent of all registered hospitals in 1910 (Bays, 1983, p. 366). However, within the for-profit sector, there has been another major shift of organizational form from the small proprietary hospital owned by a handful of doctors to the large corporate chain of for-profit hospitals. Although there is no widely accepted general theory of the behavior of nonprofit organizations (Clark, 1980) and thus no single model of nonprofit hospital behavior (McGuire, 1985), the various models of hospital behavior that have been developed provide some insights as to why this form of organization may contribute to rising costs and higher charges in the hospital sector.

Models of Hospital Behavior

The earliest models of hospital behavior focused on average cost or break-even pricing. *Average cost pricing* is based on the assumption that nonprofit organizations are interested only in serving the public and have no desire to make profits. This behavior would typically result in larger levels of output than if the hospital was only concerned with maximizing profits. Cost recovery is stressed in pricing guidelines of the American Hospital Association. However, in addition to covering costs it is recommended that prices be set high enough "to cover the funds necessary for plant expansion due to improvement of services required to keep pace with technological and scientific advances" (quoted in Davis, 1972, p. 1). Recovering costs and generating funds for new investment would require a uniform markup above costs for all services if market competition is not considered important by hospital administrators. Again, this is reflected in statements by the American Hospital Association: "The rate charged for each individual service should reflect properly the operating expenses of the service rendered plus an equitable share of the other financial needs for which the patient is responsible" (quoted in Davis, 1972, p. 2).

The situation is obviously more complex given that the hospital offers multiple services. In fact, a hospital can be considered to be a multiproduct firm. Breaking-even in the aggregate (equating total revenue and total cost) is not inconsistent with cross-subsidization—pricing some services below cost and others above cost. The excess of revenues over costs on certain services can be used to support services that might not break even on their own. The role of physicians in this model relates primarily to their ability to increase the demand for hospital services. Because patients are required to be hospitalized in hospitals where their doctors are affiliated, the demand for services depends on the number of doctors affiliated with the hospital, the size of their clientele, and the extent to which doctors are affiliated with more than one hospital.

A second model of hospital behavior is based on the concept of *utility maximization* of the hospital decision-maker—the administrator in consultation with his or her staff (Newhouse, 1970). The administrator's satisfaction or utility is related to both the quantity of services produced and to their quality. The emphasis on quality results from the decision-maker's pursuit of status and the desire to show professional excellence. The demand for services is thought to depend both on their quality and their price. Higher quality may also make it easier to attract additional staff and to serve the public better.

Increased quality, however, is more costly. If demand can be increased along with quality, the hospital can increase both its quantity and quality of output. At some point, demand will not increase as rapidly and the hospital will be forced to make a tradeoff between quantity and quality. How this tradeoff is made will depend on the preferences of the decision-maker. One implication of this model is that hospital prices will be higher than they would be in the absence of the quality increases. Furthermore, investments in new technology will be based on their contribution to the hospital's image rather than on their financial merit. This leads to the characterization of hospitals as a "Cadillac only" industry. This type of behavior may result not only in the duplication of expensive equipment but also in the existence of too many specialized services. Lower usage of more exotic procedures such as heart transplants tends to increase mortality rates (Luft, Bunker, and Enthoven, 1979). The fact that there are barriers to entry in the hospital industry means that new producers cannot simply come in and sell services at a lower price. Thus, consumers may be paying more for a higher quality of service than they desire. This model also implies the use of cross-subsidization to pay for the prestige services.

Although the utility maximization model introduces other dimensions of observed hospital behavior, it does not incorporate any significant role for physicians. Yet physicians have direct control over admissions to a hospital and over the types of treatments a patient will receive in the hospital. They also have indirect influence over hospital decisions on capital investment and the level of the nursing staff. Thus, Pauly and Redisch (1973) and Shalit (1977) have advocated models where physicians have the dominant role in decision making. These *physician-control* or *cartel models* are based on the assumption that it is the total price of hospital care that is relevant to the consumer. This total price includes the hospital charges and the fees for physician services that are usually billed separately. It is then argued that "physician staff members enjoy *de facto* control of hospital operations and see to it that hospitalization services are produced in such a way as to maximize their net incomes" (Pauly and Redisch, 1973, p. 88).

In this model, physicians are considered to be the residual claimants similar to the owner of a firm who receives the profits after all expenses are paid. Thus, decisions are made that increase their share of consumers' hospitalization expenditures. This could result in a form of cross-subsidization where lower prices are charged for hospital services that are complementary to physician services. Increases in the demand for medical care would be met by increasing hospital capacity, not by increasing the number of physicians in the hospital. Greater hospital capacity would increase physician productivity whereas a larger number of physicians would simply result in smaller per capita shares of net income.

It is also argued that the nonprofit form of hospital organization is most advantageous to maximizing physician incomes (Feldstein, 1983, pp. 219–223; Clark, 1980, pp. 1441–1447). Physicians are able to exert stronger control over decision making because there are no stockholders concerned with rates of return. The nonprofit hospital's tax advantages, ability to accept charitable contributions, and government subsidies can result in expanded hospital input to benefit the physician. The ability to cross-subsidize may also be stronger with this form of organization.

The final model of hospitals to be considered can be termed the *split organ-*

ization model (Harris, 1977). Like the physician-control model, this model emphasizes the importance of the physician in controlling the demand for hospital services. However, the supply of these services is controlled by hospital administrators. Harris argues that hospitals have a complicated set of non-price allocation rules to equate demand and supply. He also notes that doctors are concerned more about excess demand for inputs (the lack of an operating room when it is needed) than about excess supply. Thus, there is pressure to expand the size of the hospital. Administrators will comply with these demands as long as they are reasonably certain that physicians can keep hospital utilization near capacity. Therefore, incentives for new innovations and expansion are built into the internal organization of the hospital. Up until the 1980s, most hospital-rate regulations to control costs focused only on the supply side. These included certificate-of-need legislation and other restrictions on capital investment. Harris argues that effective regulation must influence both the demand and the supply sides of the split organization.

None of these models may adequately capture the complexities of the hospital organization. However, they all highlight the fact that there are competing groups within the hospital environment and that the balance of power among these groups will affect the resulting pricing and cost strategies. Hospitals have discretion in how they set prices, which is reinforced by decreased consumer sensitivity to prices given the widespread existence of both private and public health insurance. As long as the various insurers pay all charges billed, a hospital could have a differential pricing strategy or use cross-subsidization to deliberately subsidize a particular type of medical care or class of patients, to match the desires of the medical staff if they had the dominant power in the organization, or to enhance the organization's market position (Phelps, 1986). Cost-shifting or payment differentials arise from the differential relationships between hospitals and the various insurers that have evolved over time. As Ginsburg and Sloan note early in their article outlining the case study: "Insurers pay hospitals in one of three ways. Some simply pay the hospital's charges. Others, with more market power, either reimburse what they determine to be the hospital's legitimate incurred costs (this group includes many Blue Cross plans, Medicare until recently, and many Medicaid programs) or specify in advance the amounts they will pay (e.g., Medicare's new prospective-payment system)."

As Ginsburg and Sloan discuss in the section entitled "Sources of Payment Differentials" (see p. 112), the determination of costs attributable to each payer under cost-reimbursement schemes is extremely controversial. First, there is the question of the allocation of indirect costs, which are not related to a specific patient or procedure. These would include costs for building and grounds maintenance and for medical education and research. There is also the issue of capital costs. Medicare and Medicaid do not pay a return on equity to nonprofit hospitals because some of that equity is the result of charitable contributions. However, the decrease in philanthropy and government grants in recent years means that nonprofit hospitals must now compete in the capital markets with for-profit hospitals. Furthermore, reimbursement on the basis of historical costs will not cover the replacement of capital facilities in an inflationary period. Other cost-allocation issues deal with differences in the case mix between insured groups, the coverage of malpractice premiums, differences in the ease of collection of payments, the promptness of payment, and the level of amenities provided. For example, in the past, Medicare added an 8.5 percent nursing differential based on the assumption that its elderly patients required more nursing time. This practice was eliminated given the absence of research supporting this cost differential. Finally, there is the issue of indigent care and bad debts. Cost-based insurers have typically covered the costs for the bad debts of those they insured. However, most payers have argued that they should not be responsible for the care of the uninsured.

Hospitals have traditionally responded to these reimbursement constraints by engaging in cost shifting or cross-subsidization. Because not all hospital departments have equal percentages of patients insured by different payers (or insured at all), there is an incentive to shift as many indirect costs as possible to those departments that will receive cost reimbursement. Once this is accomplished, the remaining costs are covered by raising prices to the charge-based insurers and to self-paying patients (Fisher, 1980; Meyer, 1983). The ability of a hospital to engage in this type of behavior depends upon the number of patients in those latter categories and upon the continued use of cost-based reimbursement. Medicare's adoption of the diagnostic related group (DRG) prospective payment system in 1983 seriously limits the ability of hospitals to shift costs among patients. This new environment is succinctly described by Lewin and Lewin (1987, p 48):

> In an effort to reduce hospital costs, payers are moving from paying charges as billed to paying negotiated rates. The cost of charity patients, and those with large uncompensated charges, thus is spread among fewer payers. In such an environment, hospitals committed to serving the uninsured poor are forced to increase their charges, while those with low or declining charity care burdens can gain a significant price-competitive advantage solely by avoiding charity care. The result has been an erosion of the genteel arrangement of cross-subsidies (cost shifting) that historically allowed hospitals to provide charity care without serious financial penalty or competitive handicap.... The pressure to reduce uncompensated care has also intensified as hospitals in general have developed an increased preoccupation with producing "bottom lines" or total margins. In the past, most nonprofits were content to set charges to break even. Now, hospital executives and their trustees worry about producing large enough margins (profits) to retain favorable bond ratings and thus low-cost access to capital, and to ensure that they will have sufficiently deep pockets to ride out the storm of declining demand and tough competition.

Evidence on Cost Shifting and Cross-Subsidization. Now that the hospital environment and the associated issues have been described, the next stage of policy analysis involves the gathering of data on the nature and extent of cost shifting and cross-subsidization. This process involves some of the empirical issues discussed in the previous chapter—the use of simplifying assumptions, extrapolation, and deriving conclusions from limited data. Ginsburg and Sloan argue that estimating the magnitude of payment differentials is "necessarily imprecise" given the difficulty of assigning costs to various classes of patients. "The only practical way to do this for the hospital industry as a whole is to assume that the ratio of costs to billed charges (but not reimbursements) is uniform from one insurer to another. On the basis of this assumption, payment differentials are measured by comparing the ratio of reimbursements to billed charges from each insurer." Using data from a 1981 American Hospital Association survey, the authors illustrate in Table 1 of the article (p. 114) that substantial payment differentials do exist. "Although the average ratio of reimbursement to charges was 82 percent, commercial insurers had an 89 percent average, whereas the average for Medicare and Medicaid was 80 percent. Blue Cross had a ratio that was lower than that of the commercial insurers but higher than the average," the authors continue.

The authors do not have adequate data to illustrate how these percentages have changed over time. As discussed in the previous chapter, examining trends over time is an important aspect of policy analysis. When good data are not available, analysts attempt to draw conclusions from the existing evidence. Ginsburg and Sloan note that some evidence indicates that Medicare's non-recoverable charges as a percentage of billed charges increased from 1975 to 1981. The authors consider whether this could have resulted from changes in Medicare reimbursement policies or increased charity or bad debts. They reject both of these hypotheses in favor of an explanation based on hospitals raising charges faster than costs increased over this period. However, these conclusions are derived from either aggregate or very limited data. The nature of these trends and a causal explanation for them should be analyzed in much more detail.

Although the data on cross-subsidization are also somewhat sketchy and not entirely reliable for reasons discussed below, several different sources show the existence of cross-subsidization. Joseph (1976), examining the ratios of patient revenue to direct costs for selected ancillary services from a nation-wide sample survey of hospitals from 1962 to 1968, found that these ratios varied from under 1.00 for the delivery room to over 2.00 for the pharmacy. The operating room and physical therapy had revenue-direct cost ratios under 1.50, whereas the ratios for the laboratory and anesthesiology were greater than 1.50. Joseph notes that if hospitals allocated their indirect costs to departments in proportion to the direct costs incurred by the department and charged patients the sum of both costs, the ratios of patient revenue to direct costs would be the same across departments (Joseph, 1976, p. 33). These findings show the existence of cross-subsidization even in the period before the dominance of Medicare and Medicaid reimbursement.

Harris (1979, p. 225), who analyzed the relationship between prices and long-run marginal costs in a medium-size, urban teaching hospital in 1973, found that rates for routine diagnostic and therapeutic procedures and for

TABLE 4.1. **RELATIONSHIPS BETWEEN PRICES AND LONG-RUN MARGINAL COSTS.**

Service	Average Price	% Markup or Markdown of Price Over Cost
Surgery	$193.00	−44
Intensive Care Unit	211.00	−38
Special diagnostic	233.00	−16
Rooms	63.00	+49
Diagnostic X-ray	29.00	+62
Routine therapy	11.00	+69
Routine diagnostic	2.98	+158
Chest X-ray	12.00	+175

routine daily accommodations (room and board) were marked up to subsidize surgical care, special diagnostic procedures, the coronary care unit and the intensive care unit. These relationships, summarized by Bays (1983), are shown in Table 4.1.

Finally, in a study of California hospitals, Pattison and Katz (1983) found that markups and markdowns differed not only by department within a hospital but also across different types of hospitals. Certain ancillary services such as clinical laboratories, central services and supply, the pharmacy, and inhalation therapy were profitable for all classes of hospitals, whereas other ancillary services, including the blood bank, radiology, emergency and home-health services, were generally unprofitable. Routine services (room and board) were typically unprofitable for all classes of hospitals. For-profit chain hospitals tended to earn higher per-unit profits on the profitable ancillary services and to suffer smaller losses on the unprofitable ancillary services than either voluntary or public hospitals. However, the for-profit chains lost more per-unit than the public or voluntary hospitals on emergency services and routine daily services (Pattison and Katz, 1983, p. 349).

Although all of these studies provide evidence on the existence of cross-subsidization, the nature of these transfers differs considerably among the studies. For example, Harris (1979) finds routine services to be profitable while Pattison and Katz (1983) find them unprofitable. Some of these discrepancies result from differences in the samples investigated and in the data utilized. However, there is a more fundamental public policy problem here, namely the lack of uniform accounting procedures among hospitals. Harris (1979, p. 226) notes that "more than 50 percent of hospital costs is typically regarded as fixed overhead to be allocated to the hospital's products. Hospital accountants manipulate this overhead to obtain "fair shares" of revenues from each payer. The fact that each insurer specifies its own cost allocation rules makes this long-run average cost concept even more arbitrary. The distinction that some parties are paying prices and others are paying long-run average costs thus becomes illusory."

An even more caustic critique of these accounting procedures as they affect clinical laboratories in hospitals is presented by Conn (1978). He argues that hospitals treat their clinical laboratories as profit centers designed to support unrelated deficit-producing services. This behavior results from the fact that hospital labs have a monopoly on the services for hospitalized patients and from the fact that they negotiate their reimbursement rates directly with third-party payers. Laboratory profits do not appear as an explicit figure in hospital financial statements. Costs and charges become identical as inflated overhead costs are charged to the lab to transfer funds to the hospital's cost centers. Conn argues that "an Alice in Wonderland approach to laboratory cost accounting (laboratory costs mean anything I choose to have them mean) represents a serious impediment to the most efficient use of laboratory information in the patient-care process" (Conn, 1978, p. 423).

Cross-subsidization is an implication of the profit-maximizing and break-even models of hospital behavior when multiple products are considered. Each hospital service has a different demand curve. The elasticity of demand or consumer sensitivity to price changes also varies across services. Elasticity is defined as the percentage change in quantity demanded of a good relative to the percentage change in its price. Demand is inelastic (small sensitivity) when the percentage change in quantity demanded is less than the percentage change in price. Elastic demand implies a greater percentage change in quantity than the percentage change in price. Thus, if a hospital believed that the elasticity of demand was greater for room rates than for ancillary services, it would charge a lower price relative to cost for rooms than for ancillary services. Consumers should be more sensitive to changes in the room rates given the availability of out-patient treatment as a substitute for hospitalization. Once an individual is hospitalized, ancillary services are complementary to the use of rooms and there are fewer substitutes for these services. Prices that are higher relative to costs can be charged. Thus, hospitals can increase profits or output by varying their prices according to the elasticity of demand for their services.

Cross-subsidization is also consistent with the utility-maximization model. If a hospital administrator desires new technological equipment to increase the status and prestige of the hospital, any losses from this equipment can be recouped through cross-subsidization. Of course, if all hospitals behave in this manner, duplication of facilities and higher costs of services are likely to result.

Justification of Payment Differentials and Cross-Subsidization. The evidence in the previous section has demonstrated that payment differentials and cross-subsidization do exist. In the case study, Ginsburg and Sloan then turn to the issue of whether these practices are justified. Insurers have argued that they should not have to pay for certain hospital activities such as medical education, which do not directly benefit their patients. Medicare, Medicaid, and some Blue Cross plans have claimed that they should be responsible only for the bad debts of their clients. Although there may be some validity to this claim for the Medicare and Medicaid programs, which have reduced the burden of uncompensated care for hospitals, the logic would suggest "that charge-paying insurers should not be responsible for bad debts either, since the largest part of bad debts is for the care of uninsured patients." Blue Cross plans have often received a discount based on their claim of lower collection and administrative costs. Ginsburg and Sloan argue that this may be justifiable as long as narrow categories of costs are not singled out for special treatment. As noted previously, reimbursement of historical capital costs creates a problem in times of inflation. However, overly generous capital reimbursement can create incentives for unnecessary capital investment.

There are also broader issues involved when evaluating these pricing and cost-shifting policies. It may be the case that nonprofit hospitals are acting as "minigovernments" producing public goods and engaging in income redistribution (Clark, 1980, pp. 1437–1441). Public goods are goods or services whose benefits spill over to all individuals within a given geographic area. National defense is cited as a typical example of a public good. It is not possible to exclude an individual from consuming a public good once it is provided. Thus, it is usually not possible to use a market-pricing mechanism to ration goods with these public characteristics. Individuals could become "free riders" who consume the good without paying for it. Therefore, it is argued that one role for a government in a market economy is to decide on the appropriate level of public goods to be provided and to raise the revenue (typically through taxation) necessary to finance them.

Income redistribution is also considered to be another role for a national government in a market economy. It was noted above that even if a market economy is functioning efficiently, there may be a problem with the fairness or equity in the distribution of the goods and services. More generally, the distribution of income arising from the operation of the competitive marketplace may be more unequal than is desired by the individuals in the society. If income redistribution is desirable, the policy question is how should it be undertaken? It is often argued by economists that income redistribution should be a function of the national government, which can design uniform programs to benefit low-income individuals across the entire country (Hyman, 1987). These programs should be designed so as to minimize interference with the allocating and rationing roles of the pricing mechanism in a market system. However, all income-redistribution programs will create some inefficiencies in the market system and will cause some distortions in the pricing mechanism. The inefficiencies from the widespread usage of health insurance were discussed in the previous section of this chapter.

Hospitals do provide goods with public characteristics. The benefits of teaching and research undertaken in hospitals spill over into the larger society. Individuals cannot be excluded from benefiting from these activities. Hospitals also engage in income redistribution by treating patients who are unable to pay for their care. Although the Medicaid program was designed to handle the indigent-care problem, not all low-income people satisfy that program's welfare-based eligibility criteria. It has been estimated that about one-third of the nation's poor lack public as well as private insurance against the costs of illness

(Feder, Hadley, and Mullner, 1984). Cross-subsidization is a means for hospitals to finance both the provision of these public goods and the care of indigents. Charging different prices to different classes of consumers may be a method of having some care for indigents versus none at all. This would be analogous to a doctor in a small town charging larger fees to higher-income patients. This process may be the only means of guaranteeing that the town has the services of a physician. In the modern hospital, it is the various third-party payers rather than high-income patients per se who subsidize care for the indigent.

Although cross-subsidization can be used to pursue redistributional goals, it is not clear whether the observed patterns of price-cost differences support these goals. Ever since the advent of the Medicare and Medicaid programs, hospitals have had an incentive to try to pass increased costs on to these programs. Hellinger (1975) studied the pricing behavior of 17 short-term, general, nonteaching hospitals in Ohio using the combination method of reimbursement from Medicare. Hospitals using this method may increase Medicare reimbursement by increasing the charges of services in departments with high Medicare utilization. Reimbursement could also be increased by altering the original placement of costs in departments and by changing the method of allocating the cost of nonrevenue-producing departments to revenue-producing departments. Although Hellinger could not test the latter hypothesis, he did find that departments with higher Medicare utilization had relatively higher profit ratios. "This result suggests that the Medicare program subsidizes a portion of the care provided to non-Medicare patients in these hospitals" (Hellinger, 1975, p. 318). However, the distributional impact of these transfers is unclear.

Cross-subsidization is also consistent with the physician-control model of hospital behavior. Bays (1983) argues that the data presented in Table 4.1 (see p. 131) support this hypothesis rather than the income-redistribution hypothesis. He argues that there is no reason to assume that surgery, the most subsidized service, is provided more to low-income individuals than to middle- or high-income persons. However, if the hospital holds down its charges for surgery, the surgeons will be able to charge higher fees for their services. The losses to the hospital from surgery can be made up by charging prices above costs for services such as rooms and therapy, which are not as directly linked to the physician input (Bays, 1983, pp. 370–373). Joseph (1976) argues that the physician-control model could by tested by examining data on the separate billings by physicians among departments in a hospital. He hypothesizes that, other factors being equal, the ratio of patient revenue to direct cost in a department is inversely related to the magnitude of physician direct billings per patient-day. Unfortunately, the data for such an empirical test are typically not available.

It may be difficult to distinguish between these two competing hypotheses about the goals of cross-subsidization. This is unfortunate because the attitude of policymakers toward the use of cross-subsidization may depend upon which goal is being achieved. Decision-makers might be more favorably inclined toward a policy that was contributing toward national redistribution goals than one that was simply benefiting physicians. As noted previously, the limited hard data on the patterns of cross-subsidization are not always consistent. Furthermore, these goals may often be intertwined. In his study of the experiences of the Maryland Health Services Cost Review Commission, Cohen (1978) found that the commission permitted subsidization of clinics, emergency rooms, and obstetrics and related services. Clinic users were typically poor, and it was thought that they received worse care than was generally given in physicians' offices. Income redistribution was the primary motivation for this pricing below full allocated costs. "Further, there is considerable question as to whether any faith should be put into the allocation of joint costs, especially to sidelines such as clinic care" (Cohen, 1978, p. 420). Subsidization of obstetrical services was related to the lack of adequate insurance coverage for this service. These losses were recovered in radiology and pathology—"those monopolized areas where some physician is often getting a percentage of gross billings." The latter outcome is consistent with the physician-control model as is the following scenario also reported by Cohen (1978, p. 420): "The hospital requested that its clinic charge of $3.40 be increased to $34. The commission approved an increase up to costs ($17) and announced a hearing as to whether rates should be approved about costs to make up for earlier losses. At the hearing, the hospital next requested that its clinic charge be $5 with the losses to be made up in medical-surgical. It developed that certain attending physicians at the hospital were using the clinic in lieu of a private office. Their patients were happy with the $3.40 charge but not with $17. The physicians had the hospital request the reduction and reallocation. The commission eventually approved rates slightly above direct costs, or about $10 per visit."

Even if it could be demonstrated that the sole purpose of hospital cross-subsidization was to benefit the poor and to provide for indigent care, it is still questionable whether this is the best method for achieving redistributional goals. Charging certain patients prices higher than the costs of producing their services is an implicit form of taxation to finance income redistribution. This tax-transfer process is, of course, undertaken all the time by the federal government. The difference is that governmental policies are at least indirectly determined through the political process. Voters have some control over their legislators who will be making decisions on the levels of taxation and transfer programs. When this process is undertaken through hospital pricing policies, the paying patients have little knowledge of and no input into the determination of these policies. Furthermore, this form of taxation will typically not conform to the principles of horizontal and vertical equity that underlie federal government taxation policies (Clark, 1980, p. 1468). Horizontal equity requires the equal tax treatment of persons in equal positions. Vertical equity implies that persons in different positions will be treated unequally. This is often interpreted to meant that the federal income tax should be progressive, charging higher-income individuals higher rates than those applied to lower-income individuals. Cross-subsidization of indigent care in hospitals means that the burden of this care will be borne by wealthy sick people, not by higher-income persons in general (horizontal inequity). Moreover, only a crude form of progressivity is likely to result from cross-subsidization. There is also likely to be little consistency in this taxation burden among the thousands of hospitals in the country.

The evaluation of the use of explicit versus implicit taxes and subsidies may depend upon the viewpoint of the policy analyst or decision-maker. Economists generally favor explicit taxes and subsidies because they focus on "rational" decision making involving a comparison of the benefits and costs of alternative policies. Economists also typically believe in a clear distinction between efficiency and equity goals in policy-making. They often argue for the use of marginal cost pricing to achieve efficiency objectives while relying on a national pattern of income transfers to handle the distributional issues. Politicians are more likely to rely on policies whose objectives are not so clear-cut because the former are attempting to reach a consensus among the competing groups in the political process. Politicians typically like to claim the political benefits from government sbusidies, but they prefer to avoid the costs associated with taxes. They are often most responsive to their constituents and other interest groups. As Schuck (1986, p. 83) has noted, "A politician who favors a subsidy for a particular group is likely to value equity for the group more highly than he or she values efficiency for the society as a whole."

Although the preceding discussion of cross-subsidization generally results in conclusions about the inefficiencies and equity problems with this process, there is one additional complication for policy analysis to be considered. The efficiency conditions for resource allocation (prices equal to marginal costs) are derived for a theoretically "first-best" world where it is possible to attain these conditions. If, however, prices deviate from marginal costs in some sectors of the economy, the optimal allocation rules in this "second-best" world may require further deviations of prices from costs (Boadway and Wildasin, 1984; Zajac, 1978). This approach is the basis for Harris' argument that "the hospital's practice of cross-subsidization can play a critical role in compensating for distortions and inequities in existing health insurance coverage. Despite its controversial nature, this form of discriminatory pricing can be completely consistent with nonprofit objectives" (Harris, 1979, p. 240). Harris views the hospital as a regulated firm whose goal is to maximize social welfare while setting prices so as to break even financially. This would result in low prices (even below cost) for certain services (summarized by Clark, 1980, pp. 1469–1470): "(1) The service would impose a severe risk burden on an uninsured patient; that is, it is a very expensive service such as major surgery or cardiac catheterization. (2) The service is not well covered by insurance. (3) The insurance coverage that does exist imposes a high copayment risk; thus, there is some patient-directed pressure against overuse. (4) Complementary services, such as postoperative nursing care when the service in question is major surgery, are not well covered by insurance. (5) The service is consumed more heavily by lower-income patients."

Harris' argument is based on a theoretical model that contains numerous restrictive assumptions that are violated in reality. Moreover, even if hospital pricing strategies could achieve the goals postulated, there is no guarantee that the type of cross-subsidization actually utilized would do so. There is also the question about whether individual hospitals should be pursuing policies related to goals typically thought to be objectives of the federal government. Harris' argument does force us to realize that policy-makers operate in a world with multiple distortions and goals and that rules derived in a simpler framework (that is, equate price and marginal cost for efficiency) may not always be appropriate in this situation.

Recent Changes Affecting Hospital Pricing. Several recent developments in the hospital sector will have a considerable effect on hospital pricing policies and cross-subsidization. These changes include: (1) the more widespread use of prospective payment reimbursement schemes, particularly the diagnostic related groupings (DRGs) under the Medicare System; (2) the increased competition for hospitals from free-standing emergency centers (FECs) and free-standing ambulatory surgery centers (FASCs); and (3) the takeover of many nonprofit hospitals by for-profit hospital chains. All of these developments should limit the ability of hospitals to engage in cross-subsidization.

Under DRGs, hospitals are reimbursed a fixed amount for patients within each diagnostic related group. This system gives hospitals the incentive to reduce the length of a patient's stay, to increase outpatient care, and to reduce the number of ancillary services utilized. The approach should also result in less cross-subsidization because pricing strategies are constrained by government reimbursement in addition to market demand. Of course, hospitals could also consistently use the higher-priced DRG classifications in cases where there is discretion on the choice of category.

Greater competition from FECs and FASCs will also affect hospital pricing strategies. Free-standing emergency clinics, which provide episodic emergency care 24 hours per day, 7 days per week, are similar to hospital emergency rooms. Between 1978 and 1984, FECs grew at an average annual rate of 71 percent. Because 70 percent to 85 percent of hospital emergency room visits are for nonurgent health problems, the population suitable for FEC care is large (Ermann and Gabel, 1985, pp. 402, 403). Charges to patients are typically 30 percent to 50 percent lower in FECs than in hospital emergency rooms. Thus, hospitals are under competitive pressure to lower their emergency room rates. Costs are typically lower for FECs since they do not have to maintain the expensive equipment to be used in the treatment of serious illnesses and injuries. Moreover, FECs do not face any legal responsibility to treat indigent patients (Ermann and Gabel, 1985, pp. 403, 404). These factors, of course, account for many of the patterns of hospital cross-subsidization as discussed previously.

Similar competitive pressures result from the free-standing ambulatory surgical centers (FASCs). There were more than 300 FASCs in 1984. These facilities performed 371,513 surgical procedures in 1983. Growth of these facilities has been rapid, particularly in the Sun Belt region of the country

(Ermann and Gabel, 1985, pp. 406, 407). Hospitals using surgery to subsidize the production of other services will be faced with the decision to allocate more costs to the other services or perhaps eliminate them if they wish to compete with the FASCs.

Finally, the growth of for-profit hospital chains raises questions about future pricing policies and the care of the indigent. It has often been alleged that for-profit hospitals engage in "cream-skimming"—treating only those conditions that have the highest profit margins. Available evidence supports the argument that for-profits have a different case-mix than do nonprofit hospitals and that the former appear to specialize in less complicated cases (Bays, 1977). However, cream-skimming can exist only if there are certain services of nonprofits that are quite profitable. Thus, cream-skimming is related to the practice of cross-subsidization by nonprofit hospitals. It does appear that for-profit hospitals provide less indigent care than do nonprofits although the exact differences vary among research studies. In a report issued by the National Academy of Sciences in June 1986, "little difference" in indigent care was found for California hospitals whereas nonprofit facilities provided "two or three times as much uncompensated care on average" in four other states (Pear, 1986a). Public hospitals, particularly those in urban areas, provide the greatest amounts of indigent care. In the early 1980s public hospitals were estimated to provide 22 percent of all hospital care but 40 percent of all free care. Big-city public hospitals provided only 5.5 percent of all hospital care but they undertook 20.5 percent of the total amount of free care (Feder and others, 1984).

Several types of responses have been forthcoming from hospitals responding to these changes in their environment. Regarding the indigent-care problem, many hospitals have either directly prohibited or discouraged hospital use by people unable to pay. Many stories about the dumping of indigent patients have appeared in the press. Dumping has become so prevalent in some areas that state legislatures have enacted laws against it. Recent federal legislation will require Medicare-certified hospitals to provide treatment to or stabilize all emergency patients before transferring them. Violators risk termination or suspension of the hospital's agreement with Medicare, fines of up to $25,000 per violation on both the hospital and the responsible physician, and civil actions (Waldo and others, 1986). Hospitals have also been reducing or eliminating services that are heavily utilized by the poor. These include social services, hospice care, drug treatment, psychiatric care, and outpatient services (Feder and others, 1984).

In addition to cost-cutting actions, hospitals have also been undertaking strategies to increase their revenues. Hospital advertising of their services has become much more common. According to the research firm SRI Gallup, 91 percent of the hospitals in the country advertised in 1986 as compared to 64 percent in 1985. Marketing and advertising expenditures increased from $313 million to $500 million over the same period. The average hospital advertising budget grew from $64,000 to more than $100,000 (Elie, 1987). Given the previously discussed role of physicians in hospitals, it is expected that much future advertising will be directed toward influencing physicians regarding their admission decisions.

Hospitals have also been expanding into new profit-making ventures and activities. These include real estate projects such as professional office buildings near the hospital for doctors and pharmacies, nursing homes, companies that sell or rent medical equipment to home-bound patients, and health clubs. The typical change has been the creation of a parent or holding company with the nonprofit hospital as a separate subsidiary to maintain its tax-exempt status. The other business ventures, which are grouped into separate divisions, pay taxes on any profits that flow to the corporate parent and back to the hospital. Corporate ventures of the Day Kimball Hospital in Putnam, Connecticut, include a commercial cleaning business for schools and factories, a computerized billing service for doctors in the area, and a catering business that uses the hospital's kitchen at off-hours to prepare food for wedding receptions and parties. The United Hospital in St. Paul and the Metropolitan Medical Center in Minneapolis have begun a joint venture to market frozen food to the elderly in Minnesota, Florida, New York, and Indiana (Madden, 1987). These trends are expected to grow in the future.

Public Policy Options. Although hospitals have undertaken the types of actions discussed here in response to their changing environment, these may not be sufficient or desirable to handle all of the public-policy issues. As noted, federal legislation has already been enacted to limit patient dumping. Various other policies that relate to hospital cross-subsidization, pricing, and the care of the indigent have either been proposed or partially implemented.

In the case study for this chapter, Ginsburg and Sloan examine three such policy options: grants to hospitals for bad debts and charity; all-payer hospital rate setting; and an antitrust exemption to permit commercial insurers to negotiate as a group with hospitals. Each of these policies may be viewed differently by the various stakeholders in the policy process. Subsidies could be granted to hospitals meeting strict criteria regarding financial distress and the provision of care to large numbers of indigents without insurance. Ginsburg and Sloan argue that this policy would cost less than would more broad-based strategies because the grants would be targeted only on particular hospitals. Less patient dumping should occur, and access for other hospital patients should be protected given the decreased likelihood of hospital bankruptcy. Thus, consumers and the government would benefit from this policy. There would, however, be implementation problems related to the issue of distinguishing among the causes of hospital financial distress. The goal is to subsidize hospitals where the distress results from the burden of indigent care and not from poor management and inefficiencies. Hospitals might engage in creative accounting to try to increase their subsidies.

Ginsburg and Sloan argue that an alternative to a direct hospital subsidy is a public catastrophic-illness insurance plan that would reduce the amount of bad debts attributable to costly illnesses. Because this plan would focus on the patient and not the hospital, it would eliminate the implementation problem of determining which hospitals are distressed as a result of indigent care. However, this plan is likely to be much more costly. In November 1986, Secretary of Health and Human Services Otis R. Bowen proposed a wide range of new government programs and tax incentives for individuals and private industry to provide or purchase insurance for catastrophic illnesses. Central to these proposals is an expansion of the Medicare program in this area. Under the proposal, a beneficiary would pay $4.92 per month in Medicare premiums in addition to the $17.90 per month currently charged. Medicare would then cover an unlimited number of days of hospital care, and the beneficiary's out-of-pocket payments for Medicare-covered services would be limited to $2,000 per year. There is no such limit under current law. Bowen's other proposals include tax credits to people over 55 who purchase insurance for long-term care, tax exemption for insurance company reserves set aside for long-term care, and tax deductions for health insurance purchased by self-employed individuals and unincorporated businesses if the insurance covers catastrophic expenses (Pear, 1986b, 1987a). These proposals have been criticized by some officials in the Reagan Administration as too expensive and involving too large a role for the federal government in the health insurance arena. Similar criticism would be anticipated with any proposals to expand the coverage of Medicaid for the poor. Any proposals for this program would need to incorporate deductibles, co-payments, and perhaps restrictions on providers to prevent tremendous increases in program costs similar to those that occurred in the past.

Both grants to hospitals and catastrophic insurance would involve explicit taxation to finance the programs as opposed to the implicit taxation of cross-subsidization. These taxation decisions would be made through the political process and not by the pricing policies of individual hospitals. Funds could be generated through increased use of the income tax, the payroll tax, or a tax on hospitals or health insurance premiums. The choice of taxing mechanisms would, however, involve further distributional and efficiency issues. In one study it has been estimated that cost shifting places a greater burden than either the payroll tax or the individual income tax on working-class and lower-middle-income households and that the income tax burdens the highest-income households the most (Meyer, 1983). Households might also reduce their hospital use when prices increase through cost shifting or they might work less if taxes are raised to finance grants or catastrophic insurance. These distortions in people's behavior mean that the total burden of a particular financing alternative may exceed the revenue collected in taxes or the extra hospital charges. This extra or excess burden of cost shifting has been estimated to be far less than the excess burden of tax increases because labor income is already heavily taxed whereas hospital costs and health insurance are very lightly taxed (Meyer, 1983).

It has also been proposed that a fund to reimburse hospitals treating large numbers of indigents could be created through a surtax on hospital bills of patients who had insurance. If this tax is passed on to hospital patients in the form of higher charges or insurance premiums, it would be a transfer from purchasers of hospital care who buy from hospitals with a relatively low concentration of "supported" patients to purchasers from hospitals with a higher proportion of such patients. The exact distributional implications of this type of tax would depend upon the income characteristics of consumers under the various insurance programs. This type of tax might also discourage the adoption of expensive new technology by the hospital (Meyer, 1983).

Ginsburg and Sloan also examine in the case study the options of "all-payer" hospital rate-setting. Under this policy, which has been utilized in Maryland, New Jersey, New York, and Massachusetts, public agencies set rates for all third-party payers, thus making explicit the decisions concerning cost shifting or payment differentials. Although this is an advantageous aspect of this approach, rate-setting suffers from the usual lags, implementation costs, and controversy inherent in any regulatory process. Ginsburg and Sloan argue that the prospects for competitive alternatives are also reduced with this approach.

Finally, there is the argument by commercial insurers that an antitrust exemption that would permit them to negotiate jointly with hospitals would reduce their competitive disadvantage and would increase pressure on hospitals to contain costs. The obvious problem with this approach is the expected competition between commercial insurers and Blue Cross plans to see who could pay the least for reimbursement. It is unlikely that any payer would agree to cover hospital capital costs or to provide funds for the care of the indigent.

SUMMARY

This discussion of policy options illustrates the variety of conflicting goals and values in the policy process. The issues of hospital pricing and cost allocation are part of a larger set of policy issues involving both efficiency and distributional questions. In a competitive market system, prices of goods will tend to equal their marginal costs of production. This is the condition for economic efficiency in the allocation of resources. However, in the hospital sector this outcome will not typically result given the nonprofit objectives of the organizations, the uncertainty and ignorance on the part of consumers regarding the purchase of hospital services, and the widespread use of public and private medical insurance. The latter raises questions about how insurers will be reimbursed, how hospitals' financial viability will be maintained, and about who will pay for medical care for indigents who lack medical insurance.

This chapter illustrates how the tools of economic analysis are useful in analyzing both the hospital pricing-policy issues and the alternative policy options. It is clear, however, that the final policy choices will be made using criteria and values other than those of the economist alone. This interaction of economic and political factors can be clearly seen in the progress of Secretary Bowen's catastrophic health insurance proposal, which we discussed previously. House and Senate versions of this proposal, including some more protection to beneficiaries, have been proceeding through Congress in the winter and spring of 1987 (Pear, 1987b). It had been decided in the early stages of discussion that the cost of these bills, estimated to be at least $5 billion annually, could not be financed by a tax increase because it would be politically impossible to raise taxes less than a year after Congress slashed them. Thus, the financing of the bills has been based on two principles: All who benefit from the new program should pay something for the coverage, and those with higher income should pay progressively more than those with lower income. These principles represent a drastic change from previous policy, for Medicare has always had uniform benefits in return for uniform premiums. Although this plan was initially opposed by interest groups representing the elderly, they eventually softened their opposition in the face of the opportunity for expanded Medicare benefits. One lobbyist stated that a consensus was achieved on this policy because liberals saw it as a way to "protect the poor" while conservatives saw it as a means to avoid squandering federal money on the affluent. In this case economic analysis was used to provide the cost estimates of the catastrophic insurance and to outline the various means of financing the proposal. However, political factors have dominated the choice of financing options and have created the consensus needed for turning the proposal into actual public policy.

REFERENCES

Anthony, Robert N., & Young, David W. (1984). *Management control in nonprofit organizations.* Homewood, IL: Richard D, Irwin, Inc.

Bays, Carson W. 1977, March. Case-mix differences between nonprofit and for-profit hospitals. *Inquiry,* XIV, 17–21.

Bays, Carson W. (1983, Spring). Why most private hospitals are nonprofit. *Journal of Policy Analysis and Management 2,* 366–385.

Boadway, Robin W., & Wildasin, David E. (1984). *Public sector economics* (2nd ed.). Boston: Little, Brown.

Clark, Robert Charles. (1980, May). Does the nonprofit form fit the hospital industry? *Harvard Law Review 93,* 1417–1489.

Cohen, Harold A. (1978). Experiences of a state cost control commission. In Michael Zubkoff, Ira E. Raskin, and Ruth S. Hanft (eds.), *Hospital cost containment* (pp. 401–428). New York: PRODIST.

Conn, Rex D. (1978, February 23). Clinical laboratories. Profit center, production industry or patient-care resource? *The New England Journal of Medicine, 298,* 422–427.

Davis, Karen. (1972, Winter). Economic theories of behavior in nonprofit, private hospitals. *Economic and Business Bulletin, 24,* 1–13.

Elie, L. Eric. (1987, January 4). Why hospitals have to advertise. *The Atlanta Constitution,* p. 2m.

Ermann, Dan, & Gabel, Jon. (1985, May). The changing face of American health care. Multihospital systems, emergency centers, and surgery centers. *Medical Care, 23,* 401–420.

Feder, Judith, Hadley, Jack, & Mullner, Ross. (1984, Fall). Falling through the cracks: Poverty, insurance coverage, and hospital care for the poor, 1980 and 1982. *Millbank Memorial Fund Quarterly/Health and Society, 62,* 544–566.

Feldstein, Paul J. (1983). *Health care economics* (2nd ed.). New York: John Wiley & Sons.

Fisher, George Ross. (1980). *The hospital that ate Chicago.* Philadelphia: Saunders Press.

Ginsburg, Paul B., & Sloan, Frank A. (1984, April 5). Hospital cost shifting. *The New England Journal of Medicine, 310,* 893–898.

Harris, Jeffrey E. (1977, Autumn). The internal organization of hospitals: Some economic implications. *Bell Journal of Economics, 8,* 467–482.

Harris, Jeffrey E. (1979, Spring). Pricing rules for hospitals. *Bell Journal of Economics, 10,* 224–243.

Hellinger, Fred J. (1975, December). Hospital charges and Medicare reimbursement. *Inquiry, 12,* 313–319.

Hyman, David N. (1987). *Public finance. A contemporary application of theory to policy.* (2nd ed). Chicago: The Dryden Press.

Joseph, Hyman. (1976, Spring). On interdepartment pricing of not-for-profit hospitals. *Quarterly Review of Economics and Business, 16,* 33–44.

Lewin, Lawrence S., & Lewin, Marion Ein. (1987, Spring). Financing charity care in an era of competition. *Health Affairs, 6,* 47–60.

Luft, Harold, Bunker, John, & Enthoven, Alain. (1979, December 20). Should operations be regionalized? *The New England Journal of Medicine, 301,* 1121–1127.

Madden, Robert L. (1987, January 25). For hospitals, new ventures and new profits. *The New York Times,* pp. 1, 13.

McGuire, A. (1985). The theory of the hospital: A review of the models. *Social Science and Medicine, 20,* 1177–1184.

Meyer, Jack A. (1983). *Passing the health care buck. Who pays the hidden cost?* Washington, DC: American Enterprise Institute for Public Policy Research.

Newhouse, Joseph P. (1970, March). Toward a theory of nonprofit institutions: an economic model of a hospital. *American Economic Review, 60,* 64–74.

Pattison, Robert V., & Katz, Hallie M. (1983, August 11). Investor-owned and not-for-profit hospitals. A comparison based on California data. *The New England Journal of Medicine, 309,* 347–353.

Pauly, Mark, & Redisch, Michael. (1973, March). The not-for-profit hospital as a physicians' cooperative. *American Economic Review, 63,* 87–99.

Pear, Robert. (1986a, June 5). Study examines profit role in hospitals. *The*

New York Times, p. 8.

Pear, Robert. (1986b, November 21). Insurance program proposed to cover catastrophic illness. *The New York Times*, pp. 1, 13.

Pear, Robert, (1987a, January 27). Congress at work on catastrophic-illness plan. *The New York Times*, pp. 1, 7.

Pear, Robert. (1987b, June 7). Congress seeks a fair way to pay for catastrophic health insurance. *The New York Times*, p. 5.

Phelps, Charles E. (1986). Cross-subsidies and charge-shifting in American hospitals. In Frank A. Sloan, James F. Blumstein, & James M. Perrin, (eds.), *Uncompensated hospital care*, (pp. 108–125). Baltimore: The Johns Hopkins University Press.

Schuck, Peter H. (1986). Designing hospital care subsidies for the poor. In Frank A. Sloan, James F. Blumstein & James M. Perrin, (eds.), *Uncompensated hospital care* (pp. 72–93). Baltimore: The Johns Hopkins University Press.

Shalit, Sol S. (1977, January). A doctor–hospital cartel theory. *Journal of Business*, *50*, 1–20.

Waldo, Daniel R., Levit, Katharine R., & Lazenby, Helen. (1986, Fall). National health expenditures, 1985. *Health Care Financing Review*, *8*, 1–21.

Zajac, Edward E. (1978). *Fairness or efficiency. An introduction to public utility pricing*. Cambridge, MA: Ballinger Publishing Company.

CHAPTER 5

Cost-Effectiveness Analysis

INTRODUCTION

Cost-effectiveness analysis is one tool used to evaluate alternative public programs. It can show a public decision-maker either how to obtain the maximum output for a given total cost or, alternatively, how to minimize the total cost of producing a given amount of output. Although cost-effectiveness analysis is similar to benefit-cost analysis, which will be discussed in the next chapter, a significant difference exists between the two evaluation techniques. Cost-effectiveness analysis simply relates levels of output to levels of cost. It does *not* provide any information on how that output is valued by consumers (the benefits of providing it). Thus, the technique is most useful in cases where decision-makers have already decided to produce a certain output and are then trying to evaluate alternative means of doing so. It is also used in situations where the problems of determining the value or benefits of a public-sector program are so insurmountable as to make any credible estimates unlikely. Thus, cost-effectiveness analysis is a less sophisticated technique than benefit-cost analysis, but it is useful in many situations.

Cost-effectiveness analysis has long been used in the evaluation of national defense alternatives. It would be very difficult to determine the benefits that society receives from the provision of national defense. Individuals may have little idea of the monetary value they would place on the level of national defense. They also might have a tendency not to reveal that valuation if they thought they could benefit from national defense without paying for it. This is likely given the difficulty of excluding someone from being defended. Thus, it may be easier to define different levels of national defense in terms of different types of weapons systems, aircraft carriers, bombers, missiles, etc., and to compare the costs of producing these varying levels of output. Cost-effectiveness analysis of specific weapon systems has been used extensively within the Department of Defense "to estimate the relative costs of achieving specified levels of deterrent strength or force structure with a careful examination of the alternative means that are available for attaining stated objectives" (Burkhead and Miner, 1971, p. 181).

Cost-effectiveness analysis is also used in health policy areas where there are problems in placing a valuation on human lives. Although the latter issues will be discussed in the next chapter, it may be more practical to simply evaluate the differences in the number of lives saved or disabilities prevented by various public programs and the costs of doing so. This approach was used in the early years (1965–1968) of the Planning, Programming, and Budgeting (PPB) era in the Department of Health, Education, and Welfare (now the Department of Health and Human Services). This federal agency undertook a number of studies of various disease-control programs to determine which programs had the highest payoff in terms of the number of lives saved and disabilities prevented per dollar of cost (Grosse, 1970). For the cancer-control program from 1968 to 1972, it was found that the cost per death averted ranged from a low of $2,217 for uterine-cervix cancer to $6,046 for breast cancer, $43,729 for cancer of the head and neck, and $46,181 for cancer of the colon and rectum. These figures were used to compare the return from investments in these programs with other programs designed to save lives such as seat belt education and the prevention of drunk driving (Grosse, 1970, pp. 532–536).

A more recent use of cost-effectiveness analysis in the health policy area centers on the debate over investments in prevention versus the treatment of illness (Russell, 1986). Prevention is often argued to be the better policy given the advantages of avoiding disease rather than repairing the damage it causes. Pain and suffering can be avoided and possible death may be averted. Furthermore, it is typically argued that prevention costs less than treatment given the savings in medical treatment costs from the cases of disease prevented. In a 1979 Surgeon General's report, President Jimmy Carter wrote that prevention "can substantially reduce both the suffering of our people and the burden on our expensive system of medical care" (U.S. Department of Health, Education, and Welfare, 1979). However, it is unclear whether the cost-savings argument is valid in all cases. The costs of a prevention program relate to the size of the population at risk while the benefits are received only by the much smaller group which would have contracted the disease in the absence of prevention. The costs and benefits of a treatment program are focused only on those who have actually become ill. Thus, the costs per person of acute care may be much higher than those for prevention while still producing the same or lower cost per life saved or case avoided. There are also risks with the preventative treatment—side effects of vaccinations, possible misdiagnosis, etc. Whether these side effects are worth the possible gain in length of life is a question of individual values. Furthermore, the time span between preventative measures and the health benefits may be considerable, whereas there is a much more direct association between incurring costs and receiving the benefits in the treatment of disease (Russell, 1986, pp. 7–9).

Cost-effectiveness analysis is also useful in many areas of local government decision making. For example, the sanitation department might be considering the alternatives of backyard versus curbside collection of garbage. For both alternatives the outcome is the same. Differences in costs arise from the use of city sanitation workers' time to walk to the back of residents' houses versus the time costs of requiring individuals to bring the refuse out to the curb. There may also be aesthetic costs of having refuse piled out at the curb. Cost-effectiveness analysis would attempt to place monetary values on all of these costs so that decision-makers could evaluate the alternatives (Galambos and Schreiber, 1978).

In all of the above cases, cost-effectiveness analysis has been utilized to evaluate alternatives in the provision of public goods and services. However, this technique has also been applied to government income-redistribution programs (Gramlich and Wolkoff, 1979; Gramlich, 1981). Gramlich and Wolkoff examine three major types of income-transfer programs: direct cash-transfer programs such as a negative income tax; minimum wages; and job-creation programs such as public-service employment. These programs are evaluated in terms of their ability to bring families above the poverty level of income. However, the approaches differ considerably. Cash-transfer programs directly provide income to some or all families below the poverty line. Minimum wages are designed to increase the wages of those working in low-paying jobs, whereas job-creation programs attempt to provide work for those unable to find employment in the private sector. Given the assumptions and the data used in their analysis, Gramlich and Wolkoff find that a cash-transfer program such as a negative income tax raises the incomes of the poorest families more than do the other two programs. They attribute this result to the fact that "many families in these very low income categories do not benefit substantially from the other plans, either because the heads are not able to work many hours or because (for public employment) not all of the eligible workers get the jobs" (Gramlich, 1981, pp. 131, 132). Minimum wages also cause some low-income workers to lose their jobs because employers will attempt to decrease the size of their work force if they are forced to pay a higher minimum wage. These negative employment effects are typically the greatest for teenagers and the least for adult men (Mincer, 1976; Brown, Gilroy, and Kohen, 1983).

These examples show the wide range of applications of cost-effectiveness analysis. Analytical problems common to all of these cases include: (1) the issue of output measurement and the distinction between inputs and outputs in the production of public services (e.g., the measurement of deterrent strength, the number of families brought above the poverty line); and (2) the correct measurement of the costs of producing the output including all social or opportunity costs (e.g., the time costs of sanitation workers versus those of individual residents). The relevant microeconomic theory and the quantitative tools necessary for an analysis of these problems will be discussed in the next section of this chapter. Examples from a variety of public-policy areas will then be utilized to illustrate these issues.

The specific case study for this chapter begins on page 161. This case (Brinkley, 1986a, 1986b) focuses on the policy issues surrounding the release in 1986 of statistics on the mortality rates of different hospitals and the use of these rates by the general public and by the Joint Commission on Accreditation of Hospitals, the principal agency that accredits hospitals in the United States. This information policy of the Department of Health and Human Services

(HHS) was one response to the problem of variation in hospital quality and performance that affected patients as well as other stakeholders such as insurers. The policy has been praised by consumer groups as one of the most significant changes in federal health care policy in decades. However, it has also been criticized by officials in the American Hospital Association and the American Protestant Health Association, who termed it "utter folly" and the "dumbest thing" that HHS ever did (Brinkley, 1986a).

Proponents of the policy argue that it will help in the evaluation of the quality of hospitals in relation to the costs of production. Emphasis will be shifted from comparing hospitals on the basis of inputs to the measurement of their outputs. Thus, the approach of cost–effectiveness analysis is being incorporated in the hospital review and accreditation process. "Consumers and insurance companies are much more educated now and want to know if they are getting high quality care for the dollars they are spending" (Brinkley, 1986b). Critics argue that the statistics are misleading because they are often based on very small samples of patients and because they do not adjust for the severity of illness. It is feared that the statistics, which may not be correct measures of hospital output, will have an unjust adverse effect on the reputations of many hospitals. The widespread use of these statistics may unduly discourage people from using hospitals with higher than expected mortality rates. Thus, the policy is an extremely controversial attempt to improve consumer decision making and to control the costs of health care by focusing more directly on the relationship between costs and output in the hospital sector. The effectiveness of the policy depends largely upon whether the measures of hospital output utilized are credible to the various stakeholders in the policy arena. If they are not, key stakeholders or interest groups will simply spend much time and energy belittling and denouncing the statistics while consumers will be more confused than ever about the quality of their medical care. Thus, the usefulness of the cost–effectiveness approach for policy analysis and public decision making depends upon the ability of the analyst to develop measures of outputs and costs that are meaningful and believable to all interested parties.

PROBLEMS IN MEASURING PROGRAM OUTPUTS AND COSTS

Although it might seem as though measuring program outputs and costs is not a difficult task, many complexities are involved in both the definition and estimation of these concepts. Some of these problems exist for private market goods while others are unique to the public sector. The issues regarding output measurement will be discussed first. Problems in recognizing and defining all program costs will then be presented. Finally, these conceptual problems will be highlighted through the use of examples drawn from a variety of policy areas.

The relevant microeconomic concept for the discussion of output measurement is the *production function*. The production function shows the relationship between a flow of inputs and the resulting flow of outputs per unit of time. It embodies the technical knowledge about how the inputs in any production process are transformed into the resulting outputs. The concept can be applied to any type of private-sector production process ranging from a small grocery store to a large corporation. It is also relevant to activities both in the home—preparing a meal—and in the government—providing national defense, delivering the mail, etc. What differs among these production functions is the number of inputs and outputs and the technical nature of their relationship. For analysis in microeconomic theory, we may consider only a very simple production function with one output and two inputs such as labor and capital. Production functions that describe activities in the real world may involve hundreds of inputs and a variety of types of outputs (e.g., the production function for automobiles of any one of the major car manufacturers).

Using the production-function concept implies that we are able to differentiate clearly between the inputs and the outputs in the production process. For many private-sector activities, this is not a problem. Even though the process is complex, the number of hours of time of assembly line, and number of white collar and management employees in a Ford or General Motors plant can be measured. The amounts and types of capital equipment, raw materials, and other inputs can also be counted. These can then be related to a flow of automobiles differentiated by model characteristics such as color, style, number of accessories, size of engine, etc.

When the final output in the private sector is a service rather than a good, the measurement problem becomes more difficult. How do we characterize the output of a barber shop or a television repair shop, the services of a certified public accountant, or the activities of a real estate agent? Can we precisely measure the relationship between a flow of inputs and the resulting outputs in these areas? Sometimes information on the market valuation of these activities can help in defining the output. Total expenditure is simply the price per unit multiplied by the quantity of output. If data on total expenditure are available and it is known that prices do not vary substantially, inferences can be made that variations in total expenditures reflect different quantities of output.

Output measurement in the public sector is difficult because many activities of government involve the production of services and these services are often not sold in the marketplace or are not valued by market prices or their equivalent. A *service* by definition is not a physical entity but an *activity*. Activities can be counted (for instance, the number of recreation programs offered, the number of history classes taught, the number of streets patrolled) but this does not discriminate for quality differences and may not reflect the service output actually desired or intended (increased recreation activity for city residents, a better knowledge of history, safer city streets). For public-service outputs the distinction between the product and its consequences is blurred on the demand side while the distinction between the product and its production process is blurred on the supply side (Burkhead and Miner, 1971,

p. 301). Because no well-defined production functions exist for most public services, it is impossible to specify that A units of inputs X, Y, and Z produce B units of output R.

It is difficult to define indicators of output because a public-sector agency's objectives are usually vague (provide adequate recreation for all residents; improve the education level of the city's children). Furthermore, there may be multiple objectives, some of which may conflict with each other. A publicly stated goal may be to design a transportation system that maximizes the speed and comfort of the passengers while minimizing the costs of production. It is impossible to pursue all of these goals simultaneously. The objectives of a local school district may include any or all of the following: (1) maximize the achievement of the average child; (2) maximize the achievement of the very bright child; (3) increase the achievement of the handicapped child; (4) provide job skills to persons who are unskilled or unemployable (Ross and Burkhead, 1974, p. 37). Some of these objectives are likely to conflict. In cases where multiple objectives exist, there is also the question of how to weigh the different outputs. Should they all be weighted equally or are some more important than others?

The activities of a given agency are seldom the sole determinant of goal attainment (Ross and Burkhead, 1974; Anthony and Young, 1984). For example, providing recreation facilities of a given quality may be more difficult in one area than in another because of different rates of vandalism. A police force of a particular size may have a lesser impact on crime in a city with high unemployment than in a dynamic and growing metropolitan area. It may be more difficult to bring students from broken homes with little parental support to a stated education level than it is to achieve the same goal for students where there is much cultural and educational enrichment at home.

These distinctions are reflected in the definition of C-output versus D-output by Bradford, Malt, and Oates (1969). *D-outputs* are the services directly produced, whereas *C-outputs* are the "thing or things of primary interest to the citizen-consumer." D-output in police services would include the number of city blocks with a specified degree of surveillance and the number of intersections provided with traffic control, whereas C-output would be the degree of safety from criminal activity and the smoothness and rapidity of the flow of traffic. Although only C-outputs provide direct satisfaction to consumers, they are dependent upon D-outputs and other environmental variables. Costs of these types of outputs are influenced by different factors. Furthermore, while it is possible to talk about scalar multiples of D-outputs (doubling all inputs results in double the amount of output), this is not the case for C-outputs, which depend upon a larger number of factors. Further discussion of all of these issues is provided by Ross and Burkhead (1974).

Given the difficulty in measuring outputs, inputs are sometimes used as a proxy for public-sector outputs. Thus, the output of a university may be measured by the number of Ph.D.s on its faculty or the number of volumes in its library. The value of the inputs may also be used. Increases in this value may be treated as increases in output (Ross and Burkhead, 1974, p. 46). This approach, of course, prohibits any definition or measurement of productivity or productivity gains by the public agency. If productivity is measured in the average sense—output per unit of input—there can be no productivity change with this definition.

Total expenditures are also often used as a proxy for public-sector outputs. The assumption is that larger expenditures imply larger output. This assumption is valid only if prices are constant across observations. Furthermore, focusing on expenditures masks whether the factors influencing expenditure differences result from the supply or demand side of the economy.

Program costs might also seem to be a relatively easy concept to measure. Costs are listed in an agency's budget or in the financial statements of a private-sector firm. These could simply be added together and compared with program output. However, from the viewpoint of program evaluation, monetary costs listed in these types of documents may not: (1) adequately reflect the true economic costs of the program or (2) measure all of the costs to society related to the provision of the program's output.

Whether they are examining the private or public sector of the economy, economists are always concerned with measuring the *opportunity costs* of producing various types of output. These are the costs that must be included in both cost–effectiveness and benefit–cost analysis. Therefore, this discussion is relevant for both this chapter and the one that follows. Opportunity costs measure the cost of using society's resources in one activity in terms of the opportunities foregone or the activities not undertaken. In some cases these costs are equal to the monetary costs found in an agency's budget. However, in other cases budgetary costs reflect an accounting definition rather than an economic definition of costs. Furthermore, some opportunity costs are not found in a given agency's budget and may not be easily evaluated in monetary terms. By definition, certain external costs such as those resulting from pollution are imposed on other individuals from the production of a given output and are not recognized by the producer. The measurement of opportunity costs will first be discussed in general terms. These costs will then be related to several specific examples.

Opportunity costs must truly reflect the value of using a resource in a particular activity. This value must be included in a cost–effectiveness analysis even if the agency conducting the analysis does not have to pay this cost. For example, a city might be considering two alternative sites for a proposed park. In one case the city already owns the vacant plot of land while it has to purchase the land in the other case. It might be tempting to argue that the cost of providing the first alternative is lower than for the second option. Although it is true that the monetary cost to the city is lower in the first case, the opportunity cost of using the first plot of land is not necessarily lower. The city needs to determine the value of that first plot of land in its next best alternative use or what price it would command in the marketplace. This opportunity cost must be included in a cost–effectiveness analysis because the city could lease or sell that plot of land. The cost of using that land to provide park and recreation services is not zero unless there is no alternative use for the land. Of course, the city might not want to include this implicit opportunity cost if, for political or other reasons, decision-makers were already in favor of the one park option. They might also argue that since this is not an out-of-pocket cost, it is not understandable by, nor relevant to, their constituents. This is another case where the perceptions of the various stakeholders are important to the final policy outcome.

A similar example from the private sector would be the treatment of the time incurred by the owner of a company in the production of a good or service. In a family-operated business the owner may not explicitly be paid a salary so that the costs of his or her time may not be included as a cost of production. This practice will result in an overstatement of the firm's profits. If the owner could earn $25,000 per year by working in some other activity, that figure represents the opportunity cost of the individual's time in the family business. This cost may not be reflected in any existing financial statement.

In a competitive market economy where resources are fully employed, the market price that an agency must pay for its inputs typically reflects their opportunity costs. For example, if the wages of construction workers are determined by the forces of supply and demand and if all workers who want to work are able to do so, the monetary cost of hiring those workers for a public-sector program, which is reflected in the agency's budget, should equal the opportunity cost of employing the workers. The only way to draw workers into the public sector is to pay them what they could have earned in the private sector. However, if certain types of workers face the prospect of continued unemployment, the opportunity cost of employing them for a public-sector project may be less than the monetary cost in the agency's budget.

In a detailed study of construction projects, Haveman (1983) estimated the proportion of labor and capital that was drawn from an idle pool of these resources by comparing the pattern of resource demands with the occupational and regional pattern of labor unemployment and the industrial pattern of excess plant capacity. He argued that the opportunity cost of the expenditures for these projects in 1960 varied between 70 percent and 90 percent of the monetary costs. The validity of adjusting monetary costs to reflect problems of unemployment depends upon whether the opportunity cost of using unemployed labor is zero or extremely low. The value of that nonworking time may not be zero if it is used for family activities, going to school, etc. Furthermore, macroeconomic conditions also influence the rates of unemployment. Gramlich (1981, p. 67) argues that the opportunity cost of unemployed labor is less than its monetary cost only if: "(1) The reduction in unemployment can be sustained. Inflationary pressures will not be set up which require other cutbacks in spending demand, generating corresponding increases in unemployment somewhere else in the economy. (2) The project is responsible for reducing unemployment. Tax reductions, monetary policy, or price flexibility would not have done so anyway. (3) It can be persuasively argued that the supply curve or some other notion of social externality makes the opportunity cost *below* the market wage. . . ." Since valuing labor costs below their monetary costs makes a public-sector project look more favorable, advocates of a project will often be tempted to follow this procedure. Gramlich argues that this approach must be resisted if the above three conditions are not met. Otherwise, public-sector projects either do not really create jobs, are not the only way to create jobs, or they create jobs which do not have much social value (Gramlich, 1981, p. 67).

Certain costs of producing output in either the private or public sector are not faced directly by the producer. One of the costs of production involves the disposal of waste materials. If a company dumps its wastes into a river, these costs of production are borne by other individuals living downstream and are classified as external costs. Economists argue that resource misallocations occur when these external costs are not considered by decision-makers because they are part of the total opportunity costs of production. Thus, costs must be counted regardless of who actually pays them or where they actually appear. Most of the costs of government air and water pollution control programs are not borne by the regulating agency and are not even reflected in the agency's budget. They appear as increased costs for the regulated companies, increased prices for consumer products, and greater social costs such as those associated with unemployment. The costs of controlling air pollution through the use of emission-control devices and inspections of automobiles include higher car prices, the possible unemployment of automobile workers if consumers buy fewer cars, and the time spent by consumers in getting their cars inspected. These costs do not appear in the budget of a regulating authority such as the Environmental Protection Agency.

A good example of both the problems of adjusting budgetary costs and of measuring all costs associated with a program is given by Weisbrod (1983) in his comparison of hospital- versus community-based treatment of the mentally ill. Weisbrod argues that the costs of inpatient care at the Mendota Mental Health Institute (MMHI) provided by the State of Wisconsin differ from the true social or opportunity costs in three respects: "(1) *the opportunity cost of the land* on which the hospital is located had been disregarded; (2) *the depreciation of the hospital buildings* was based on historical cost rather than replacement cost; and (3) *research* carried out at MMHI was included in the per diem cost figure for the hospital" (Weisbrod, 1983, p. 237). The land valuation problem was discussed above. Depreciation presents a problem because accounting procedures typically involve the use of historical costs. Yet it is the current cost of replacing the asset that best reflects the opportunity cost of using the asset to provide output. Research costs were included in the per diem figure for accounting purposes, but these costs were not directly related to the treatment of patients. Thus, the per diem cost estimated by the state "was adjusted upward to allow for an opportunity cost of 8 percent on the estimated value of the land and the depreciated replacement cost of the physical plant, and it was adjusted slightly downward to account for research activities . . ." (Weisbrod, 1983, p. 237).

Other costs that Weisbrod attempted to measure included secondary treatment costs by other agencies, institutions, and professions; law enforcement costs associated with the different modes of treatment; external costs caused by the patients' illnesses; and patient maintenance costs. Secondary costs included those of other hospitals and psychiatric institutions, halfway houses, visiting nurses, and counseling services. Law enforcement costs were obtained from patient interviews on the number of police and court contacts, the number of nights spent in jail, and the number of contacts with probation and parole officers. External costs related to members of the patients' immediate families or other individuals who suffered from the illegal or disruptive behavior of the patients. It was impossible to place monetary values on these costs. However, family members were asked whether they had experienced work or school absences, disruption of domestic or social routines, trouble with neighbors, or stress-related physical ailments as a result of the patient's illness. They were also questioned about expenses incurred that were related to the patient. These responses were used to categorize each family as suffering a "severe," "moderate," "mild," or "no" burden from the patient's illness. Although the attempt was made to count only the incremental patient maintenance costs associated with the outpatient program, data limitations meant that all maintenance costs were actually included in the analysis (Weisbrod, 1983, pp. 239–241). Thus, implementation problems may prevent analysts from calculating all costs as theoretically desired or from valuing all costs in monetary terms. These problems should be noted and their implications should be discussed so that decision-makers have full information about the limits of the analysis.

SPECIFIC EXAMPLES OF COST-EFFECTIVENESS ANALYSIS

In this section we will discuss three specific examples of the use of cost-effectiveness analysis that were mentioned briefly in the introduction to this chapter: national defense; the prevention-versus-treatment controversy in health care policy; and the evaluation of alternative types of income redistribution programs. These examples will illustrate the conceptual issues discussed in the preceding section.

National Defense

Cost-effectiveness analysis has long been utilized by the Department of Defense in terms of developing military strategy (Berg, 1967; Hitch and McKean, 1965; Niskanen, 1967). Defense Department objectives have typically been stated in terms of deterrence, defense, and offense (Niskanen, 1967, pp. 22–32). *Deterrence* relates to the provision of military forces capable of damaging a potential enemy to discourage the enemy from initiating military action. *Defense* involves reducing the unfavorable consequence of enemy military action that has not been avoided by deterrence. *Offense* implies the capability to undertake direct military action. Measures of the effectiveness of a strategic deterrent force relate to its capability to inflict fatalities on the enemy in various scenarios that depend upon the opponent's level of defense, whether our forces strike first, etc. Defense effectiveness is typically measured by the capability of an opponent to inflict fatalities on the United States. Niskanen (1967, pp. 27–30) argues that a number of measures of effectiveness should not be used in strategic analysis. For example, the number of targets potentially destroyed is not useful because "cities of different sizes should be weighted by the potential population destroyed." The number of offensive vehicles (missiles or bombers) intercepted is not an appropriate measure because a defense force can serve an important purpose even if it never intercepts any missiles. Ratios of the numbers of fatalities in this country relative to those of the enemy are also not useful. Niskanen argues that for ground forces, the "single best measure of effectiveness is probably the population in 'free' territory.... For tactical air forces in general, one should use a measure of effectiveness which reflects the enemy capability after the employment of our tactical air forces.... For defense systems, such as an interceptor air-defense system or a surface-to-air missile system, one should almost always use the capability of one's own side after the enemy's attack, rather than some measure of how many offensive weapons are shot down" (Niskanen, 1967, pp. 28, 29).

In their classic study, *The Economics of Defense in the Nuclear Age*, Hitch and McKean present an example of a specific military choice and the alternatives available to decision-makers (Hitch and McKean, 1965, pp. 133–142). The problem is that of choosing an intercontinental military air transport fleet for the decade 1958 to 1967. It is noted that the larger question of whether we should have such an air transport fleet is *not* being considered in this analysis. There are two tasks—routine worldwide resupply of United States' military bases at all times and deployment in the event of a peripheral war. The tasks are stated in terms of cargo and passenger tonnages to be delivered via 20 channels—origin and overseas destinations. For most channels, several round-trip routes are available for delivering the required tonnage. Four different types of aircraft, which differ in terms of their cargo and range, are considered. Some of the aircraft are presumed to be available while others can be procured within specified production limits. The problem is analyzed over time so that the alternatives are not just fleets, but fleet sequences. What is sought is the best Period I–Period II sequence of fleets.

The costs to be measured in this example include the following: (1) procurement costs, (2) installations and training costs, (3) attrition costs, and (4) annual operating costs (Hitch and McKean, 1965, pp. 136–139). One of the conceptual issues to be faced in this case is the allocation of costs between peacetime and wartime usage. Since a mothballed fleet would not be ready for a quick response in a wartime situation, the operating costs of practice time during periods of peace must be included in the analysis. The authors assume that "six hours daily flying for each aircraft in the fleet is necessary to a capability of immediately achieving ten hours daily flying whenever the occasion warrants." Thus, the costs of six practice-hours per day over the 10-year period are included in the analysis.

Procurement costs of the aircraft include both the costs of the airframe and an initial outlay for spare parts. There are two sets of these costs, which decline as the number of aircraft produced increases. Certain fixed costs of tooling are incurred regardless of the number of aircraft produced. These costs per unit decrease with increased production. Furthermore, there is a "learning" process that occurs as production is undertaken. This also increases efficiency and lowers costs as production increases. Installations and training costs are also initial rather than recurring costs. The purchase of a vehicle requires an outlay for facilities such as buildings, kitchens, and ground-handling equipment and for the training of crews and maintenance personnel. How specific these costs are to a particular type of aircraft and how quickly they depreciate are major questions to be answered. Attrition costs result from the practice operations that occur in peace time. These costs can be troublesome given the concern with fleet design and with constraints on how many aircraft different manufacturers can provide at different times. If production of certain types of aircraft is stopped, they must be replaced with newer models, which change the composition of the entire fleet. Yet the latter is what is being costed. Annual operating costs are proportional to the peacetime practice activity and include factors such as wages, fuel, and maintenance. Hitch and McKean note that *sunk costs*—procurement costs of aircraft already in the fleet—are not included in the analysis because they cannot affect future decision making (Hitch and McKean, 1965, pp. 138, 139).

The results of this analysis indicate that the least-cost fleet sequence includes some aircraft that were not available at the beginning of the period under study (Hitch and McKean, 1965, pp. 140–142). The analysis also showed the inefficiency of the "least-procurement" policy—buying no more new aircraft than would be necessary to carry out the task. The cost-effectiveness procedure for a sequence of decisions over time is not necessarily the one that minimizes current expenditures. Hitch and McKean also performed a sensitivity analysis by examining alternatives that excluded certain types of aircraft. They recognize that manpower constraints and uncertainty may affect the validity of the analysis. Is the mission analyzed truly representative of reality? How do technological developments affect cost and performance estimates? These types of political-value questions, which are inherent in all cost-effectiveness and benefit-cost analyses, lead to differences in stakeholder positions on the results of the analyses.

Health Care Policy

The second example to be discussed is the prevention-versus-treatment debate in health care policy. The health effects or output for a vaccination program for a disease such as measles are typically measured by the number of deaths, cases of retardation caused both by the measles and by vaccine side effects, the number of cases hospitalized, and by days lost from school or work. Estimates of these effects are made both with and without a vaccination program (Russell, 1986, pp. 34, 35). No attempt is made to produce a composite measure of all health effects particularly since the side effects of the vaccine are similar to those of the disease. This approach is less useful when there are a large number of health effects and when the effects of different alternatives are not directly comparable. For example, if hypertension is untreated, people's lives may be shorter. The gain from treatment is the years of added life. However, the treatment often causes unpleasant side effects. Therefore, people who take antihypertensive drugs may live longer but they may not feel as well as without the treatment. Simply counting years of additional life does not fully account for all of the relevant health effects. Furthermore, this approach is not relevant for treatments that increase the quality of life without necessarily lengthening it.

These quality-of-life issues have long been recognized in the literature, and there have been various attempts to deal with them. For example, a year of life with a transplanted kidney has typically been weighted more heavily than a year on a dialysis machine (Klarman, Francis, and Rosenthal, 1968). More recently there have been attempts to develop overall indices of health effects or health status (Russell, 1986, pp. 66–70; Warner and Luce, 1982, pp. 91–93, 148–149). The goal has been to find a common unit to measure different health effects and to be able to translate these different effects into the common unit. A unit typically utilized is the quality-adjusted life-year or the year of healthy life. A year of healthy life is given a value of 1.0. These years are weighted the same no matter who gains them. Thus, no judgments are made regarding increases by the young versus the old, workers versus nonworkers, etc. A 10-year gain to one individual is counted the same as two 5-year gains to two individuals. Years of life with illness or disability are weighted at some fraction of a year of healthy life and are given a value between 0.0 and 1.0. Death is given a value of zero although some would argue that severe disability is even a worse state.

Warner and Luce (1982, p. 92) argue that health-status indices suffer from the problems of reliability (do repeated measurements provide the same information?), validity (is the relative weighting system correct?), and definitional consistency (what constitutes health?). Sometimes arbitrary measures are utilized. In their study of hypertension, Weinstein and Stason (1976) decided that most people would value a year of life with side effects from hypertensive medication as worth just under 0.99 of a year of healthy life. By this definition, an average person would be willing to give up about 1 percent of his or her remaining life span, or about four days per year, to be free of the side effects of the medication. It would be preferable to have data that are directly related to individual preferences. These data might be elicited from surveys asking how much time individuals would be willing to trade off in return for excellent health in their remaining years. However, the problems in obtaining reliable information here are similar to those in benefit-cost analysis in which individuals are asked about their willingness to pay for longer life. Survey responses in both areas may be very dependent on the phrasing of the questions. The ability of individuals to provide reasoned answers to these types of questions is also unclear.

More recently, researchers have been defining healthy years in terms of ability to function rather than in terms of specific diseases. "Specific diseases can be described in terms of the levels of function and symptoms, and the length of time each of those levels of function and symptoms lasts. For example, if the person confined to bed [the level of function] with shortness of breath [the symptom] has a cold, the impairment will last only a few days; if he or she has chronic bronchitis, much more time will be affected. By defining different conditions in terms of a common set of elements, this approach helps to maintain and test the consistency of valuations of diverse states of health" (Russell, 1986, p. 69). Researchers have found that valuations placed on various combinations of functions and symptoms vary little among different social and economic groups, correlate well with medical tests of the problem, and have the same effect on overall health evaluation regardless of the combination of other symptoms or functions (summarized by Russell, 1986, pp. 69, 70). Other researchers have developed a Sickness Impact Profile, while attempts to measure not only physical functions but also emotional state, mental alertness, and willingness to participate in social activities (Bergner and others, 1981).

For the prevention-versus-treatment decision for measles vaccination, two types of costs were estimated for each alternative: direct medical expenses and net expenditure for institutional care (Russell, 1986, pp. 32–34). In the absence of vaccination it was assumed that the number of measles cases would continue to increase at the same rate as in the past. Costs of this alternative include those costs incurred for medical treatment and for the lifetime institutionalization of children left retarded by the illness. Vaccination costs include administrative costs, treatment costs for those children who were missed by the program and for those where the vaccine failed to produce immunity, and institutionalization costs for any children left retarded. Researchers were unable to measure the costs of treating the side effects and the retardation caused by the vaccine. Expenditures for long-term institutional care were estimated net of normal maintenance costs to determine the additional costs to society from this factor. Because the costs of institutionalization are estimated over 40 years in the future, these costs were discounted to adjust for the time-value of money. Because this procedure is necessary for the estimation of both benefits and costs extending into the future, it will be discussed in the next chapter.

The results of this analysis indicate that measles vaccination during the period 1963–1968 increased direct medical expenditures by $31 million, compared with no vaccination, but reduced expenditures on institutionalization by $201 million. The net saving of approximately $170 million may be high because several procedures in the analysis probably resulted in an overestimate of the costs of not vaccinating and an underestimate of the costs of vaccination—the number of measles cases in the absence of vaccination is probably overestimated, the net cost of institutionalization is probably overestimated, and the cost of treating vaccine side effects has been omitted (Russell, 1986, p. 34).

In the case of treating hypertension, the costs per year of healthy life gained vary considerably with the characteristics of the patient, the choices made about the treatment, and the assumptions about the areas of uncertainty (Russell, 1986, pp. 71–76). For individuals whose diastolic pressure is reduced from 110 to 90, the estimates range from a low of $3,270 per year of healthy life for 20-year-old men to $16,330 for men aged 60 (in 1975 dollars). The cost for women appears to fall with age because hypertension seems to cause less damage in women, particularly when they are young. In this study sensitivity analysis is also employed regarding several of the key assumptions in the analysis.

Income Redistribution Programs

Output measurement for income redistribution programs, the third example to be discussed in this section, must deal with the differential causes of poverty in order to define the success of the program. Poverty can result from a variety of reasons: (1) families earn very little money; (2) there are a large number of children to care for, which may prevent a mother from working; (3) the primary worker is unemployed; (4) the primary worker is employed but earns only a low wage. Earning poverty-level income may also be either a temporary or a chronic phenomenon. Gramlich and Wolkoff (1979) define the family as their unit of observation for their analysis of the effect of income redistribution programs. Family income is to be averaged over the number of mouths to be fed. These researchers use the Department of Health and Human Services poverty standard for families of various sizes—the amount of income these families need to be at a very minimum standard of living. This standard was $6,000 for a family of four in 1978. Gramlich and Wolkoff then compute a family welfare ratio, Z, which equals Y/N where Y is a family's total income (including all money income after taxes and all food stamps or transfers in kind) and N is the government poverty or needs standard for a family of that size. If Z equals 1.0, the family's income is just at the poverty line. Values of Z greater than 1.0 indicate income above the poverty line. Gramlich and Wolkoff use a 9-year average of this ratio to deal with the fact that both Y and N vary significantly over time (Gramlich, 1981, pp. 123–125). The effect of different income redistribution programs is then measured by their impact on families with varying Y/N ratios. In particular, the percentage change in income from different programs in the 0.0–0.5, the 0.5–1.0, and the 1.0–1.5 Y/N classes is of greatest importance. Various income redistribution programs may have different concentrations of output among these income-needs classes in the population.

The costs associated with the alternative income redistribution programs analyzed by Gramlich and Wolkoff are quite different from those in the military and health care examples discussed above. Under a negative income tax program, families are paid a certain guaranteed income if no work is performed. A marginal tax rate is applied to every dollar earned in the marketplace. Thus, the net subsidy from the government is reduced as earned income increases. The break-even level of earned income is that level where the net subsidy from the government is zero. Both the plan's guaranteed income and the marginal tax rate may cause family members to work less. Receipt of the guaranteed income may cause them to increase their consumption of leisure time. Furthermore, since they receive only some fraction of each dollar earned in the marketplace, they may want to work less than if they received the full dollar of earnings. This increased consumption of leisure (or decreased work) may make the negative income tax program appear less cost-effective. However, the gain in leisure time has value to the family and probably also to society. Adults can spend more time with children, individuals can attend school longer, etc. Thus, an attempt must be made to place a value on this gain in leisure time to make a correct comparison with the costs of the program. Costs of a minimum wage program relate to the fact that employers are forced to pay a higher wage under the program than they would wish to do so. Costs of a public employment program include both the direct costs to the government and wage changes faced by private employers (Gramlich, 1981, pp. 128–131). Gramlich and Wolkoff's analysis of these three types of income redistribution programs, each costing $5 billion, showed that the negative income tax achieved the greatest increases in income for the lowest income families.

Following Case Study No. 4, analysis of it begins on page 165.

Case Study No. 4
Hospitals and the Cost-Effectiveness Approach to Policy-Making

U.S. Releasing Lists of Hospitals With Abnormal Mortality Rates
(Joel Brinkley. Copyright © 1986 by The New York Times Company.
Reprinted by permission.)

Washington, March 11—The Health and Human Services Department is preparing to release lists of the nation's hospitals that have mortality rates significantly higher or lower than the national average, the first such lists ever compiled.

The lists, provided to The New York Times and scheduled for general release on Wednesday, show that more than twice as many patients died at certain hospitals than would have been expected under national norms.

But Federal officials warned that the statistics were suggestive, not conclusive. They said that perhaps half the hospitals shown might have acceptable explanations for their abnormal death rates that had nothing to do with the quality of the medical care.

"This is not meant to point an accusing finger," said Dr. Henry R. Desmarais, Acting Administrator of the Health Care Financing Administration, the agency that compiled the lists. The list was intended to help state medical review agencies indentify hospitals with problems, he said. "It is not a report card on the nation's hospitals," he added.

Action is Welcomed

Even with that warning, releasing the data brought protests from the medical profession. "It's the dumbest thing I've ever seen H.H.S. do," said Jack Owen, executive vice president of the American Hospital Association. "It's utter folly," said Frederick Graefe, counsel for the American Protestant Health Association.

But consumer groups lauded the move, calling it one of the most significant changes in Federal policy for health-care consumers in decades. Whether or not the statistics are valid, they said, releasing the material is an important precedent.

"We've been waiting for this for a long time," said Dr. Sidney Wolfe, head of the Public Citizens Health Research Group, which has spent a decade lobbying for fuller disclosure of evaluative information on doctors and hospitals. "We're not worried about misuse of the data; people are too bright to do that."

Even with possible flaws in the statistics, said Cyril F. Brickfield executive director of the American Association of Retried Persons, "it is better to err on the side of providing more information to consumers. We applaud H.H.S. for taking this step."

The principal list shows 269 hospitals with abnormal overall mortality rates, 142 with death rates higher than average and 127 with rates lower than average. The Government said a lower than average death rate could mean the hospital provides better than average care, or it could mean that the hospital routinely discharges especially sick patients before they die. A higher than average death rate could mean that the hospital treats sicker than average patients, or it could suggest high levels of malpractice.

In addition, the department released other lists showing hundreds of hospitals with higher than average or lower than average death rates for nine common medical problems, from pneumonia to coronary-artery bypass operations. Again those lists show that patients are several times more likely to die when treated for certain illnesses in some hospitals as compared with others.

Ten other lists show which of the nation's hospitals have discharge rates higher or lower than average. An unusual discharge rate could indicate that hospitals are releasing patients before they are well or keeping them hospitalized longer than necessary.

The lists were prepared for private use by Professional Review Organizations, the federally financed agencies in each state charged with monitoring the quality and necessity of care given to patients whose bills are paid by Medicare, the Federal health program for the elderly and disabled.

As part of the Federal Government's program to reduce the cost and improve the quality of health care, the review agencies were to use the list to see if problems existed at certain hospitals and to take corrective action if there were problems. The review agencies have the power to withhold payment for medical treatment they consider unnecessary or of poor quality.

The Government said it made the lists public only because it had no choice under the Federal Freedom of Information Act. "This was never meant to be used by consumers," Dr. Desmarais said. "I don't think it is really useful for making judgments."

But after an article about the lists appeared in *The New York Times* last week, Dr. Desmarais said, the department received hundreds of requests for the data, "and it was the opinion of our counsel that, despite our concerns, the public had a right to view it."

Now that the lists have been made public, there is disagreement over who should answer questions from consumers about hospitals that have abnormal death rates.

Dr. Desmarais said people should ask their state-based review organizations about hospitals that appear to have problems. Federal law requires the review agencies to make public information they may have in evaluating the quality of care at individual hospitals, after allowing the hospitals time to attach comments.

But Andrew Webber, executive vice president of the American Medical Peer Review Association, the umbrella agency for the state agencies,

said: "They're sticking us with interpreting their analysis that, quite honestly, a lot of our folks don't even understand."

"We're going to refer people to the hospitals," or back to the Federal agency, he said.

The lists were derived using case records from all 10.7 million patients treated in 1984 whose bills were paid by Medicare. Nearly all the nation's hospitals treat Medicare patients.

The mortality lists show the percentage of the Medicare patients who died, compared with the percentage that would be expected to die using national statistics. For each hospital, the comparative national statistic was adjusted for 89 possible variables that could affect the death rates. A hospital that treats a large number of elderly patients or stroke victims would be expected to have more deaths than average, as an example. So that hospital's "predicted" death rate would be adjusted upward accordingly.

But Dr. Henry Krakauer, the Federal official who compiled the lists, said the statistics could not be adjusted to account fully for two significant variables.

The first is the severity of the patients' illnesses. If a hospital routinely treats patients who are significantly sicker than average, it will have more deaths.

Illustrating that, the Nevada hospital shown with the highest death rate—88 percent of its Medicare patients died in 1984—was actually a hospice that cares for terminally ill patients.

Oak Forest Hospital of Cook County, near Chicago, had the second highest rate; 26 percent of its Medicare patients died in 1984 when the prediction was that only 9 percent should have died. Today the hospital's administrator explained that most of Oak Forest's patients were elderly people with chronic illnesses.

The second major variable Dr. Krakauer cited was hospital record-keeping errors. Some hospitals fail to note patient deaths on their forms, making the mortality rate appear better than it acutally is.

Some state review agencies said they were not equipped to sort out which of the hospitals on the list have malpractice problems and which have legitimate explanations for unusual death rates.

David McIntyre, chief executive officer of Wisconsin's review agency, for example, said: "We don't have the manpower to go over each medical record in these death cases and make a final judgment."

The Federal list shows that Wisconsin has three hospitals with higher than average death rates; at one, the death rate was nearly 50 percent higher than predicted, using the Government's analysis.

Although one hospital has come up with an explanation, for the others, "the only thing we can do is use the statistics and assume there is a problem," Mr. McIntyre said. "We'll have more intensive reviews, look very closely at the deaths they have to see if the problem is resolved or if the behavior has changed."

Key Hospital Accrediting Agency To Start Weighing Mortality Rates
(Joel Brinkley. Copyright © 1986 by The New York Times Company. Reprinted by permission.)

Washington, Nov. 3—The principal agency that accredits the nation's hospitals said today that it would soon being using surgical mortality and complication rates, along with other measures of medical outcome, as a central tool in accreditations.

The change, to be gradually introduced over several years, starting next year, represents a fundamental shift in the way the nation's hospitals are evaluated. The medical authorities say this could be the most important step yet in the broad national movement toward holding doctors and hospitals directly accountable for the quality of the care they provide.

Now accreditation is based on whether hospitals are properly equipped and managed so they have the capacity to provide high-quality care.

Methods for Fair Evaluation
Under the new policy, hospitals will also be judged on whether they actually provided care at least equal to local and national standards. That conclusion will be based on analyses showing how many patients recovered from treatment quickly and without complications and how many did not, among other measures.

Agency officials say they believe the methodology now exists for adjusting statistics to account for any differences between the patients in different hospitals that might explain variations in different mortality rates.

In an interview today, Dr. Dennis O'Leary, president of the Chicago-based accrediting agency, the Joint Commission on Accreditation of Hospitals, called the change "controversial but inevitable."

The commission, a semiprivate agency, accredits more than 80 percent of the nation's 6,000 acute-care hospitals as well as 2,500 other health care facilities, including nursing homes, psychiatric hospitals and outpatient clinics. Commission accreditation is critical for most hospitals because without it they are not eligible to receive money from the Federal Medicare program, which pays for the care of about 40 percent of the nation's hospital patients.

Nearly all the commission's directors are appointees from the nation's major health care organizations, such as the American Medical Association and the American Hospital Association, both of which support the change. The agency's financing comes from hospitals that pay to be accredited.

Dr. Alan Nelson, chairman of the medical association's board of trustees, who also sits on the commission board, said today that the new plan was "a very important change and a difficult task." In the past, he said, hospital accreditation "was based too much on structure, paper work, minutes of staff meetings and other boilerplate stuff; it didn't really reflect on the quality of the care, the outcome of the treatment."

Numerous public and private studies have shown wide variations in mortality and complication rates for certain medical and surgical procedures in essentially similar hospitals. In essence the studies, which include a large-scale analysis by the Department of Health and Human Services earlier this year, show that patients may be significantly more likely to die in one hospital than in another.

But hospitals and other medical professionals have argued that the studies are flawed because they have not been adjusted completely to account for differences in the hospitals' patient mixes. For example, in the Government study of mortality rates last March, even though the statistics had been adjusted for differing patient mixes, the hospital with the highest mortality rate turned out to be a hospice for the terminally ill.

Dr. O'Leary and Dr. James Prevost, director of the agency's research and development department, said the commission's board decided that the statistical methodology for measuring treatment outcome had improved significantly in the last two years and decided in a private meeting in September to introduce the new accrediting procedure gradually, starting next year. The decision was not widely publicized.

Dr. Prevost said: "Answering the question 'does the hospital have the capacity to provide high quality care' is no longer sufficient. Consumers and insurance companies are much more educated now and want to know if they are getting high quality care for the dollars they are spending."

A number of public and private agencies, including health consultants and insurance agencies, have already devised several methods for measuring mortality and complication rates, adjusted to account for unique features of an individual hospitals' patients.

"We don't know which method is best," Dr. Prevost said. "So we are going to convene a number of work groups and task forces early next year to study all the existing methodologies and select the best indicators."

"The intention," Dr. Nelson said, "is to develop national norms, adjusted for local conditions, for such things as neonatal mortality, infection rates, mortality rates and other measures, particularly for certain high-risk procedures."

Once the best system is chosen, the commission will continually monitor hospitals, rather than simply subjecting them to an inspection once every three years, as is the usual practice now. Hospitals with problems will receive advice and warnings at first but could lose their accreditation if the problems do not improve.

Dr. O'Leary said the commission would probably establish another study group to determine what new information will be released to the public. Under the commission's current policy, none of its survey material is made public unless the hospital authorizes its release. But Dr. O'Leary said, "We will have a data base here which is of broad national interest, and our policy could change, at least as it refers to aggregate data" for groups of hospitals.

Professional Review Organizations, the federally financed oversight agencies in every state that monitor the care given to Medicare patients, gather some statistical data on treatment outcomes for Medicare patients. Despite strenuous objections from the health care industry, the Government said last year that much of the data should be made available to the public. But medical officials now say publicizing the data has not caused acute hardships.

Analysis of Case Study No. 4

The case study for this chapter focuses on the use of mortality rates as a measure of hospital output by both the public in general and by hospital accrediting agencies. This switch to a cost-effectiveness approach became the center of public-policy controversy in March 1986 when the Department of Health and Human Services released lists of the nation's hospitals with mortality rates both above and below the national average. These lists were derived from case records of all 10.7 million patients treated in 1984 whose bills were paid by Medicare. They show the percentage of Medicare patients who died compared with the percentage who would be expected to die calculated from national norms. The national statistics were adjusted for 89 possible variables that could affect death rates in individual hospitals. The principal list showed 269 hospitals with abnormal overall mortality rates, 142 with death rates higher than average, and 127 with lower than average rates (Brinkley, 1986a).

The lists had been prepared for private use by Professional Review Organizations, the federally financed agencies that review the quality and necessity of care provided to Medicare patients. The review agencies were to use the lists to determine if there were problems with particular hospitals as part of the federal government's overall concern with the costs and quality of hospital care. The government was forced to make the lists public under the provisions of the federal Freedom of Information Act. In the first case cited, Dr. Henry R. Desmarais, Acting Administrator of the Health Care Financing Administration, the agency that compiled the lists, is quoted as saying that the information was "never meant to be used by consumers. I don't think it is really useful for making judgments." The significance of this information became even greater when, in November 1986, the Joint Commission on Accreditation of Hospitals, a semiprivate agency that accredits more than 80 percent of the nation's 6,000 acute-care hospitals as well as 2,500 other health care facilities (second case cited), announced that it would begin using mortality and complication rates when evaluating hospitals for accreditation (Brinkley, 1986b). Hospitals will be judged in part on whether they provide care at least equal to local and national standards. This represents a shift from current policy, which focuses on inputs to one emphasizing outputs and the costs of providing them. A Joint Commission official has stated that past hospital accreditation "was based too much on structure, paper work, minutes of staff meetings and other boilerplate stuff; it didn't really reflect on the quality of the care, the outcome of the treatment" (Brinkley, 1986b).

The controversy surrounding the policy issues in this case relates to the output measurement issues discussed previously. What do hospitals produce? Is it possible to derive an output measure that is independent of the inputs of production? Can output measures be developed that are comparable among different types of hospitals and that can be compared with the costs of production? Furthermore, are these measures credible to the various stakeholders in this policy arena? The policy has been described as one of "utter folly" by one hospital official. Even the executive vice-president of the American Medical Peer Review Association, the umbrella agency for the state review organizations, stated: "They're [the Health Care Financing Administration] sticking us with interpreting their analysis that, quite honestly, a lot of our folks don't even understand" (Brinkley, 1986a).

In response to criticisms about the public's use of this data to make quality judgments about hospitals, federal officials warned that the statistics were "suggestive, not conclusive" (Brinkley, 1986a). Officials acknowledge that "perhaps half the hospitals shown might have acceptable explanations for their abnormal death rates that had nothing to do with the quality of the medical care" (Brinkley, 1986a). The statistics were *not* adjusted for two significant variables: (1) the severity of a patient's illness and (2) hospital record-keeping errors. Hospitals treating patients who are sicker than average will have higher mortality rates from that factor alone. Little could be implied about the quality of care in these cases. Some hospitals may also fail to note patient deaths on their forms, thus making their mortality rates appear better than average. Lower than average rates could also result from a policy of discharging patients before they die.

The sample size can have an effect on the interpretation of the mortality statistics. For example, in Georgia the number of Medicare patients treated at many rural hospitals is very small. The government-predicted death rate among patients with pacemaker implants was 3 percent at one 147-bed rural hospital. The actual death rate at the hospital was 50 percent because two of the four patients with this condition died (Seabrook, 1987). Although it may appear to be unfair to compare these statistics with those from large urban hospitals, the small number of patients does raise questions about the appropriateness of performing that procedure in a hospital where there is only a small demand for the operation. Repeated performance of complex surgical procedures may increase the quality of the output. Luft, Bunker, and Enthoven (1979) found that for complicated types of surgery, the greater the volume of surgery performed, the lower the surgical mortality rates. This study controlled for other factors affecting mortality rates such as the patient's age, sex, and health status.

Officials at the Joint Commission on Accreditation of Hospitals argue that the statistical methodology for measuring treatment outcomes has improved enough recently to justify the new policy of focusing on outcomes. Futhermore, they believe that answering the question "Does the hospital have the capacity to provide high quality care?" Is no longer sufficient (Brinkley, 1986b). These officials will be using a number of different methods for measuring mortality and complication rates adjusted for the unique features of an individual hospital's patients until they determine which methodology is best. They then intend to monitor hospitals on a continuous basis rather than once every three years as in the past. Decisions will also be made on how much of this information will be released to the public.

Any methodology designed to implement a cost-effectiveness approach to hospital accreditation must deal with the alternative methods of measuring hospital output and with the variety of goals that hospitals may be pursuing.

Research studies have shown that mortality rates by themselves are misleading unless the other dimensions of hospital output and the multiple goals of hospitals are taken into account. In a classic study of hospital behavior, Sylvester Berki outlined six definitions of hospital output: (1) patient days, weighted or unweighted, (2) hospital services, (3) episode of illness, (4) end–results and health levels, (5) intermediate inputs, and (6) composites of one or more of the above (Berki, 1972, pp. 33, 34). The advantages and disadvantages of each of these measures will be discussed in turn.

One of the earliest measures of hospital output was simply *patient days*. The problems with this measure are obvious and relate to its aggregate nature. Two patients can spend an equal number of days in the hospital and receive quite different types and intensities of treatment. Thus, the problem is that of the heterogeneity of the output measure. Berki (1972, p. 34) argues that there are three distinct types of *hospital services* patients receive: admission–specific, stay–specific, and diagnostic–specific. "*Admission-specific* services, such as chest X–ray examinations and blood tests, are independent of the diagnosis on admission or discharge or of the length of stay. *Stay-specific* services, such as routine nursing care and hotel–type services, are determined by the length of stay, again largely independent of the nature of illness. *Diagnostic-specific* services, such as laboratory, inhalation therapy, physical therapy, surgical operations, vital functions monitoring, radiation, and other specialized services are determined neither by the act of admission nor by the length of stay but by the suspected or defined diagnosis, modified by case severity." Although stay–specific services may be adequately measured by unweighted patient days, admission–specific services are related to patient turnover while diagnostic–specific services vary greatly among individual patients.

Attempts have been made to deal with the latter problem by adjusting patient days for case–mix variation. The International Classification of Diseases Adapted for Use in the U.S. has often been utilized for this purpose (Berki, 1972, p. 35). The use of this classification system implies that some specific set of medical services corresponds to each diagnostic category. Other researchers have simply defined output as patient days and then attempted to control for case–mix, facility and service complexity, and the actual number of special services performed. If only the latter is controlled, there is the implicit assumption that the same set of services provided to two patients results in the same output.

Closely related to weighted patient days are output measures that focus on the sum of weighted services. While services are directly measured in physical units, the major question with this approach is the weighting issue. Some researchers have weighted services by their average cost of production (Berki, 1972, p. 37). This approach presents a problem for cost–effectiveness analysis, for the correlation between hospital costs and this measure of output should be almost perfect. Others have attempted to define weights for narrowly specified procedures based on "the professional qualifications of the individual performing the service, the health status of the patient (case severity), and the estimated difficulty of the diagnostic or treatment procedure" (Berki, 1972, p. 38). It is also possible to control explicitly for case-mix variation by selecting a sample of hospitals that offer the same types of services.

A few studies have focused on the treatment of an *episode of illness* (Berki, 1972, pp. 40, 41). In some cases the emphasis has been more on the cost of treatment than on the use of the episode as a measure of output. Others have defined output as the "number and categories of episodes of illness given adequate treatment." The problem here is the definition of "adequate," which is often used synonymously with "successful." Quality of treatment and heterogeneity of illness problems are inherent with this approach.

Berki's fourth measure of output, *end results* or *health levels*, is the factor most closely related to the case study for this chapter. "To the extent that disease remission (and prevention) contribute to increased health levels, the output of the system, and hence of the hospital, is its contribution to the successful termination of illness episodes" (Berki, 1972, p. 41). Thus, higher mortality rates may represent an "unsuccessful contribution" to output. This measure of output raises all of the questions discussed in the case study for this chapter. Furthermore, it incorporates Berki's fifth measure—hospital output as an *intermediate input* in the production of health. Hospital and all other medical services can be characterized as the outputs of a production process with various labor and capital inputs. However, these medical services can also be seen as one of the inputs to the production of health. This is analogous to Bradford, Malt, and Oates' (1969) D-output versus C-output, which was discussed earlier. Because this is an important alternative viewpoint of the role of hospital and medical services, it will be discussed in more detail in the following section of the chapter.

Berki's last measure of output, *composite units*, reflects the complexity of the measurement problem being discussed (Berki, 1972, pp. 43–44). Some researchers have used a "veritable smorgasbord of output definitions ranging from patient days to laboratory activities, X-ray activities, maternity activities, medical education, and ambulatory care." Others have focused on the number of days hospitalized, the weighted sum of services delivered, and the amount of the patient's bill.

More recent analyses have attempted to relate these multiple measures of output to a model of the hospital as a multiproduct firm (Goldfarb, Hornbrook, and Rafferty, 1980; Hornbrook and Goldfarb, 1983). Goldfarb and colleagues (1980, p. 186) assume that the goal of hospital decision making is the "maximization of an objective function that is defined over the level of admissions, their diagnostic mix, and the quality and revenue implications of each patient type, subject to the constraints of reimbursement, technology, patient availability, and general resources." Although these researchers define quality as "the probability of a successful outcome to the inpatient phase of the illness episode, as produced by the appropriate length of stay and appropriate mix of ancillary services," they are forced to measure quality by an implicit approach based on the length of hospital stay, which is related to the hospital's discharge policy.

Hornbrook and Goldfarb (1983) argue that hospitals are concerned with six factors: net operating surplus, total admissions, level of emergency stand-by capacity, diagnostic mix of patients admitted for treatment, quality of patient care outcomes, and the hospital's style of practice. Hospitals may attach different weights to each dimension. "The relative realizations of these six objectives will depend not only on the nature of the particular utility function, but also on such constraints as the community's ability to pay for hospital care, community epidemiology, and availability of substitute sources of care" (Hornbrook and Goldfarb, 1983, p. 668). Hospitals can either choose aggressive admissions policies or they can choose to provide higher quality care for a more limited range of cases. These choices are reflected in the establishment of trauma, burn, coronary care, and intensive care units by certain hospitals. Hornbrook and Goldfarb do define quality of hospital output as mortality rates measured on a diagnosis-specific basis. From a study of 63 hospitals in the New England area, they conclude that "patient preferences and ability to pay have strong impacts on the type of medical care hospitals are expected to provide. Highly educated communities tend to prefer risk averse, service-intensive hospital output. Teaching hospitals are shown to prefer higher protection levels, service-intensive patterns of care, and higher admissions levels" (Hornbrook and Goldfarb, 1983, p. 676). Thus, recent research indicates that focusing on a single measure of output such as mortality rates, even when adjusting for numerous other factors, may not fully capture all of the dimensions of hospital output and behavior. The mortality rates unadjusted for case-mix severity, which are the focus of this chapter's case study, are probably not very useful by themselves as guidelines either for consumer decision making or for the accreditation and regulation of hospitals by policymakers.

THE PRODUCTION OF HEALTH OUTPUT

It was noted above that hospital and other medical services can be considered as intermediate inputs in the overall production of health (Berki's fifth measure of hospital output). This viewpoint raises a larger set of issues when applying cost-effectiveness analysis to the health care sector. If both medical and nonmedical inputs are used in the production of health, it may be more cost-effective to spend society's resources on the nonmedical inputs if they result in a larger gain in health output. Answers to these questions require knowledge about health-production functions and about the marginal product of each input.

The marginal product of an input is the additional output achieved from a single-unit increase in the input. Thus, if health output is measured by a health status index, the gain in health status from increased medical expenditures can be compared with the increase resulting from changes in life style such as decreased smoking or increased exercise. The marginal product of an input will eventually decline as the amount of the input is increased. If the costs of increasing the inputs in two programs are the same, resources should be allocated so that the marginal product of the first program is equal to the marginal product of the second program. If the marginal product of one program is greater, more resources should be allocated to it because the additional gain in output is larger. If the costs of increasing the inputs in the two programs differ, the ratio of additional gains to additional costs should be equalized. This, of course, is another way of looking at cost–effectiveness analysis. Note that attention is focused on the additional or marginal product and not on the average product–output per unit of input. Two programs could have equal number of lives saved per unit of input and yet have very different increases in lives saved for additional increases in inputs. Policy analysis must center on what can be gained by moving from the status quo.

Grossman (1972) has argued that consumer concern for health lies behind the demand for medical and hospital services. The demand for medical services is derived from the demand for health. Consumers demand health because it is both a consumption commodity (you feel better) and because it is an investment commodity (your state of health determines the time available for work and leisure). The return to the investment in health is the monetary value of the decrease in sick days suffered. Individuals can improve their state of health by purchasing medical services and by using nonmedical inputs such as changes in life style. They are constrained by restrictions on both the amount of money and time available. Thus, individuals with higher wages may demand more medical care because they place a higher value on sick days lost from work. They may also be working longer hours and have less time available for exercise and other fitness programs. Education is often said to have a negative impact on the demand for medical care because individuals with higher levels of education may be more efficient producers of health themselves.

Regarding the production of health, there have been both macro and micro studies of health-production functions (Feldstein, 1983, pp. 22, 23). Macro studies take counties, states, or countries as the unit for analysis and use mortality rates adjusted for age and sex as the measure of output. Micro studies focus on individuals as the unit of measurement. Output is characterized by the number of work-loss days, self-evaluation of health status, the number of chronic conditions, etc.

One often-cited macro health-production function study is that by Auster, Leveson, and Sarachek (1969). These researchers examined interstate differences in age-sex adjusted mortality rates in 1960. They estimated the elasticities or percent changes in the health output resulting from a 1 percent change in each of the inputs. Medical inputs were represented both by expenditures on medical care per capita and by a separate medical-production function using the number of physicians, paramedical personnel, medical capital, and prescription drug expenditures per capita as inputs. Other variables included in the analysis were the level of income and education, the percent of the state's population in metropolitan areas, the percent employed in manufacturing, alcohol and cigarette consumption, the percent in white collar occupations, the percent of females not in the labor force, and the presence of a medical school in the state (Auster and others, 1969, pp. 414–418). Income may have either a positive or negative effect on health status. Higher-income individuals have a greater ability to purchase medical services. However, they may also have more stressful life styles and less exercise, which would have a negative impact. The percent employed in manufacturing and in white collar occupations also pick up these job-related effects on health status. The percent of the population in metropolitan areas measures the effects of urbanization—increased pollution, congestion, etc. Higher alcohol and cigarette consumption per capita should have negative effects on health status. The percent of females not in the labor force controls for work patterns and for the production of health in the home. The presence of a medical school in the state is a crude attempt to control for the quality and technology of medical care available.

The empirical results of this study accounted for more than 50 percent of the interstate differences in mortality rates. The elasticity for medical inputs was found to equal 0.1. Thus, a 1 percent increase in medical inputs would result in a 0.1 percent decrease in a state's mortality rate. However, the elasticity coefficient for education was 0.2—twice as large as that for medical inputs. Although higher education levels appear to be associated with lower mortality rates, it is not clear what type of education is the most important. Increases in cigarette smoking and in income both have a negative effect on health. The elasticity coefficient for cigarette consumption is 0.1, whereas that for income is 0.2. Thus, higher income appears to be associated with greater stress and less-healthy life styles. Alcohol consumption did not have a consistent effect on mortality rates, and urbanization was not important when the other factors were held constant. The percent of employees in both manufacturing and in white collar occupations had a negative impact on health, whereas the percent of females not in the labor force and the presence of medical schools had positive effects (Auster and others, 1969, pp. 422–431).

Feldstein (1983, pp. 27–29) has shown how these results on health-production functions can be used in policy analysis. In 1980 the economic cost of mortality in the population was estimated at $152.6 billion, the estimated cost of morbidity was $90.7 billion, and total medical expenditures were $235.6 billion. If a 1 percent increase in medical expenditures results in a 0.1 percent decrease in mortality and presumably morbidity, an expenditure of $2.356 billion on medical services would result in cost savings of $243.3 million. Because the elasticity for the education input was found to be twice as large by Auster and colleagues (1969), education expenditures would have to be increased by only 0.5 percent to achieve the same effect on mortality rates. One-half percent of the 1980 education expenditures was $831 million. Thus, if the production function results are correct, the same gains in health output could be achieved by either a $831 million expenditure on education or by a $2.356 billion expenditure on medical services. This type of analysis is, of course, only suggestive, for it assumes that there are no other significant effects from either of these investments. This aggregate analysis also does not give any indication of what types of education or medical-service programs should be increased.

Feldstein (1983, pp. 28, 29) also updated these production-function results for the period 1965 to 1980 to compare the expected change in mortality rates from several of the inputs with the actual changes in mortality rates over the period. There was a 19.6 percent decrease in the death rate over this period. Based on the estimated elasticities, the actual changes in real health care expenditures per capita, education, and cigarette consumption should have reduced mortality rates by 9.1 percent. Increased median family income would have increased mortality rates by 3.1 percent if the production-function estimates were correct. Thus, Feldstein argues that a 13.6 percent decrease in mortality rates was not accounted for by these factors. He hypothesizes that decreases in infant mortality rates and reductions in heart disease from changes in life styles and increases in the number of coronary-care units may have contributed to this unexplained decrease in mortality rates.

In a recent study, Hadley (1982) has estimated age-sex-race-specific health-production functions from 1970 Census data for a more disaggregated sample—county groups consisting of one or more whole counties with a minimum population of 250,000 people. His results, holding a number of socioeconomic, behavioral, and environmental factors constant, suggest that "a 10 percent increase in per capita medical use is associated with about a 1.5 percent decrease in mortality rates. This result was obtained for the four infant cohorts, for all adult female cohorts, and for elderly (65 and older) male cohorts. Increased medical care use appears to have about twice as large an impact on white, middle-aged (45 to 64 years old) males and about half as large an impact on black, middle-aged males as on the other cohorts" (Hadley, 1982, p. 169). Education was found to have a consistently negative association with mortality rates as in earlier studies, whereas the effect of income varied among the cohorts examined and with the type of income.

Hadley used his results to analyze several cost-effectiveness policy questions. The allocation of medical resources among geographic areas and population groups was explored. Hadley also compared the effect on mortality rates of increasing medical care use by 10 percent with two other policies—reducing cigarette consumption by 10 percent and increasing income transfers to low-income families and individuals so as to increase the incomes of the poorer half of the population by 10 percent (Hadley, 1982, pp. 170–174). The number of deaths averted per $100,000 of policy cost was calculated for each alternative. The inverse of this figure, the cost per death averted, was then used to rank each policy in terms of its efficiency in reducing mortality rates. Hadley's results indicated that "reducing cigarette consumption was the most efficient policy, with a cost per death averted of roughly $9,000. Increasing medical care use was estimated to cost about $85,000 per death averted. Finally, the income-transfer policy is the least efficient of the three, with a cost of almost $3,000,000 per death averted" (Hadley, 1982, p. 174). These results, of course, are only suggestive. Hadley notes that changing three key assumptions would increase the first estimate of $9,000 per death averted to $72,000. These results also raise issues of government involvement with individual rights and freedoms, and they do not take into account other goals of the policy. However, they are illustrative of the types of questions in the health care sector for which cost-effectiveness analysis is the appropriate tool for policy evaluation.

SUMMARY

This chapter has focused on cost-effectiveness analysis, one of the important analytical tools in public-policy analysis. This technique is useful for comparing alternative outcomes or outputs with the costs of achieving them. It does not deal with the more sophisticated question of valuing the output or estimating the benefits people place on producing the output. That question is the focus of benefit-cost analysis, which will be discussed in the next chapter.

Conceptual and empirical problems arise in measuring both output and costs of public programs. As in the case of hospitals, there may be a variety of dimensions to the output produced that cannot be adequately captured in a single measure. This can be seen conceptually in the distinction between the D-output and C-output of Bradford, Malt, and Oates (1969) and, more specifically, in the controversy over the use of mortality statistics for consumer decision making and hospital accreditation in the case study for this chapter. The use of output measures that are not credible to the major stakeholders in the policy process can only serve to increase confusion and to decrease confidence in the goals of that policy.

Similar problems exist regarding the measurement of the costs of public programs. The costs to be measured are the opportunity or social costs of the program. These may not all be monetary costs nor are they likely to all be included in the budget of the agency undertaking the project. Thus, various stakeholders are likely not to recognize all the costs of providing various outputs either because the costs are incurred by other parties or because the costs are not explicit out-of-pocket payments. However, it is the goal of cost-effectiveness analysis to make decision-makers aware of the true social costs of any particular program.

Cost-effectiveness analysis has been applied in a wide variety of public-policy areas as illustrated in this chapter. These range from national defense to health care to income redistribution. Although the technique can not answer the question of whether the program output is worth producing (that is, what the benefits are to society of having it), it does help decision-makers determine how to obtain the most output per dollar spent when comparing alternative policy options. This alone can help increase the effectiveness of public policy, especially in a period of tight budgets and great concern over the amount of spending by all levels of government.

REFERENCES

Anthony, Robert N., & Young, David W. (1984). *Management control in non-profit organizations*. Homewood, IL: Richard D. Irwin, Inc.

Auster, Richard, Leveson, Irving, & Sarachek, Deborah. (1969, Fall). The production of health: An exploratory study. *The Journal of Human Resources, IV*, 411–436.

Berg, R.S. (1967). Armed Forces' use of cost-effectiveness analysis. In Thomas A. Goldman (ed.), *Cost-effectiveness analysis: New approaches in decision-making* (pp. 91–103). New York: Praeger Publishers.

Bergner, Marilyn & others. (1981, August). The sickness impact profile: Development and final revision of a health status measure. *Medical Care, 19*, 787–805.

Berki, Sylvester E. (1972). *Hospital economics.* Lexington, MA: Lexington Books.

Bradford, D.F., Malt, R.A., & Oates, W.E. (1969, June). The rising cost of local public services: Some evidence and reflections. *National Tax Journal, 22*, 185–202.

Brinkley, Joel. (1986a, March 12). U.S. releasing lists of hospitals with abnormal mortality rates. *The New York Times*, pp. 1, 12.

Brinkley, Joel. (1986b, November 4). Key hospital accrediting agency to start weighing mortality rates. *The New York Times*, pp. 1, 26.

Brown, Charles, Gilroy, Curtis, & Kohen, Andrew. (1983, Winter). Time-series evidence on the effect of the minimum wage on youth employment and unemployment. *The Journal of Human Resources, 18*, 3–31.

Burkhead, Jesse, & Miner, Jerry. (1971). *Public expenditure.* Chicago: Aldine-Atherton.

Feldstein, Paul J. (1983). *Health care economics 2nd ed.* New York: John Wiley & Sons.

Galambos Eva C., & Schreiber, Arthur F. (1978). *Making sense out of dollars: Economic analysis for local government.* Washington, DC: National League of Cities.

Goldfarb, Marsha, Hornbrook, Mark, & Rafferty, John. (1980, February). Behavior of the multiproduct firm: A model of the nonprofit hospital system. *Medical Care, 18*, 185–201.

Gramlich, Edward M. (1981). *Benefit-cost analysis of government programs.* Englewood Cliffs, NJ: Prentice-Hall.

Gramlich, Edward M., & Wolkoff, Michael J. (1979, Summer). A procedure for evaluating income distribution policies. *The Journal of Human Resources, 14*, 128–160.

Grosse, Robert N. (1970). Problems of resource allocation in health. In Robert H. Haveman and Julius Margolis (eds.), *Public expenditure and policy analysis*, (pp. 518–548). Chicago: Markham Publishing Company.

Grossman, Michael. (1972, March/April). On the concept of health capital and the demand for health. *Journal of Political Economy, 80*, 223–225.

Hadley, Jack. (1982). *More medical care, better health?* Washington, DC: The Urban Institute Press.

Haveman, Robert H. (1983). Evaluating public expenditure under conditions of unemployment. In Robert H. Haveman and Julius Margolis (eds.), *Public expenditure and policy analysis*, (3rd ed.) (pp. 167–182). Boston: Houghton Mifflin.

Hitch, Charles J., & McKean, Roland N. (1965). *The economics of defense in the nuclear age*. New York: Atheneum.

Hornbrook, Mark C., & Goldfarb, Marsha G. (1983). A partial test of a hospital behavioral model. *Social Science and Medicine, 17*, 667–680.

Klarman, H., Francis, J., Rosenthal, G. (1968). Cost effectiveness analysis applied to the treatment of chronic renal disease. *Medical Care, 6*, 48–54.

Luft, Harold, Bunker, John, & Enthoven, Alain. (1979, December 20). Should operations be regionalized? *The New England Journal of Medicine, 301*, 1121–1127.

Mincer, Jacob. (1976, August). Unemployment effects of minimum wage changes. *Journal of Political Economy, 84*, S87–S104.

Niskanen, William A. (1967). Measures of effectiveness. In Thomas A. Goldman (ed.), *Cost-effectiveness analysis: New approaches in decision-making* (pp. 17–32). New York: Praeger Publishers.

Ross, John P., & Burkhead, Jesse. (1974). *Productivity in the local government sector*. Lexington, MA: Lexington Books.

Russell, Louise B. (1986). *Is prevention better than cure?* Washington, DC: The Brookings Institution.

Seabrook, Charles. (1987, February 8). Medicare deaths high in 27 Georgia hospitals, officials say. *The Atlanta Constitution*, pp. 1A, 8A.

U.S. Department of Health, Education and Welfare. (1979). *Healthy people: The surgeon general's report on health promotion and disease prevention*. Washington, DC: U.S. Government Printing Office.

Warner, Kenneth E., & Luce, Bryan R. (1982). *Cost-benefit and cost-effectiveness analysis in health care*. Ann Arbor, MI: Health Administration Press.

Weinstein, Milton C., & Stason, William B. (1976). *Hypertension: A policy perspective*. Cambridge. MA: Harvard University Press.

Weisbrod, Burton A. (1983). Benefit-cost analysis of a controlled experiment: Treating the mentally ill. In Robert H. Haveman and Julius Margolis (eds.), *Public expenditure and policy analysis*, (3rd ed.) (pp. 230–259). Boston: Houghton Mifflin.

CHAPTER 6

Benefit–Cost Analysis: The 55 MPH Speed Limit

INTRODUCTION

Benefit-cost analysis is a program–evaluation tool closely related to cost-effectiveness analysis. All of the problems involved in measuring of costs of public programs discussed in Chapter 5 also apply to this evaluation technique. However, whereas cost-effectiveness analysis is used to determine how to produce the maximum output for a given cost or how to minimize the costs of producing a given level of output, benefit-cost analysis attempts to answer a more difficult question: How much is the output worth to society? This dollar value of the output is then compared with the costs of producing it. If the benefits exceed the costs, the program is considered to be an efficient use of society's resources.

Benefit–cost analysis has long been used by various government agencies to evaluate different public programs. The Army Corps of Engineers was one of the earliest users of the tool to evaluate physical-investment projects involving the dredging of harbors, the construction of canals and waterways, and flood control. Indeed, the U.S. Flood Control Act of 1939 specified the standard that "the benefits to whomever they accrue [be] in excess of the estimated costs" (Gramlich, 1981, p. 7). In the 1960s benefit-cost analysis began to be applied to a much wider range of projects involving investment in human beings (human capital) as well as physical-investment projects. This was related to President Johnson's "Great Society" efforts to get the federal government actively involved with fighting poverty, creating jobs, providing education and training, etc. As the government moved into these new areas of activity, concern arose about which type of program provided the greatest return for the dollars invested. The use of benefit-cost analysis was also related to the formal installation of the Planning, Programming, and Budgeting System (PPBS) in federal government agencies. Developed in the Defense Department, this system had five major elements: "(1) A careful specification of basic program objectives in *each* major area of governmental activity. (2) An attempt to analyze the *outputs* of each governmental program. (3) An attempt to measure the *costs* of the program, not for one year but over the next several years. (4) An attempt to compare alternative activities. (5) An attempt to establish common analytic techniques throughout the government" (Gramlich,

1981, p. 8). These are the basic features of benefit-cost analysis. Although the formal use of the PPBS system had died out by the mid-1970s, the use of evaluation techniques such as benefit-cost and cost-effectiveness analysis has survived. Indeed, in areas such as the health care sector there has been a greater emphasis on these techniques as concern has increased over rising health care costs (Warner and Luce, 1982; Avorn, 1984).

In this chapter we will discuss the basic issues relating to the measurement of benefits and costs of public programs. The major focus will be on benefit estimation as the cost-analysis issues presented in the previous chapter are still relevant here. However, there are some situations in which it is unclear whether a program effect should be treated as a benefit or a cost. Thus, the two sides of the question are interdependent. A secondary question in this chapter will be the proper role of benefit-cost analysis as a decision-making tool. In many cases these issues become intertwined with the technical issues of benefit and cost estimation because it may either be impossible to place monetary values on all benefits and costs or the estimates derived may not be credible to the major stakeholders in the policy arena. Furthermore, neither all of the costs nor the benefits may impact the agency undertaking the project. These factors relate back to the issues of problem definition and the role of political elements in the policy-making process discussed in earlier chapters of this book.

THE 55 MPH SPEED LIMIT

The general principles of benefit-cost analysis will be related to the specific case study for this chapter, the 55 MPH speed limit, which begins on page 191. The issues are presented in an editorial by Senator John C. Danforth of Missouri (Danforth, 1987) and in a *New York Times* article by Isabel Wilkerson discussing the impact of the change in the speed limit in 1987 (Wilkerson, 1987). The 55 MPH speed limit was imposed in 1974 as a measure to limit gasoline consumption in response to the Arab oil embargo of 1973. Although early estimates of fuel saved were less than expected, it was soon observed that the lower speed limit reduced the number of traffic fatalities. However, from its inception, opposition to this legislation has been voiced by truckers and other heavy users of the highway system and from individuals living in rural states, particularly in the western part of the country. The lower speed limit increases transportation time costs. It is also argued that the speed limit is not needed in rural areas and that it is not observed there anyway. Thus, the issues in this case study center on the benefits of saving lives and fuel versus the costs of increased time for travel.

These issues came to the forefront of public policy again in 1987 when Congress passed a highway and mass transit bill that raised the speed limit to 65 MPH on rural interstate highways. Most of the controversy surrounding this bill, which was passed despite a veto by President Reagan, focused on the amount of highway funding and over the alleged "budget-busting" nature of the legislation (Greenhouse, 1987). However, the time-saving versus life-saving arguments also resurfaced in Congress and on the editorial pages of the country's major newspapers (Danforth, 1987; Weinraub, 1987). A *New York Times* editorial of March 21, 1987 argued that Congress has supported "an intelligent amendment to let states raise the limit to 65 miles per hour on rural interstates." However, on March 15, 1987 the editors of the *Washington Post* argued against increasing the speed limit: "The equation is minutes versus lives. It's not even close. . . . A hundred miles at 55 mph take about 17 minutes longer than at 65. That's the price of those lives. It ought to be the easiest vote the House takes this year."

In the second article of the case, it can be seen that increasing both the national and local speed limits has caused the various stakeholders affected by these changes to move into action (Wilkerson, 1987). While several state governments have reluctantly given in to their constituents' desire for the higher speed limit, they have attached conditions such as a lower speed for trucks and increased enforcement. In Michigan the state police did not want the speed limit raised at all. The state senate approved a bill that would raise the limit only for cars and light trucks but that would also ban the use of radar detectors by motorists. But under intense lobbying by the manufacturers and users of radar-detection equipment, a Michigan House committee rejected the latter provision. Individual truckers have called the differential car-truck limit "one of the worst things the state of Michigan could do" while a survey of the American Trucking Association members has indicated support for the differential limit. Both sides of the truck-speed debate have raised the safety issue.

Not all of the speed limit controversy is found at the state and national level of government. Wilkerson (1987) also reports on the town of Leonidas, Michigan (population 300) where the speed limit on the state highway through the town has been raised from 40 MPH to 50 MPH. "The Michigan Department of Transportation changed the signs after it found that the old limit, decades old, was being ignored by most motorists anyway. Residents immediately began protesting. Schoolchildren wrote letters to the Michigan Department of Transportation and . . . about 100 protesters held a rally on Route 60. Now there are makeshift signs coming and going . . . urging drivers to slow down." This controversy arose because the road through the town is filled with truck drivers trying to avoid the weigh stations on nearby interstate highways and motorists who are taking a detour to Indiana. Residents complained of accidents, near-accidents, and rattling furniture from the speeding traffic. They offered to pay $1,000 per year for a crossing guard but there have not been any takers for the job. On the other side of the controversy, a Michigan transportation department official stated that, "The bulk of drivers don't pay attention to speed limit signs unless they know there are patrols. They generally drive what they feel is safe and comfortable speed." A state patrol officer observed that "Everyone wants 25 miles per hour in front of their house and not anywhere else." Thus, these cases involve both issues of the measurement of the relevant benefits and costs and the differential impact of these benefits and costs on the various stakeholders in the policy process.

AN OVERVIEW OF BENEFIT-COST ANALYSIS

Benefit-cost analysis is not simply a comparison of the "good" and "bad" aspects of a public program. Both benefits and costs have very specific meaning derived from economic theory. They are related to the basic economic concept of efficiency in resource allocation—making the best use of society's limited resources. A program is said to be efficient if its benefits, that is, the total amount of money that people are willing to pay for the output of the program, are greater than program costs—the real opportunity costs reflecting what is sacrificed to product the output. The benefits and costs are to be added up over all the individuals receiving and paying them. This aspect of the technique can create a decision-making problem if some of the benefits and/or costs flow to individuals other than those undertaking the analysis. Whittington and MacRae (1986) call this the problem of "standing" in benefit-cost analysis: Whose preferences are to count when summing benefits and costs. A given agency may want to count only the benefits to itself or its constituency. This may result in an underestimation of the total benefits from the project. For example, the benefits of a water-pollution-control project may flow to individuals across an entire metropolitan region. However, the agency financing the project may be concerned only with the benefits accruing to its taxpayers. Not counting the benefits (or costs) to other parties may significantly bias the resulting benefit-cost calculation. This is a decision-making problem that can affect the technical results of the analysis. Whittington and MacRae (1986) raise questions about whether benefits should include those flowing to illegal aliens or to criminals. These issues can raise significant policy questions. For example, the U.S. Nuclear Regulatory Commission has concluded that approximately one-third of the benefits of controlling radon gas emissions would accrue to individuals outside the United States. In its analysis the Nuclear Regulatory Commission included the effects on Canadians and Mexicans but ignored the benefits to the rest of the world. Subsequently, the Environmental Protection Agency assigned a zero weight to everyone outside the borders of the country (Whittington and MacRae, 1986, p. 675).

The benefits or costs of a project may bear no particular relationship to the flow of revenues or tax receipts to the agency undertaking the project. For many government projects, there are no direct revenues to the agency. This does not mean that there are zero benefits from the project. These issues focus on the *distribution* of the benefits and costs, namely, who receives the benefits and who pays the costs. These issues may be very important from a decision-making point of view. Indeed, they may determine whether the project is funded or not. In the controversy over Westway, the proposed West Side highway in New York City, construction options with less favorable benefit-cost ratios were favored over more efficient projects because the federal government was willing to finance a large share of the total costs of the former. The costs to New York City taxpayers were lower in these cases (Herzlinger, 1979). However, distributional issues are typically not incorporated in the formal estimation of benefits and costs. Sometimes separate data are presented on how the benefits or costs are distributed by income group, region of the country, etc., so that decision-makers can see how different groups of people will be affected by the project. It has also been argued that distributional weights should be applied when the total benefits are being summed (Gramlich, 1981, pp. 118–122). This approach directly incorporates the distributional or equity issues with the efficiency calculations. However, it is not clear what weights should be applied. Should benefits to low-income groups be weighted twice, five times, or one-half as heavily as benefits to high-income groups? This approach makes the estimation of program costs directly dependent on the method of financing the project. Many have argued that these issues should remain separate.

Benefit-cost analysis involves a "with and without" comparison as opposed to a "before and after" comparison (Haveman and Weisbrod, 1983). The attempt is made to calculate what are the benefits and costs of having the program versus what would have happened without the program. Thus, if a program provides job skills and training to teenagers, the *increased* wages these individuals will earn over their lifetime compared to what they would have earned otherwise are considered to be one of the benefits of the program. This is a more complex calculation than simply examining wages before and after the program. This example also illustrates the fact that benefits and costs of a public program may extend many years into the future. A teenager's working life may be 40 years or more. The life of a physical-investment project may be a hundred years or more. Thus, benefit-cost analysis involves not only the technical details of benefit and cost estimation but the projection and comparison of the dollar values over time. Issues relating to the timing of benefits and costs will be discussed after the basic techniques for estimating benefits are presented.

It may be extremely difficult if not impossible to place dollar values on some of the benefits and costs of particular projects. For example, the damming of a river may produce recreation benefits in terms of increased days of recreation by individuals. Although in the 1950s arbitrary dollar values were assigned to these recreation-days, there have been major advances over the past two decades in developing more sophisticated methods of estimating these benefits (Clawson, 1959; Clawson and Knetsch, 1966). However, there may also be increased aesthestic pleasure associated with the project. It is not clear how this benefit should be valued. In vocational-rehabilitation projects the increased wages earned may be the primary benefit of the program. However, an increase in the participants' self-esteem may be an equal or even more important outcome of the project. Again, it is unclear how this benefit could be measured (Conley, 1969). In the case of the 55 MPH speed limit, the controversy centers on the valuation of lives saved versus the value of time. Many would argue that it is difficult if not impossible to derive meaningful monetary estimates of these factors. These real but unmeasured effects of a project are called *intangible benefits*. The goal of benefit-cost analysis is to make all benefits and costs tangible (measured in dolllar terms). It may not be possible to do this given the state of the art.

This issue can create a decision-making problem similar to those involved with equity or distributional issues. Suppose that one project has a less favorable benefit-cost ratio than another but greater intangible benefits. If the projects are mutually exclusive, which one should be undertaken? It has been suggested that intangible benefits could be put in common, undefined units for comparison among projects (Freeman, 1970). However, if different intangible benefits can be valued in terms of a common unit, that unit should probably be dollars. Decision-makers do implicitly place a weight on the intangible benefits when making a choice among projects. Although the results of this decision-making process might be useful for weighting intangible benefits in future projects, they are not helpful for the current project. Questions also arise about the consistency of this weighting process over time. Recent benefit-cost analyses have typically included unmeasured or intangible benefits and costs along with those measured in dollar terms. The study of inpatient versus outpatient treatment of the mentally ill by Weisbrod (1983), discussed in the previous chapter, uses this procedure. External costs caused by patients' illnesses are measured as the number of families reporting physical illness and the percentage of family members experiencing emotional strain due to patient behavior. Improved consumer decision making by patients is measured by the amount of insurance expenditures and by the percentage of the groups having savings accounts (Weisbrod, 1983, pp. 248, 249). These intangible costs and benefits are included because they are considered to be important, but they are not measured in dollar terms.

Another important distinction in the calculation of benefits is the difference between real and pecuniary benefits (Haveman and Weisbrod, 1983, pp. 92, 93). The goal of benefit-cost analysis is to measure the real net gains to society that result from a project in terms of the valuation of the increased output produced. However, there may also be other changes in prices and profits in the economy that occur as a result of the project. Many of these changes may simply represent transfers of income among individuals in the economy and not real gains to society. These transfers or pecuniary benefits should *not* be counted in benefit-cost analysis. For example, if a rapid rail system is constructed in a city, there is likely to be increased business activity and profits for those stores and restaurants located near the rail stations. Yet these increases may be offset by decreased business activity in other areas of the city. Thus, there may be no net gain to the economy. It is also often argued that job-training programs will produce benefits in the form of decreased welfare and unemployment compensation payments. Although this reduction represents a benefit to the federal government and should decrease its expenditures, it does not represent a social benefit from the program. Welfare and unemployment compensation payments are simply transfer payments. They represent shifts of income from taxpayers to the recipients of the benefits. If recipients receive fewer benefits and, thus, have lower transfer incomes, taxpayers must have lower taxes and higher private disposable incomes. Thus, the gains and losses cancel out and no net gain accrues to society. The real benefits from the job-training programs would be the increased output and income of the participants that directly result from the training itself.

This is the same issue as was discussed in the previous chapter in comparing the social versus monetary costs of utilizing unemployed labor for a project. Arguing that the social costs of using unemployed labor are less than the monetary or budgeted costs is equivalent to arguing that increased employment represents a real and not a pecuniary benefit to the economy. In each case an adjustment is being made either to costs or benefits that would make the project look more favorable. This adjustment should be made only if it can be argued that a real benefit actually exists. This example also illustrates that fact that some program effects can be treated as either decreases in costs or increases in benefits. It does not matter which approach is taken as long as both are not utilized. That would result in double counting.

In some cases pecuniary benefits are used as proxies for the real benefits of the project. The development or improvement of a recreation area in a city may increase land values around the area. These increases would typically be pecuniary benefits for there should be decreases in land values in other areas of the city. However, if it should prove to be impossible to find another measure of the real benefits of the recreation project, the increases in land values could be used as a measure of individuals' willingness to pay for the project (Darling, 1973). These increases should, of course, be counted only once to avoid artificially inflating the dollar benefits of the project. Other examples of the difficulties of distinguishing between real and pecuniary benefits are discussed by Gramlich (1981, pp. 58–67).

METHODS OF ESTIMATING BENEFITS

The benefits of a project are defined as the total amount of money individuals are willing to pay for the output of the investment project. *Benefit analysis* attempts to use an approach similar to that used in the marketplace to evaluate private goods and services. As discussed in Chapter 4, market prices perform an allocating and rationing function in a market economy. If an individual is willing to buy a particular good, that action gives us an estimate of how the person values the good. The goal of benefit analysis is to use that same approach in the valuation of public-sector goods and services that may not be sold in the market or have any prices directly associated with them.

In Figure 6.1, suppose that P_1 is the price of the good and Q_1 is the quantity demanded at that price. The amount of money spent on the good is price times quantity, or the area of the shaded rectangle. However, this area does not represent the total amount consumers would be willing to pay for the good rather than go without it. That total willingness to pay is represented by the area underneath the demand curve up to quantity Q_1. This results from the fact, discussed in Chapter 4, that the prices along the demand curve represent

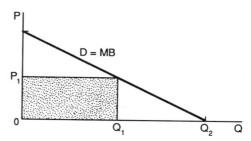

Figure 6.1. The Demand Curve for a Particular Good

consumers' *marginal* benefit or evaluation, the dollar value they attach to each additional unit of the product. If we add up all of these evaluations for each of the units, we get the total valuation, or the amount consumers are willing to pay for all of the units. This dollar amount represents the benefits to consumers of producing the output. If we looked only at the actual consumer expenditure (the area of the shaded rectangle in Fig. 6.1), we would typically underestimate the total willingness to pay or the benefits to society of producing the output. Furthermore, if the good was provided by the government free of charge, there would be no consumer expenditure to measure. In this case the quantity demanded would be Q_2 and the total willingness to pay would be the monetary value of the entire area underneath the demand curve up to quantity Q_2.

Although *willingness to pay* is the term used in the benefit–cost literature, it must be remembered that income is one of the factors influencing the position of a demand curve. Therefore, the demand curve for a city recreation project could be further from the origin, and thus the total benefits larger, for a high-income neighborhood than for a low-income neighborhood simply because the high–income residents have a greater ability to pay for the recreation output. This is an example of the income distribution problem discussed above. In this case city officials might want to weight the benefits to the low-income neighborhood more heavily or to otherwise adjust for the distributional considerations. Thus, even though benefit-cost analysis primarily focuses on efficiency issues, the distributional questions are never far away.

This discussion shows that benefit estimation is directly connected with the economic concept of demand. Thus, the goal of benefit measurement is to estimate the demand or willingness to pay for the output of the project. Estimating the shape and position of a demand curve for any product is not an easy task. As discussed in the chapter dealing with pricing, demand is the relationship between price and quantity demanded, holding all else constant. The problem is how to hold all else constant. In marketing research and consumer surveys, an attempt is made to hold income and the socioeconomic characteristics of consumers constant while charging different groups of consumers different prices and observing the quantities they demand at each price. This same approach is taken when utilizing statistical techniques such as multiple-regression analysis (Chapter 3). Estimating a demand relationship with multiple-regression analysis would show the effect of changing price on the quantity demanded while statistically holding all else constant. Both the marketing and the statistical approach assume that there is enough variation in prices and quantities to be able to estimate a significant portion if not the entire demand curve.

The problem with this direct-demand approach to estimating benefits for public-sector projects is that there may be no data on prices and quantities available. It has been argued in the previous chapters that prices may not be charged for public-sector goods and services either because it is impossible to do so (the public-good problem) or because society has made a conscious decision not to do so (the income distribution or equity question). Thus, for many government investment projects indirect methods must be utilized for benefit estimation given the lack of data on prices and quantities. These methods will be catalogued under several broad headings in the following discussion. More detailed presentations of these issues are found in Merewitz and Sosnick (1971), Mishan (1976), Anderson and Settle (1977), Thompson (1980), and Gramlich (1981).

The first indirect approach to benefit estimation can be termed the *discounted future earnings approach*. It focuses on the increased stream of future earnings from either individuals or land as a result of a government investment project. Thus, a health, education, or job-training program may make an individual more productive and increase his or her wages above what they would have been in the absence of the project. Land values may increase as a result of urban renewal, recreation, or transportation projects (subject to the real versus pecuniary distinction discussed above). This increased earning stream is a proxy for the valuation of the increased output to society by the more productive individuals. Thus, the increased earnings of the inpatient versus outpatient group of patients was one of the benefits measured by Weisbrod (1983) in his study of alternative means of treating the mentally ill. A similar approach was taken by Kemper, Long, and Thornton (1983) in their study of the Supported Work Experiment, a program providing work experience for individuals with severe employment problems such as ex-drug addicts, ex-offenders released from prison, young school dropouts, and long-term recipients of Aid to Families with Dependent Children. The Upward Bound program, established by the U.S. Office of Economic Opportunity to give underprivileged youths a special college preparatory education, has also been evaluated in this manner (Garms, 1972). Because these earnings extend over a future period of time, they must be discounted to reflect this time pattern. This discounting process or calculation of the present value of the future stream of earnings will be discussed below. Discounted future earnings are also related to valuation of life problems, discussed in the next section of the chapter.

The next major indirect approach to benefit estimation focuses on the *costs* to society that are *saved* as a result of the government investment project. This approach is utilized in evaluating transportation, pollution-control, and disease-control projects. The costs to society that would have been incurred in the absence of the project are considered to be the benefits of the investment project. For transportation projects, the emphasis is on time-cost savings. The goal of a transportation project (bus, rapid rail system, etc.) is to move people from one point to another. Since the "final" good or output is having passengers arrive at their desired destination, the transportation investment lowers the "price" of this final output. Thus, cost savings are related to the basic willingness-to-pay concept of benefit-cost analysis. Transportation improvements would provide cost-saving benefits to those individuals who are currently using the system and they would attract additional users to the system. Both of these gains must be measured. These projects involve valuation of time questions, which will be discussed in more detail in the following section of the chapter.

For pollution-control projects, the costs of pollution (cleaning, physical damage, health-related problems) that would have been incurred without the project are considered to be the benefits of the project. These costs to be avoided would be calculated in several steps. For example, a report of the Organization for Economic Co-Operation and Development (Maler and Wyzga, 1976) develops the medical costs of pollution-caused bronchitis in the United States in 1958. The number of chronic bronchitis patients is first identified. An estimate is then made of the total number of bronchitis cases that result from air pollution. To translate physical damage into monetary damage, the cost of treating patients with bed-disability days was assumed to be the same as the cost of hospital inpatients suffering from chronic bronchitis. An adjustment was then made for the cost of treating the bronchitis patient with no bed-disability days. This methodology resulted in an estimate of $44.8 million as the cost of treating pollution-caused bronchitis in the United States in 1958.

A third approach to benefit estimation is the *substitute good approach*. Although the benefits of a public-sector project may not be directly observable, there may be private-sector substitutes that are adequate proxies for the public-sector program. Thus, certain private recreation areas may closely resemble public-sector projects. If prices are being charged in the private areas, this may provide enough information for direct-demand estimation. If the private area is then a reasonable substitute for the public project, the area underneath that demand curve can be considered as an estimate of the benefits of the public project. Thus, ridership and fare data for an existing bus system might be used to estimate the benefits of a proposed subway or rapid rail system. The crucial issue here is the closeness of the two types of projects regarding consumer demand. A private golf course or swimming pool may not be similar to a municipal course or pool if it is providing benefits (exclusivity, association with the "right" people) other than direct recreation activities. The individuals who would be using the two facilities could be quite different in terms of the socio-economic and income characteristics affecting their demands.

A final method of benefit estimation is the *associated cost approach*. This has been widely used in evaluating the benefits of wilderness recreation areas (Clawson, 1959; Clawson and Knetsch, 1966). For many state and national parks, either direct prices are not charged or these prices are not high enough to influence consumer decision making. Thus, it is not possible to directly estimate demand curves for these projects. However, individuals do incur significant costs associated with reaching these recreation areas. These would include the money and time costs of traveling to these areas. These costs could be used as proxies for differences in "prices" faced by different groups of consumers. It would be expected that consumers facing higher associated costs would demand smaller quantities or have fewer visits to the recreation areas. Thus, differences in these associated costs could be used to derive an indirect measure of willingness to pay. Use of this method would involve defining the areas from which visitors attend the facility and then collecting data on visits, distance, time costs of travel, size of the population, income, and other variables affecting the number of visits. The demand function would be estimated under the assumption that people would react to increases in the entrance fee as they react to increases in travel costs. The relevant area underneath the demand curve would then be the estimate of recreation benefits. This approach is far more sophisticated than the use of recreation-day values, which was common in the 1950s and 1960s. For example, the Army Corps of Engineers had used a value of $1.60 per visitor-day, which originated from an old study of average recreation expenditures by participants. This figure was used uniformly regardless of the relative scarcity of recreation opportunities or differences in any other factors affecting demand (Merewitz and Sosnick, 1971, pp. 148–153).

Many studies use a combination of these methods to try to capture different types of benefits. For example, in addition to measuring the increased wages of the mentally ill in the experimental and control programs, Weisbrod (1983) also attempted to measure increased work stability and improved consumer decision making. Data on absenteeism and on the number of "beneficial" and "detrimental" job changes were incorporated in the analysis. The subjects' expenditures on insurance and the percentage of the groups having savings accounts were included as a measure of forward thinking. In the analysis of the Supported Work Experiment, Kemper and colleagues (1983) focused on the increase in the participants' earning streams, the reduction in criminal activity (reduced property damage and injury, stolen property, and justice system costs), the reduction in drug treatment costs, and the reduced use of alternative services. These researchers also note the increased tax payments and the reduced dependence on transfer programs that could be considered "negative benefits" or costs from the viewpoint of program participants but that have no impact from the viewpoint of social benefit-cost analysis (Kemper and others, 1983, pp. 272, 273). A study of the benefits of prison reform (Holahan, 1974) focused on the reduction in physical injury, property damage, and expenditures on the criminal justice system. It was argued that a reduction in the other social costs of crime—private expenditures, migration, the avoidance of normal activities—was also important but was too difficult to measure. This study attempted to estimate the benefits from a program that reduced recidivism by one person who otherwise would have committed another property crime.

Although the above discussion has focused on the alternative methods for estimating the benefits of a project, the time pattern of the benefits (and costs) also affects the overall benefit–cost ratio or resulting net benefits. This result occurs because benefits and costs in the near future are weighted more heavily than those in the distant future. A dollar that I receive next year is worth more than a dollar received 10 years from now because I can reinvest next year's dollar so that it will be worth more than one dollar in 10 years. This argument relates to the productivity of capital and investments and has nothing to do with the inflation rate. It would be relevant in a world of zero inflation. Given that most projects involve a stream of benefits and costs off into the future, it is necessary to calculate the present value of these benefits and costs to make them comparable in terms of the time dimension. This present value calculation involves the choice of a discount rate. What discount rate to choose is an extremely controversial question that can have a major impact on the results of the analysis.

The calculation of the present value of a flow of benefits is the reverse of a compound-interest problem. Compound interest attempts to determine what a given amount of money will be worth at n years in the future at a given interest rate for compounding. Thus, $100 will be worth $110 one year from now if the interest rate is 10 percent. If this amount is left to compound for another year, it will grow to $121. Alternatively, the present value of $110 received one year from now is $100 using a discount rate of 10 percent. This can be calculated from the following formula: Present Value = $110/(1 + 0.10) = $100. The present value of $121 received two years from now is also $100 and can be calculated as $121/(1 + 0.10)^2$. Thus, the present value of an annual stream of benefits flowing n years in the future can be derived as follows: Present Value = $R_1/(1 + i) + R_2/(1 + i)^2 + \ldots + R_n/(1 + i)^n$ where i is the discount rate.

The choice of the discount rate can have a significant impact on the resulting present-value calculation. Suppose that the benefits from Project A equal $100 in year one and zero thereafter, whereas the benefits of Project B are zero for the first 19 years and $100 in year 20. This is an extreme example of a short-term versus a long-term project with equal monetary benefits. Using the above formulas and a discount rate of 5 percent, the present value for Project A is $95.23 while for Project B it is $37.89. Thus, benefits one year from now are weighted much more heavily than benefits received 20 years from now. If a discount rate of 20 percent is used, the present value of the benefits of Project A is $83.33 while the present value for Project B is only $2.61. While the present value of the benefits of both projects decreases, there is a much larger drop for Project B. Thus, raising the discount rate favors the short-term investment project. Low rates favor long-term investments.

The following more realistic example shows how changing the discount rate can make a project look either efficient or inefficient (Table 6.1). Suppose that the project life is 25 years and that the initial cost is $5 million. The annual cost is $100,000 per year for 25 years and the annual benefits are $600,000 per

TABLE 6.1. **THE EFFECTS OF DISCOUNT RATES ON PROJECT EFFICIENCY**

	Discount Rates			
	0%	*3%*	*5%*	*10%*
B	$15,000,000	10,448,000	8,456,000	5,442,000
C	7,500,000	6,741,000	6,409,000	5,906,000
B/C	2.00	1.55	1.32	0.92
B−C	7,500,000	3,707,000	2,047,000	−464,000

B, benefits; C, costs; B/C, benefit-cost ratio; B−C, net benefits.

year. Table 6.1 shows the benefits, costs, net benefits, and benefit–cost ratio calculated for four different discount rates ranging from zero (no discounting) to 10 percent.

It can be seen that the undiscounted net benefits of $7.5 million drop to $3.7 million when a discount rate of only 3 percent is used in the example. The net benefits keep decreasing with a higher discount rate and become *negative* when a 10 percent rate is utilized. Thus, raising the discount rate can change a project from appearing efficient to one that is inefficient. These issues are of particular importance for projects such as the previously discussed Upward Bound program, whose benefits extend over a significant period of time.

Given this importance of the discount rate, the question becomes, What rate should be used in benefit–cost studies? This question is controversial both in theory and in actual practice. It is often argued that opportunity cost or the rate of return that resources could earn in the private sector is the appropriate choice (Baumol, 1970; Gramlich, 1981). If resources are going to be drawn from the private sector of the economy into the public sector, they should provide a rate of return in the public sector at least as great as what could have been earned in the private sector. However, the question still remains of what rate measures the opportunity cost since it varies with the source from which the project's resources are drawn. A variety of interest rates in the private sector reflect differences in risk, the impact of distortionary taxes, imperfections in the marketplace, etc. Other government monetary and fiscal policies in pursuit of various macroeconomic goals also have an influence on interest rates. A weighted average of different rates may be most appropriate although the choice of weights is also unclear. There is also the question of whether a below-market social discount rate should be utilized given the above problems. This rate reflects concern about whether society overvalues present consumption, and it relates to optimal values of saving and investment for a country (Baumol, 1970; Gramlich, 1981).

Government policy on the use of a discount rate has always been ambiguous. Even in the period of the Planning, Programming, and Budgeting System, the choice of discount rate varied tremendously among federal agencies. Merewitz and Sosnick (1971, pp. 120, 121) show that in the late 1960s the discount rates utilized by different agencies ranged from 0 percent to 12 percent.

Attempts have been made to standardize the choice of rate over time but not always with great success. The choice of a discount rate was one of the factors in the debate between President Jimmy Carter and the Congress over the deletion of 19 water-resource projects in the 1978 budget. Carter wanted to reject some projects that were discounted at 6.38 percent whereas some in Congress argued that this rate was higher than the rate provided by law at the time the projects were authorized (Mikesell, 1978).

Let us now turn to the case study. (Analysis follows on page 195.)

Case Study No. 5
The Value of Time and the Value of Life

Maintain 55 MPH as Speed Limit and Arrive Alive
(Senator John C. Danforth, *Atlanta Constitution*, February 12, 1987)

Danforth, a Republican, is a U.S. senator from Missouri.

Washington — The 55 MPH speed limit saves lives—a lot of them.

Raising the speed limit above 55 MPH will cost lives—a lot of them.

The Senate has passed legislation that would permit states to increase the speed limit to 65 MPH on rural interstate highways.

This is a question of weighing time saved against lives saved.

According to the National Academy of Sciences, when the speed limit was reduced to 55 MPH in 1974, fatalities on the nation's highways fell by 9,100 the first year. The overall fatality rate dropped 32 percent while remaining unchanged on roads that were not affected by the speed limit reduction. Since that time, the 55 MPH speed limit has continued to save lives. The National Safety Council estimates that the proposed speed limit increase on rural interstates would result in 600 to 1,000 additional highway fatalities a year.

The 55 MPH speed limit also prevents injuries.

The National Academy of Sciences estimates that the lower speed limit prevents 65,500 injuries a year. The American Medical Association estimates that the lower speed limit has reduced spinal column injuries by 60 percent. As a result, motor vehicle crashes are no longer the No. 1 cause of spinal injuries in the United States.

Far less compelling an argument, but a fact, is that the 55 MPH speed limit saves money. According to the National Academy of Sciences, the current speed limit saves approximately 167,000 barrels of oil per day, $2 billion worth of oil per year. Other savings include reduced medical expenses, legal fees, costs of motor vehicle damage and costs to the federal government from Medicare, Medicaid, Social Security disability payments and lost income tax revenues.

It has been argued that regulating the speed limit on interstate highways is a states' rights issue. Underscore the word "interstate."

Congress funds the Interstate Highway System. It is an INTERstate highway system, not a state highway system. There is no constitutional right of states to regulate interstate commerce. It is the role of Congress to address matters of interstate commerce. The federal government regulates the length, width and weight of trucks on interstate highways. It regulates interstate highway design and construction. The 55 MPH speed limit is not a constitutional issue.

It is said that many drivers exceed the 55 MPH speed limit, but many drivers will exceed whatever limit is set. The chance of being killed in an accident increases exponentially as speed increases. For example, a collision at 40 miles an hour is 10 times as likely to kill as one at 20 MPH. The likelihood of death at 50 MPH is 20 times as great as it is at 20 MPH.

It is said that enforcement of the 55 MPH speed limit diverts police resources that could be more productively employed. The assistant superintendent of the Ohio State Patrol disagrees. In testimony before the Senate Commerce Committee, he said that the single most important thing that Congress can do to improve highway safety is to maintain the 55 MPH speed limit.

Finally, it is said that rural interstates are safer than urban interstates. That simply is not true. It is not true in Colorado. It is not true in Montana. It is not true in Nebraska. It is not true in Utah. In those states, the fatality rate on rural inter-states is two to three times the fatality rate on urban interstates.

The National Academy of Sciences estimates that if the speed limit is increased from 55 MPH to 65 MPH, an average of one minute a day per driver will be saved.

A minute a day means nothing. Six hundred to 1,000 lives annually mean a great deal.

The choice is clear. Keep the speed limit at 55 MPH.

Increased Speed Limits Beginning to Encounter Opposition in Some States

(Isabel Wilkerson. Copyright © 1987 by The New York Times Company. Reprinted by permission.)

Town in Michigan Seeks Slowdown

LEONIDAS, Mich., May 3—At a time when most states are scrambling to raise the speed limit on rural highways, people in this tiny Michigan town are protesting an increase of the speed limit on a state highway that cuts through Leonidas.

Residents awoke one morning late last January and found that the speed limit on their stretch of Route 60, near Kalamazoo, had suddenly been raised to 50 miles an hour from 40. The Michigan Department of Transportation changed the signs after it found that the old limit, decades old, was being ignored by most motorists anyway.

Residents immediately began protesting. Schoolchildren wrote letters to the Michigan Department of Transportation and, last week-end, about 100 protesters held a rally on Route 60. Now there are makeshift signs coming and going—four-by-four-foot placards next to the official speed limit signs and banners across the pump supply shop—urging drivers to slow down.

"We didn't even like 40 miles per hour," said Terry Moyer, an automobile worker who is a leader of the protest. "There was no way we would sit back with 50."

Decision is Expected

The Michigan State Police and Department of Transportion are scheduled to decide the matter on Tuesday. Earlier attempts at a compromise with residents were unsuccessful. "They won't even consider 45 miles per hour," said Jim Burge, a district engineer in the Department of Transportation.

Highway speed limits have been a topic of national debate since Congress first took up the popular highway bill allowing states to raise the speed limit on Interstate highways in rural areas to 65 miles an hour. The bill became law early last month after Congress overrode President Reagan's veto, to the delight of the Western and Middle Western states.

But here in Leonidas, people are furious about the change on the state highway. Route 60 is bustling with truck drivers trying to avoid weigh stations on the nearby interstate and motorists taking a detour to Indiana. The highway runs straight through the two-block downtown, past the antique shop and grocery store, and, residents said, traffic endangers dozens of children who must cross the street to get to school.

Even with the old speed limit, people here complained of accidents and near-accidents and of furniture rattling as cars whizzed through town at up to 60 or 70 miles an hour. Residents fear that the new limit will encourage motorists to drive even faster.

Leonidas is a town with one stoplight and 300 people. "They're aren't that many of us, and we want to keep all we got," Mr. Moyer said.

Since the speed limit was raised, the town

voted to spend $1,000 a year for a crossing guard to help people get across the highway. But so far, said Suzanne Moyer, who helped organize the protest and paint the placards with her husband, "we haven't been able to get anybody to take the job." She explained, "Nobody wants to go out there and try to stop traffic."

About 4,000 vehicles pass through Leonidas on Route 60 every day, volume comparable to "any busy alley in Detroit," Mr. Burge said. He added that the old speed limit was "artificially low" and that most people were driving about 50 miles an hour anyway.

"People want to get where they're going," he said. "The bulk of drivers don't pay attention to speed limit signs unless they know there are patrols. They generally drive what they feel is safe and comfortable speed."

Residents complained that speed limits should not be changed to accommodate people who break the law. But Lieut. Wes Hubers of the Michigan State Police traffic division said, "Everyone wants 25 miles per hour in front of their house and not anywhere else."

Since January, average driving speeds on Route 60 in Leonidas have fallen to 43 miles per hour, according to town and state police records. Residents say that is because of the placards they have posted along the roadway, bearing slogans like, "Please slow down in town or go around." Sometimes truck drivers honk their horns as they rumble through and sedans and station wagons can be seen braking as they pass a gallery of signs.

State officials say the signs could be a problem if they block official speed limit signs. "Technically, they may be an obstruction, but we don't believe we want to get into that right now," said Lieutenant Hubers.

Residents say they are determined to get their point across. "The signs aren't coming down, even if the speed limit does," Mrs. Moyer said.

Surge in Death Toll Feared
(Isabel Wilkerson. Copyright © 1987 by The New York Times Company.
Reprinted by permission.)

Lansing, Mich., May 4—The legal speed limit is catching up to the drivers on thousands of miles of the nation's interstate highways. But the move to 65 miles per hour from 55 in rural areas is far from universal, and in some states the higher limit is being accompanied by new measures to mitigate what officials say may be a surge in deaths and serious injuries.

Several state governments, while bowing to their constituents' desire for the higher limit, are attaching conditions such as a lower speed for trucks and toughened enforcement.

Illinois, for example, coupled the increase with the temporary reassignment of 300 State Police officers to highway duties, where they are to enforce strictly both the new 65 MPH limit and a state law requiring the use of seat belts. Illinois also kept the limit at 55 MPH for larger trucks, motor homes and trailers.

The Congressional measures permitting states to raise the speed limits on Interstate highways in rural areas became law at the beginning of April when President Reagan's veto was overridden. Twenty states, most of them west of the Mississippi, had done so as of April 30, according to David M. Seiler, an analyst at the National Highway Traffic Safety Administration. Legislation is pending in nine other states, Mr. Seiler said.

Issue of Radar Detectors
The debate here in Michigan illustrates how contentious the issues can be. State Police officials dislike raising the limit at all. The state Senate has approved a bill that would raise the limit only for automobiles and light trucks, and would also ban radar detectors.

"By allowing motorists to use a device that

subverts the law, we're saying we're not really serious,'' said Thomas O. Reel, executive director of the Traffic Safety Association of Michigan.

But after a lobbying campaign by manufacturers and users of radar detectors, a Michigan House committee last week rejected the provision to outlaw the detectors. The measure goes to the full House this week, and it is not clear how the difference with the Senate bill will be resolved. Gov. James Blanchard has said that he would not sign the speed-limit legislation without the ban on radar detectors.

Some truckers are upset with Michigan's likely enactment of a car-truck speed differential. A lower limit for trucks "would be one of the worst things the state of Michigan could do,'' Barry Pfister, a trucker, told the House committee at a hearing.

But preliminary results from a membership survey of the American Trucking Association, which represents motor-carrier companies, indicate support for a lower limit for trucks even if automobiles are allowed to go faster, according to William Johns, the association's managing director of technical services.

Both sides of the truck-speed debate raise the safety issue. Those who favor 55 MPH stress among other things, that trucks cannot stop as quickly as cars. It would be folly, they say, to increase the already substantial stopping distance. But those who favor 65 MPH say cars traveling faster than trucks would have more frequent rear-end collisions with the trucks.

At its enactment in 1974, the national 55 MPH speed limit was primarily an energy-saving response to the Arab oil embargo. But the oil glut of the 1980's blunted that argument, which was replaced by another: safety.

Study after study has shown that the rate of death and serious injury drops with the average speed of vehicles. And even though motorists have routinely exceeded 55 MPH—the average speed on Michigan's rural interstates last year was 63.8—many officials say they fear that raising the limit will increase the problem.

According to the National Highway Traffic Safety Administration, as of April 30 the following states had decided to raise the speed limit on rural interstates to 65 MPH for some or all vehicles: Arizona, Arkansas, Colorado, Florida, Idaho, Illinois, Kansas, Louisiana, Mississippi, Missouri, Montana, Nevada, New Hampshire, New Mexico, North Dakota, Oklahoma, South Dakota, Vermont, Washington and West Virginia.

There are no plans to increase the speed limit in Eastern states, including New York, New Jersey, Connecticut, Maryland, Massachusetts and Virginia, said Mr. Seiler of the National Highway Traffic Safety Administration. Delaware and Rhode Island are ineligible to increase the speed limit under the Federal legislation because their Interstate highways are all within areas designated as urban.

"There's a lot more to consider in the Eastern states,'' said Chris Pattarozzi, senior research analyst at the National Conference of State Legislatures in Denver. "The roads are older and traffic volumes are heavier.''

Analysis of Case Study No. 5

The case for this chapter focuses on the issue of returning the speed limit on interstate highways to 65 miles per hour. Although Congress has voted in favor of this policy and has overridden a veto by President Reagan (Greenhouse, 1987), the issues in this policy area are still controversial because they involve the benefits from saving lives versus the benefits from saving time. Senator John Danforth pleads that "A minute a day means nothing. Six hundred to 1,000 lives annually mean a great deal. The choice is clear. Keep the speed limit at 55 MPH." Others have argued that the speed limit should be increased on rural portions of the interstate highway system because the 55 MPH limit is being ignored in any case and that law enforcement resources could be better devoted to other activities. Supporters of the change also argue that traffic fatalities have dropped because of seat belts, better automobile design, and other safety measures. They claim that truck drivers and other rural drivers who spend long hours on the road lose "considerable time" (Weinraub, 1987). As of April 30, 1987, 20 states, most of them west of the Mississippi, had increased their speed limits on interstate highways. Eastern states such as New York, New Jersey, Connecticut, Maryland, Massachusetts, and Virginia had no plans to do so. Federal legislation makes Delaware and Rhode Island ineligible to increase the limit because their interstate highways are all within areas designated as urban (Wilkerson, 1987).

The issues in this case study center on the following questions: (1) What reductions in traffic fatalities and increases in travel time can be attributed to the 55 MPH speed limit? (2) What monetary valuation can be placed on each of these factors? (3) Are there other costs (enforcement, evasion, etc.) or benefits (reduced gasoline consumption) that should be considered in the analysis? This chapter will focus primarily on the complex issues involved in the first two questions. However, research attempts to answer question 3 will also be noted. This section will explore both the conceptual issues involved with these questions and some of the empirical methodology utilized. Thus, the analysis of the case study relates to material discussed both earlier in this chapter and in the previous chapters of the text.

Placing a value on the lives saved is a central issue in many health, disease control, safety, and transportation programs. In an early discussion of the issues, Schelling (1968) pointed out that the question is not the worth of human life but of life-saving or preventing death. Also, the concern in this policy area is not with a particular death but with a statistical death. When a situation arises involving particular individuals—the collapse of a building, a liver transplant for a child, etc.—hundreds of thousands of dollars may be voluntarily collected in response to media attention. However, there may be quite different responses when the issues involve a bill to increase construction safety standards or to devote more resources to medical research. Thus, the issue is the valuation of unidentified, statistical lives in public programs.

There have been two major approaches to the valuation of life in the benefit-cost literature. The first is termed the *discounted future earnings* or the *human capital* approach (Rhoads, 1978; Gramlich, 1981; Warner and Luce, 1982;

Landefeld and Seskin, 1982; Avorn, 1984). Under this approach, researchers take the average age at which death occurs and then compute the expected future income individuals would have received if they had lived a normal term. This flow of expected income is then discounted by using the procedures discussed above. This approach is based upon the idea of maximizing society's present and future production. The value of an individual's life is reflected in his or her contribution to the gross national product. Sometimes an individual's earnings net of consumption have been utilized. This approach is based on the concept that death results both in the loss of future production and consumption. Labor earnings are usually evaluated before taxes, reflecting society's viewpoint, as opposed to after taxes, which would be most relevant to the individual. Non-labor income is generally excluded because capital holdings are not affected by an individual's continued existence (Landefeld and Seskin, 1982, p. 556).

This approach appears to place a market value on lives saved. However, as Gramlich (1981, p. 69) notes, it is the wrong market. The market focuses only on the productive activities of the individual. It cannot value how much the individual actually enjoys life. The approach also implies that a low valuation should be placed on those individuals who have low market wages. This means that there will be different valuations for children versus adults, the working versus the retired, men versus women, those with high education and training versus others, etc. Any differences in wages resulting from labor market discrimination and other institutional factors will be transmitted into the valuation of lives saved under this approach. Nonmarket activities are typically not included. If the discounted future earnings represent the decedent's utility loss from death, there are also losses to the individual's spouse, family, friends, etc. Some estimate of these losses would need to be made. This approach also ignores all costs of the fear of the risk of death and of nonmonetary suffering (Rhoads, 1978).

The choice of a discount rate for computing the present value of these income streams can have a major impact on the analysis given that life expectancies up to 70 years may be involved. The present value of the future earnings of males ages 1 to 4 in 1977 were calculated to be $405,802 using a real discount rate of 2.5 percent, whereas they were only $31,918 using a 10 percent discount rate. The choice of discount rate can also affect the relative valuations between different age groups. At a real rate of 6 percent, males aged 20 to 24 are valued higher than males ages 40 to 44. The reverse is true using a 10 percent discount rate (Landefeld and Seskin, 1982, p. 556). Despite all of these problems, this approach has been widely used given the relative ease of gathering the data necessary for the calculations.

The second approach focuses on estimating society's *willingness to pay* to reduce the probability of a statistical death. This approach follows directly from the methodology discussed earlier in this chapter. The major problem is how to apply the willingness-to-pay concept to the valuation of life. Consumer polls and surveys have been utilized to try to answer these questions. However, there is a preference-revelation problem with this method. Individuals may not correctly state their preferences if they believe they will be taxed or assessed accordingly to support the program. This is likely to be the case if the program is a public good whose benefits spill over to everyone. More important, it is unclear whether individuals can understand and give consistent answers to these types of questions. An individual's answer may depend upon the wording of the question. Individuals may be willing to pay more to eliminate a risk than to achieve an equivalent reduction in the risk. They may also demand much more money to give up something than they would be willing to pay to acquire it (Thaler, 1983).

These problems result in a wide range of estimates for the valuation of lives. In one study, individuals were asked open-ended questions about their willingness to pay for a coronary care unit that would reduce the risk of death from heart attack by 0.002. The average person in the sample was willing to pay $76 for the unit. This translated into $38,000 per statistical life saved. In a survey concerning safety and airline travel using similar methods, a value of $8.4 million per statistical life was calculated. Another survey on the willingness to pay to reduce cancer mortality found a value of $1.2 million per statistical life saved (Landefeld and Seskin, 1982, p. 557). This wide variation in the estimates obviously raises substantial problems when applying these estimates to public-policy problems such as the 55 MPH speed limit.

Rather than directly attempting to estimate willingness to pay from surveys, it is also possible to examine the decisions made by individuals in the marketplace. Suppose that there were two jobs which were alike in every respect except that there was no risk of death in one job whereas there was a positive risk in the other job. In a competitive market with a large number of available jobs and full information about the risks associated with each job, the only way companies with risky jobs could attract workers would be to pay them higher wages. Thus, these compensating wage differentials could be used as a measure of individuals' willingness to pay to reduce the risk of death. These differentials would have to be measured after controlling for education, race, experience, unionization, region, and all other factors that would also contribute to differences in wage rates. The problems with this approach are also obvious. Workers may not have freedom of choice among jobs. They may be forced to take a particular job regardless of the risks involved if the only alternative is unemployment. Workers may not have accurate information on the magnitude of the risks involved. Moreover, as in the case of certain chemicals, no one in society may have adequate knowledge of the risks to human life in working with these products. Workers may also have different attitudes or preferences toward risk. Those in risky jobs may exhibit less risk aversion than the population as a whole. Even with good data, estimates based on wage differentials would typically omit the willingness to pay of most white-collar workers and of all nonworkers. Society's willingness to pay may also depend upon how painful the pre-death stages of a disease are or upon whether the program is preventative or curative (Rhoads, 1978; Gramlich, 1981; Landefeld and Seskin, 1982).

The range of life-saving valuations from this approach is also very large.

Studies have calculated estimates from $277,000 up to $5.9 million (Landefeld and Seskin, 1982, p. 558). In many cases all the important characteristics of workers affecting wage rates may not have been adequately controlled for in the analysis. It is also often the case that aggregate rather than individual data are utilized. Job risks may not be uniform across occupations when the data are aggregated.

Equally controversial issues are involved when attempting to place a valuation on an individual's time. Typically an individual's wage rate is taken as a measure of the opportunity cost of his or her time. If workers have a choice about the number of hours to work, the wage rate would measure the value of the leisure time given up by working. This approach is not useful for workers who are unemployed or who are not able to work as many hours as they would like. A wage rate, as discussed above, also reflects a job's risk, unpleasantness, fringe benefits, working conditions, etc., as well as the valuation of leisure time lost. These other effects should be disentangled to get a true measure of the time valuation. It is also the case that the valuation of time varies over different periods—peak hour versus nonpeak hour commuting, weekday versus weekends, etc. A standard wage rate should not be applied in all of these cases (Gramlich, 1981, pp. 72, 73). It is also the case that a wage rate is not very appropriate for evaluating time costs in recreation-benefit studies. Cesario (1976, p. 34) argues that "it seems farfetched to assume that the recreation tripmaker is trading off time for travel with time for work. It seems much more likely that the trade-off is between time for travel and time for leisure activities."

Most of the research on the valuation of time has been undertaken in connection with transportation studies examining consumers' choice of transportation mode. The time valuations from these studies have been summarized as follows: "Wage earners with annual incomes greater than about U.S. $30,000 value an hour of time in intracity transit at about half their equivalent hourly wage rates. For wage-earners with annual incomes less than about $30,000, the ratio of the value of time in transit to income increases approximately linearly from zero at zero income to about .5 at $30,000. The value of waiting time is about two to three times that of time in transit. The connection between the incomes of a household's wage earners and the travel-time values of its non-wage earners has not been firmly established in this literature" (Mohring, Schroeter, and Wiboonchutikula, 1987, pp. 40, 41). The differences between the valuation of waiting time and time in transit have been found to be especially important in the evaluation of rapid rail systems. Many cities have constructed these systems (BART in San Francisco, MARTA in Atlanta, etc.), which minimize the time in transit between two points. However, if individuals value wait-time much more heavily than transit time, it can be argued that the resources on the rail systems would have been better spent on improving bus systems, which have longer transit times but less wait-times (Webber, 1976).

These valuation issues are combined with measures of impact when evaluating the 55 MPH speed limit issue. In a benefit-cost analysis of the speed

limit, Forester, McNown, and Singell (1984) first estimate the number of reduced fatalities from annual time series data for the United States from 1952 to
1979 using a three-equation recursive-regression model relating fatalities,
average speed, variability of speed, and the speed limit. Traffic fatalities are
hypothesized to be a function of real earned income, vehicle miles travelled, an
age variable measuring the number of youths relative to the number of adults,
the number of imported cars as a fraction of all cars purchased, the average
speed, the concentration of speed (the percentage of cars traveling between 45
and 60 miles per hour), and the speed limit. The effect of several of these variables on fatalities is ambiguous (Forester and others, 1984, pp. 632–633). For
example, an increase in income could represent an increase in the opportunity
cost of travel time. This could make individuals reduce the time spent driving
safely and, thus, increase fatalities. On the other hand, safety could be considered to be a good that people demand in larger quantities as their incomes
increase. Young drivers have typically been assumed to be greater accident
risks. However, they may be more resilient if injured and they may place a
lower value on time, both of which could result in decreased fatalities. Although
imposition of the 55 MPH speed limit lowers average speed, it might contribute to increased fatalities if drivers then become less safe in their driving habits
or if the longer driving times increase fatigue and carelessness. The effect of
these variables must be tested empirically in a regression model because the
hypothesized effect is uncertain. Furthermore, the net impact of the speed limit
on total fatalities must also include the indirect effect of the law on reducing
average speeds and the variability of speed. Thus, Forester and colleagues
(1984, pp. 633–634) estimate two additional equations, with the average speed
and the concentration of speed as the dependent variables. The independent
variables in these equations are similar to those discussed above.

Forester and colleagues conclude that the 55 MPH speed limit reduced
fatalities by 7,466 lives per year. However, it is the greater concentration of
speed (the extent to which cars travel at similar speeds) resulting from the
speed limit and not the reduction in average speed that contributes the most to
lowering fatality levels (Forester and others, 1984, p. 635). This conclusion is
reached by analyzing the indirect impact of the speed limit on fatalities through
its effects on average speed and the concentration of speed (the second and third
equations in the model). Indeed, the estimated coefficients of the first equation
(traffic fatalities) imply that the imposition of the speed limit, controlling for
the other variables included in the equation, actually increases the number of
fatalities. However, the overall impact is a reduction in the number of fatalities
resulting from the lower speed limit. Regarding the other variables, higher real
income is associated with greater fatalities. Thus, there appear to be reduced
safety habits at higher levels of income. Young people also appear to be more
prone to riskier driving habits.

The estimated reduction of 7,466 fatalities annually represents a gain of
316,000 years of life based upon the average age of individuals killed on the
highways (33.5 years old) and life expectancy in the United States (42.4 addi-

tional years of life for those 33.5 years old). This saving of lives requires that 456,300 additional years of life be spent on the highways annually, given the total vehicle miles in 1978, the reported average vehicle occupancy, and the reduction in average speeds estimated from the regression equations (Forester and others, 1984, pp. 636, 637). Although most of these calculations were based on 1981 data, no such data on vehicle miles were available for that year. The researchers argued that there was a leveling of total vehicle miles driven in the late 1970s so that the use of 1978 data for this variable would not bias the results of the analysis. This is an example of the data problems that analysts face and that were discussed in more detail in Chapter 3 of this text.

Using three different measures of the value of lives saved (discounted lifetime income, lifetime income less personal consumption, and a revealed preference approach), these researchers found that the 55 MPH speed limit would *not* be economically efficient (a benefit-cost ratio greater than 1) unless time was valued at less than one-quarter of the average wage. This is a much smaller valuation of time than has been typically used in the benefit-cost literature (Forester and others, 1984, pp. 638, 639). These researchers do attempt to examine the additional benefits associated with reduced gasoline consumption and reduced injuries. The impact of the speed limit on gasoline consumption was estimated from a regression equation that included such variables as the price of gasoline, the number of vehicle miles, the average speed and concentration of speed, and the mix of vehicles on the road. The estimated reduction in gasoline consumption was approximately 600 million gallons per year or about one-half of 1 percent of 1979 total consumption. This reduction, valued at the 1980 average price of $1.20 per gallon of unleaded fuel, resulted in a cost savings of $716 million, 12 percent to 18 percent of the value of lives saved. Regarding injuries, the authors state that they "were unable to determine the value of reduced injury levels under the law without a breakdown of the incidence of the types of injuries from which a cost of injury could be imputed. Using estimates of an injury equation similar to the specification of the fatality equation and a cost per injury of $15,504 based on National Safety Council estimates, a rough valuation of the savings from reduced injuries is $3.07 billion" (Forester and others, 1984, p. 640). These researchers argue that even when the benefits of reduced gasoline consumption and the value of reduced injuries are added to the value of the lives saved, "the benefit-cost ratios range between .35 and .42 when the average wage rate is used to value time. Such results do not make a strong case for maintaining the 55 MPH limit. Indeed, the results of this study suggest that much of the gain in lives saved results from a smaller variability in speeds. It might be therefore that a minimum speed may be more important than a reduced maximum speed" (Forester and others, 1984, p. 640).

Policy analysis is always complicated by the fact that different researchers reach varying conclusions on any policy issue given differences in methodology and the data sources utilized. In benefit-cost analyses, researchers are not always able or do not attempt to measure the same benefits and costs. Thus, policymakers need to examine carefully the differences among studies. They may need to form their own judgments about the significance of the benefits or costs *not* measured in a given study. Castle (1976), Lave (1979), and Jondrow, Bowles, and Levy (1983) conclude, as do Forester and co-workers, that the benefits of the 55 MPH speed limit do not justify the costs. However, Clotfelter and Hahn (1978) argue for the opposite conclusion. This study will be discussed briefly to contrast their results with those of Forester and colleagues (1984).

Clotfelter and Hahn (1978, p. 285) argue that while their study "is by no means intended as a full cost-benefit analysis of the law, the analysis below attempts to provide rough estimates for the major costs and benefits using readily available data." They focus on the actual costs and benefits resulting from implementation of the 55 MPH speed limit between 1973 and 1974 in contrast to Castle's (1976) approach, which analyzes the potential costs and benefits that could be obtained if all drivers obeyed the new speed limit. They also recognize that all of the relevant data to analyze a problem may not be readily available. Thus, the problem-definition issues discussed in Chapter 2 of this book can have a major impact on the empirical studies supporting various policy options. Clotfelter and Hahn (1978) also note that some of the decreased driving speeds during this time period may have resulted from the higher gasoline prices. Because they believe that this effect is small, however, they *assume* that all of the decreased speed results from the new speed limit. In contrast, Forester and colleagues (1984) attempt to *model* this effect by including the price of gasoline in their average speed equation.

Clotfelter and Hahn focus both on the time costs of the new speed limit and on the compliance and enforcement costs of the law. Regarding the time-cost issue, Clotfelter and Hahn (1978) criticize Castle (1976) for measuring these costs simply by multiplying the number of additional hours spent driving by the average value of time. They argue that motorists decreased the amount of driving in response to the law and that using the beginning-year mileage would overstate the social cost of the law while using the second-year mileage would understate the cost. They use each of these figures to determine upper and lower-bound estimates of the time lost because of the speed limit (Clotfelter and Hahn, 1978, p. 286). They also use two difference estimates of the value of travel time drawn from the existing literature, namely, 42 percent and 33 percent of the wage rate for those in the labor force. Other drivers and riders are assumed to have the same value of time as those in the labor force. Clotfelter and Hahn (1978, p. 287) emphasize the following qualifications to their estimates: "First, the estimates of the value of travel time employed above are based on studies of commuters. To the extent that vacation and other long-distance travelers may have lower values of time, the values used may provide overestimates. Second, the opportunity cost of increased transport time for commercial vehicles is not adequately reflected in these values of time. The costs of additional travel time for these vehicles are likely to be more, rather than less, than the values used in the calculations.

Although Clotfelter and Hahn term the measurement of enforcement costs "problematical," they attempt to provide some rough estimates. Forester and colleagues (1984) did not address this issue at all in their study. Clotfelter and Hahn focus on the costs associated with the modification of speed limit signs by examining the amounts of money that states requested from federal highway funds for this purpose. They project an amount for all states based on filed reports from only 25 states. The researchers also argue that the federal government spent funds on advertising to encourage compliance with the speed limit. Although no direct costs of these activities were available, Clotfelter and Hahn (1978, p. 288) assume these costs to be 10 percent of the $2.0 million advertising and public information budget of the U.S. Department of Transportation. Thus, the judgmental forecasting of Chapter 3 in this book and other reasonable assumptions play a role in benefit and cost estimation.

In their benefit estimation, Clofelter and Hahn focus on valuing the gasoline saved, the fatalities and injuries averted, and on reduced property damage. Reduced gasoline consumption was based on vehicle-mile estimates similar to those discussed above. The valuation problem of determining the true social costs of the gasoline saved was more difficult given the extensive government regulation and controls in the gasoline market. The market price of gasoline "failed to reflect the social cost of gasoline due to the government's price control of "old" domestic oil and to the entitlements program . . . the social marginal cost for gasoline would be . . . the market price that would prevail in the absence of price controls and entitlements. In other words, the value of resources used up when a gallon of gasoline was consumed not the artificially low price paid by consumers, but rather the value of goods and services foregone in this country as a result of using one gallon of gasoline made from foreign oil" (Clotfelter and Hahn, 1978, p. 289). These researchers used a weighted average of the wholesale prices of gasoline refined from domestic and foreign oil to reflect these social costs. The conceptual issues supporting this procedure were discussed earlier in the chapter.

Regarding fatalities and injuries averted and reduced property damage, Clotfelter and Hahn essentially took measures of the changes in these factors for this period of time from other sources and then attributed some proportion of these changes to the new speed limit. They used a National Safety Council estimate that the reduction in traffic speed accounted for 46 percent to 59 percent of the total reduction in fatalities. The social costs saved of $240,000 per traffic fatality averted were drawn from a 1972 study conducted by the U.S. Department of Transportation. These figures did compare closely with other independent estimates. The authors used the same 46 percent and 59 percent figures for the reduction in injuries attributable to the law. Cost figures for injuries avoided were derived from estimates by the National Highway Traffic Safety Administration. Alternative assumptions of 50 percent and 25 percent were used to estimate the proportion of the reduction in the total number of incidents involving property damage that were attributed to the change in the speed limit. Average costs of $300 and $363 per incident, drawn from government studies, were used to place a valuation on the reduction in property damage (Clotfelter and Hahn, 1978, pp. 289–291). Once again, it can be seen that judgment, arbitrary assumptions, and statistics drawn from a variety of sources are typically utilized in deriving plausible benefit and cost figures.

Clotfelter and Hahn conclude that the total costs of the reduced speed limit range from $2.89 billion to $3.96 billion, whereas the total benefits measured vary from $4.40 billion to $5.21 billion (Clotfelter and Hahn, 1978, pp. 291, 292). Although these figures make the program appear to be efficient, the researchers do stress the limitations of much of the data used in the analysis. They also note that the speed limit may not be "the only or the best policy for achieving the goals of conservation and highway safety. Indeed, a speed limit appears to be a second- or third-best policy for achieving both safety and conservation goals. It is quite possible that other policies, aimed directly at these goals, would be more effective. Alternative policies could also eliminate the present inequity of penalizing, in terms of time costs, drivers of efficient compacts and gas guzzlers alike" (Clotfelter and Hahn, 1978, p. 293). Thus, these researchers emphasize the important fact that policy analysis cannot simply focus on just one policy option. Decision-makers must use tools such as benefit-cost and cost-effectiveness analysis to compare alternative programs to determine which, among a variety of options, is the most appropriate for achieving a given policy goal. Given the limitations of all of the research tools, the final choice is and must be influenced by the political and judgmental factors discussed in the earlier chapters of this text.

SUMMARY

In this chapter we discussed both the conceptual and empirical issues regarding the use of benefit-cost analysis as a tool for analyzing alternative public-policy options. These issues were illustrated through the case study of the 55 MPH speed limit, an example that shows the valuation problems common to all benefit-cost analyses and the alternative positions of the different stakeholders in the policy arena. Benefit-cost analysis relates to the problem–definition issues discussed in Chapter 2 of the book. Which benefits and costs are relevant and which should be measured depends on how the policy problem is defined. Various empirical techniques, ranging from judgmental forecasting to the more sophisticated-regression techniques examined in Chapter 3, are then utilized to derive plausible estimates of the benefits and costs. The most appropriate data are often not available; hence, simplifying assumptions must be used to draw upon data sources that are in existence.

All benefit-cost analyses are imperfect given the state of the art in estimating benefits and costs. Furthermore, even if these factors could be measured perfectly, questions relating to the distribution of the benefits and costs and to the overall political support for the program arising from the vested interests of the major stakeholders might still be the dominant factors affecting the policy outcomes. However, benefit-cost analysis can provide estimates of the program costs and the value that individuals place on the resulting outputs, which should be useful to decision-makers as they consider alternative policy options and as they work through the diverse and complex elements of the policy process.

REFERENCES

Anderson, Lee G., & Settle Russell F. (1977). *Benefit-cost analysis*. Lexington, MA: Lexington Books.

Avorn, Jerry. (1984, May 17). Benefit and cost analysis in geriatric care: Turning age discrimination into health policy. *The New England Journal of Medicine, 310*, 1294–1301.

Baumol, William J. (1970). On the discount rate for public projects. In Robert H. Haveman and Julius Margolis (eds.), *Public expenditures and policy analysis* (pp. 273–290). Chicago: Markham Publishing Company.

Castle, Gilbert H. (1976, January). The 55 mph speed limit: A cost/benefit analysis. *Traffic Engineering*, 11–14.

Cesario, Frank J. (1976, February). Value of time in recreation benefit studies. *Land Economics, 52*, 32–41.

Clawson, Marion. (1959). *Methods of measuring the demand for and the value of outdoor recreation*. Washington, DC: Resources for the Future.

Clawson, Marion, & Knetsch, Jack L. (1966). *Economics of outdoor recreation*. Baltimore: The Johns Hopkins University Press.

Clotfelter, Charles T., & Hahn, John C. (1978, June). Assessing the national 55 mph speed limit. *Policy Sciences, 9*, 281–294.

Conley, Ronald W. (1969, Spring). A benefit-cost analysis of the vocational rehabilitation program. *The Journal of Human Resources*, 226–252.

Danforth, John C. (1987, February 12). Maintain 55 mph as speed limit and arrive alive. *The Atlanta Constitution* p. 23A.

Darling, Arthur H. (1973, February). Measuring benefits generated by urban water parks. *Land Economics, 49*, 22–34.

Forester, Thomas H., McNown, Robert F., & Singell, Larry D. (1984, January). A cost-benefit analysis of the 55 mph speed limit. *Southern Economic Journal, 50*, 631–641.

Freeman, A. Myrick, III. (1970). Project design and evaluation with multiple objectives. In Robert H. Haveman and Julius Margolis (eds.) *Public expenditures and policy analysis* (pp. 347–363). Chicago: Markham Publishing Company.

Garms, Walter I. (1972). A benefit-cost analysis of the Upward Bound program. In Robert H. Haveman, and others (eds.), *Benefit-cost analysis 1971* (pp. 171–185). Chicago: Aldine Publishing Company.

Gramlich, Edward M. (1981). *Benefit-cost analysis of government programs*. Englewood Cliffs, NJ: Prentice-Hall.

Greenhouse, Linda. (1987, April 3). Senate rejects Reagan plea and votes 67–33 to override his veto of highway funds. *The New York Times*, p. 1, 9.

Haveman, Robert, H., & Weisbrod, Burton A. (1983). Defining benefits of public programs: Some guidance for policy analysts. In Robert H. Haveman and Julius Margolis (eds.), *Public expenditure and policy analysis (3rd ed).* (pp. 80–104). Boston: Houghton Mifflin.

Herzlinger, Regina. (1979, Spring). Costs, benefits, and the West Side Highway. *The Public Interest*, 77–98.

Holahan, John. (1974). Measuring benefits from prison reform. In Robert H. Haveman, and others (eds.), *Benefit-cost and policy analysis, 1973* (pp. 491–516). Chicago: Aldine Publishing Company.

Jondrow, J., Bowles, M., & Levy, R. (1983, July). The optimal speed limit. *Economic Inquiry*, 21, 325–336.

Kemper, Peter, Long, David A., & Thornton, Craig. (1983). A benefit-cost analysis of the supported work experiment. In Robert H. Haveman and Julius Margolis (eds.), *Public expenditure and policy analysis (3rd ed.)* (pp. 260–300). Boston: Houghton Mifflin.

Landefeld, J. Steven, & Seskin, Eugene P. (1982, June). The economic value of life: Linking theory to practice. *American Journal of Public Health*, 72, 555–566.

Lave, C. (1979). Energy prices as public policy. In R.A. Fazzolare and C.B. Smith (eds.), *Changing energy use futures*. New York: Pergamon Press.

Maler, Karl Goran, & Wyzga, Ronald E. (1976). *Economic measurement of environmental damage*. Paris: Organization for Economic Co-Operation and Development.

Merewitz, Leonard, & Sosnick, Stephen H. (1971). *The budget's new clothes*. Chicago: Rand McNally College Publishing Company.

Mikesell, John. (1978). *The discount rate for public projects*. Washington, DC: American Enterprise Institute for Public Policy Research.

Mishan, Edward J. (1976). *Cost-benefit analysis, New and expanded edition*. New York: Praeger Publishers.

Mohring, Herbert, Schroeter, John, & Wiboonchutikula, Paitoon. (1987, Spring). The value of waiting time, travel time, and a seat on a bus. *The RAND Journal of Economics*, 18, 40–56.

Rhoads, Steven E. (1978, Spring). How much should we spend to save a life?" *The Public Interest*, 74–92.

Schelling, Thomas C. (1968). The life you save may be your own. In Samuel B. Chase, Jr. (ed.), *Problems in public expenditure analysis* (pp. 127–176). Washington, DC: The Brookings Institution.

Thaler, R. (1983, Fall). Illusion and mirages in public policy. *The Public Interest*, 60–74.

Thompson, Mark S. (1980). *Benefit-cost analysis for program evaluation*. Beverly Hills, CA: Sage Publications.

Warner, Kenneth E., & Luce, Bryan R. (1982). *Cost-benefit and cost-effectiveness analysis in health care*. Ann Arbor, MI: Health Administration Press.

Webber, Melvin M. (1976, Fall). The BART experience—What have we learned? *The Public Interest*, 79–108.

Weinraub, Bernard. (1987, March 19). House backs a 65–mph limit for rural interstates by 217–206. *The New York Times*, p. 1, 11.

Weisbrod, Burton A. (1983). Benefit-cost analysis of a controlled experiment: Treating the mentally ill. In Robert H. Haveman and Julius Margolis (eds.), *Public expenditure and policy analysis (3rd ed.)* (pp. 230–259). Boston: Houghton Mifflin.

Whittington, Dale, & MacRae, Duncan, Jr. (1986, Summer). The issue of standing in cost-benefit analysis. *Journal of Policy Analysis and Management*, 5, 665–682.

Wilkerson, Isabel, (1987, May 5). Increased speed limits beginning to encounter opposition in some states. *The New York Times*, p. 17.

Index